Social Epistemology and Relativism

This is the first book to explore the connections and interactions between social epistemology and epistemic relativism. The essays in the volume are organized around three distinct philosophical approaches to this topic: 1) foundational questions concerning deep disagreement, the variability of epistemic norms, and the relationship between relativism and reliabilism; 2) the role of relativistic themes in feminist social epistemology; and 3) the relationship between the sociology of knowledge, philosophy of science, and social epistemology.

Recent trends in social epistemology seek to rectify earlier work that conceptualized cognitive achievements primarily on the level of isolated individuals. Relativism insists that epistemic judgements or beliefs are justified or unjustified only relative to systems of standards – there is not neutral way of adjudicating between them. By bringing together these two strands of epistemology, this volume offers unique perspectives on a number of central epistemological questions.

Social Epistemology and Relativism will be of interest to researchers working in epistemology, feminist philosophy, and the sociology of knowledge.

Natalie Alana Ashton is a postdoctoral researcher at the University of Stirling. Before this she was a postdoctoral researcher at the University of Vienna, and before that completed her PhD at the University of Edinburgh. Her research concerns the political and social aspects of epistemology – specifically the effects of oppression and power on epistemic justification. She has published papers on feminist standpoint theory, hinge epistemology, and epistemic relativism, and on the connections between all of these. Her latest work investigates what these topics can tell us about online epistemic environments.

Martin Kusch has been Professor of Philosophy of Science and Epistemology at the University of Vienna since 2009. He has published research monographs with OUP, Routledge, MIT Press, and Acumen. His main current area of research is epistemic relativism, past and present. He is currently writing two monographs: a defence of epistemic relativism, and a study of the first 20th-century defender of relativism, Georg Simmel.

Robin McKenna is Lecturer in Philosophy at the University of Liverpool. Before coming to Liverpool he worked in Austria (at the University of Vienna) and Switzerland (at the University of Geneva). He completed his PhD at the University of Edinburgh. Most of his work is in epistemology, but he is also interested in the philosophy of language, philosophy of science, and ethics. Within epistemology, he works on various topics in applied epistemology, feminist epistemology, and social epistemology more broadly. Current topics of interest include the epistemology of persuasion, the epistemology of climate change denial (and of "dysfunctional epistemologies" more broadly), epistemic injustice, and social constructivism.

Katharina Anna Sodoma is a doctoral candidate at the University of Vienna. She wrote her dissertation on moral relativism and the possibility of moral progress as part of the ERC project "The Emergence of Relativism" and has published on this topic.

Routledge Studies in Epistemology
Edited by Kevin McCain
University of Alabama at Birmingham, USA
Scott Stapleford
St. Thomas University, Canada

Pragmatic Encroachment in Epistemology
Edited by Brian Kim and Matthew McGrath

New Issues in Epistemological Disjunctivism
Edited by Casey Doyle, Joseph Milburn, and Duncan Pritchard

Knowing and Checking
An Epistemological Investigation
Guido Melchior

Well-Founded Belief
New Essays on the Epistemic Basing Relation
Edited by J. Adam Carter and Patrick Bondy

Higher-Order Evidence and Moral Epistemology
Edited by Michael Klenk

Social Epistemology and Relativism
*Edited by Natalie Alana Ashton, Martin Kusch,
Robin McKenna and Katharina Anna Sodoma*

For more information about this series, please visit: www.routledge.com/
Routledge-Studies-in-Epistemology/book-series/RSIE

Social Epistemology and Relativism

Edited by Natalie Alana Ashton,
Martin Kusch, Robin McKenna
and Katharina Anna Sodoma

LONDON AND NEW YORK

First published 2020 by Routledge

2 Park Square, Milton Park, Abingdon, Oxon OX14 4RN

605 Third Avenue, New York, NY 10017

Routledge is an imprint of the Taylor & Francis Group, an informa business

First issued in paperback 2022

Copyright © 2020 Taylor & Francis

The right of Natalie Alana Ashton, Martin Kusch, Robin McKenna and Katharina Anna Sodoma to be identified as the authors of the editorial material, and of the authors for their individual chapters, has been asserted in accordance with sections 77 and 78 of the Copyright, Designs and Patents Act 1988.

All rights reserved. No part of this book may be reprinted or reproduced or utilised in any form or by any electronic, mechanical, or other means, now known or hereafter invented, including photocopying and recording, or in any information storage or retrieval system, without permission in writing from the publishers.

Notice:
Product or corporate names may be trademarks or registered trademarks, and are used only for identification and explanation without intent to infringe.

Publisher's Note

The publisher has gone to great lengths to ensure the quality of this reprint but points out that some imperfections in the original copies may be apparent.

Library of Congress Cataloging-in-Publication Data
A catalog record for this book has been requested

ISBN: 978-0-367-18938-9 (hbk)
ISBN: 978-1-03-233686-2 (pbk)
DOI: 10.4324/9780429199356

Typeset in Sabon
by Apex CoVantage, LLC

Contents

Acknowledgements	ix

1. Introduction
NATALIE ALANA ASHTON, MARTIN KUSCH, ROBIN MCKENNA, AND KATHARINA ANNA SODOMA

1

PART I
Foundational Issues in Social Epistemology

9

2. Hinge Disagreement
ANNALISA COLIVA AND MICHELE PALMIRA

11

3. Norms of Inquiry in the Theory of Justified Belief
SANFORD C. GOLDBERG

30

4. Relativism: The Most Ecumenical View?
ALEXANDRA PLAKIAS

47

5. Naturalism, Psychologism, Relativism
HILARY KORNBLITH

66

PART II
Feminist Epistemology and Social Epistemology

85

6. Relativism in Feminist Epistemologies
NATALIE ALANA ASHTON

87

7. Feminist Epistemology and Pragmatic Encroachment
ROBIN MCKENNA

103

viii *Contents*

8. Charity, Peace, and the Social Epistemology of Science
    Controversies   122
    SHARYN CLOUGH

9. Epistemic Responsibility and Relativism   143
    KRISTINA ROLIN

PART III
**Social Epistemology and the Sociology of Scientific
Knowledge**   159

10. Sociologism and Relativism   161
     DAVID BLOOR

11. Sociologistic Accounts of Normativity   174
     PAUL BOGHOSSIAN

12. Relativism in the Sociology of Scientific
     Knowledge Revisited   184
     MARTIN KUSCH

     List of Contributors   204
     Index   207

Acknowledgements

This volume is a product of the ERC Advanced Grant Project "The Emergence of Relativism: Historical, Philosophical and Sociological Issues," which was hosted by the Philosophy Department of the University of Vienna between 2014 and 2019. The main objectives of the project were threefold. First, to *retrace the intellectual history of the emergence* of important forms of relativism (and counterpart forms of anti-relativism) in 19th and early 20th-century German-speaking philosophy and science, giving proper attention to the various influences of French- and English-speaking authors. Second, to *explain* key junctures of this history in *sociological terms*. Third, to *critically evaluate* the central arguments for and against specific relativistic ideas, both as they were formulated in the period under investigation and as they have been further developed in more recent discussions. The project was *interdisciplinary* in that it brought together expertise from intellectual history, the history of science, the sociology of knowledge, and philosophy. All three strands of the project were the topic of international workshops and conferences. This volume belongs with the third strand of the project, the critical evaluation of arguments for and against epistemic relativism.

We are grateful to the participants of a 2018 workshop in Vienna in which several of the papers collected here were first tried out. The workshop was one of the key events during an ERC-funded "Advanced Grant Project" entitled "The Emergence of Relativism" (2014–2019, grant number 339382). We thank the other project members – Katherina Kinzel, Johannes Steizinger, and Niels Wildschut – for their support. Input from Delia Belleri and Anne-Kathrin Koch was also crucial. This is our third volume with Routledge, and we greatly appreciate the editors' support of our work.

1 Introduction

*Natalie Alana Ashton, Martin Kusch,
Robin McKenna, and Katharina
Anna Sodoma*

1.1. Social Epistemology and Relativism

This volume critically evaluates arguments for and against epistemic relativism. Specifically, it focuses on relativistic themes in different forms of *social epistemology*.[1] Social epistemology investigates the epistemic effects of social interactions and social systems. It has been developed against the background of and through critical engagement with the individualistic approach of much of analytic epistemology. Traditional analytic epistemology's rigid focus on the beliefs of individuals in isolation led to a distorted picture of our epistemic situation, which is, after all, heavily influenced by social factors. Social epistemology seeks to rectify this picture and has become very influential over the last decades.

The relativist regarding epistemology insists that epistemic judgments or beliefs, about knowledge or justification, for example, are true or false, justified or unjustified, *only relative to systems of standards*.[2] For the relativist there is more than one such system, and there is *no neutral way* of adjudicating between them. Some relativists go further and claim that all such systems are *equally valid*. Relativism – whether as threat or panacea – has frequently galvanized debate in both philosophy and the sciences. It was a central topic throughout the twentieth century, and the discussion continues unabated in the twenty-first. Today the debate extends to all areas of philosophy: e.g. epistemology, ethics, political philosophy and philosophy of science.

Although philosophers have worked on relativistic themes since antiquity, and on social epistemology intensively for the past 30 years or so, this volume is the first place where philosophers explore the intersection of these influential fields and topics. Our contributors address the question of relativism as it arises in the context of social epistemology from three different directions:

1. foundational questions concerning deep disagreement, the variability of epistemic norms, the relationship between relativism and reliabilism;
2. the role of relativistic themes in feminist social epistemology; and

2 *Natalie Alana Ashton et al.*

3. the debate over the relationship between the sociology of knowledge and social epistemology.

More specifically, they address the following questions:

- Does the phenomenon of deep disagreement provide support for relativism, and if so, what sort of relativist position emerges (Coliva and Palmira)?
- Do norms of inquiry vary from community to community, and if so, does this variation support a form of relativism about norms of inquiry (Goldberg)?
- Does the empirical evidence support or refute epistemic and other forms of relativism (Plakias)?
- Is a reliabilist epistemology committed to a form of epistemic relativism (Kornblith)?
- How is the feminist epistemologists' claim that "knowledge is socially situated" best understood? Does the best version of this claim lead to relativistic implications (Ashton, McKenna)?
- Do feminist values in scientific inquiry lead to relativism (Clough)?
- If feminist considerations in philosophy of science and social epistemology lead to relativism, what kind of relativism do they lead to (Ashton, Clough, McKenna)?
- How strong is the case for a "sociologistic reductionism", i.e. the thesis that the social sciences are social epistemology enough? And how good are the arguments for and against sociological reductionism (Bloor, Boghossian, Kusch)?
- How do epistemic and moral-political considerations interact in public attempts to scrutinize scientific knowledge (Rolin)?

While our contributors may disagree amongst themselves on whether epistemic relativism emerges as a viable view from its encounter with social epistemology, we think that, taken as a whole, this volume demonstrates the fruitfulness of the encounter.

1.2. Overview of the Volume

For ease of exposition, we have divided the chapters into three parts: foundational issues, feminism and relativism and the social epistemology of science.

Part I looks at the problem of relativism in relation to four "foundational issues" in social epistemology: disagreement, norms of inquiry, experimental epistemology and reliabilism. Relativism is very much a live issue in the literature on disagreement (e.g. the idea that "deep disagreements" are rationally irresolvable),[3] norms of inquiry (e.g. the idea that different communities have different norms)[4] and experimental

Introduction 3

epistemology (e.g. Stephen Stich's work on "cognitive diversity").[5] Annalisa Coliva and Michele Palmira, Sanford C. Goldberg, and Alexandra Plakias take up these issues in their contributions.

Coliva and Palmira discuss deep disagreement in connection with Wittgenstein's *On Certainty*. They take up two problems for a Wittgensteinian "hinge epistemology": can we disagree over hinges, and if so, can we rationally resolve these disagreements? They argue for a positive answer to both questions, which builds on Coliva's "constitutivist" version of hinge epistemology. The thought is that disagreements over hinges can be rationally resolved by considering what is constitutive of epistemic rationality.

While it is arguably true that our epistemic practices vary widely between communities and have varied widely over time, "orthodox epistemologists" have not taken this to provide any support for epistemic relativism. Goldberg aims to identify a form of intercommunity variation in epistemic practices that, even by the lights of orthodox epistemology, provides support for a (mild) form of epistemic relativism. The idea is that orthodox epistemology focuses on "norms of belief" (what one should believe given the evidence one has) and ignores "norms of inquiry" (how one should get evidence in the first place), but norms of inquiry may vary between communities, and this has implications for what individuals should believe. The upshot is that, while "standards of rationality" may not be interculturally variable, what one should believe can depend on the epistemic practices of one's community.

Plakias takes up the question of whether relativism is a commitment of ordinary normative discourse. It is common – particularly in the normative domain of ethics – to assume that relativism runs contrary to our ordinary normative commitments. The "folk" are not relativists, so relativism must be understood (and defended) as a revisionary account of our normative practices. Plakias argues that, if we take a closer look at work in "philosophical ethnography", we can see things are far more complicated. While the "folk" may have some anti-relativist commitments, they also have some pro-relativist commitments. Further, she argues that the relativist may do a better job of making sense of our normative commitments than the anti-relativist.

But what about reliabilism? While one might think the sort of reliabilism pioneered and defended by Alvin Goldman as a centrepiece of his "veritistic" approach to social epistemology is entirely inhospitable to epistemic relativism, Kornblith argues that a form of epistemic relativism is a natural consequence of the fact that Goldman views *doxastic* justification as prior to *propositional* justification.[6] Goldman's view is that some subject S is (doxastically) justified in believing some proposition p just in case p is produced by a reliable belief-forming process. He then defines propositional justification (roughly) as follows: S is propositionally justified in believing that p just in case S's cognitive state is

4 *Natalie Alana Ashton et al.*

such that S could become doxastically justified in believing that p. This means that whether p is propositionally justified for some S depends on whether S could believe that p. Because we can imagine subjects who are psychologically incapable of beleiving certain propositions, this in turn means that propositional justification is relative to our psychological makeup.

Part II brings together different strands of research at the intersection of feminist epistemology, social epistemology and philosophy of science.[7] Being concerned with the effects of gender on knowledge production and certification, feminist epistemology has contributed important insights to understanding the social dimensions of knowledge. One of the central theses of feminist epistemology is that "knowledge is situated", i.e. that social location affects what we can come to know and how. This invites the question of epistemic relativism. Moreover, the political consequences of adopting a relativistic stance are debated in feminist epistemology: Would a commitment to epistemic relativism help or hinder the emancipatory goals of feminist epistemology? Finally, much important work in feminist epistemology focuses on scientific knowledge and scientific objectivity. The basic gist of this work is that, not only is a feminist perspective entirely consistent with a deep respect for science, it can also help us understand science better. The contributions by Natalie Alana Ashton, Robin McKenna, Sharyn Clough and Kristina Rolin address these questions drawing on recent developments in feminist epistemology.

While critics of feminist theorizing often view it as committed to an objectionable form of relativism, feminist theorists themselves have often taken the view that feminist projects and goals are badly served by relativism. Ashton explores the reasons some feminist theorists have given for thinking this and finds them largely wanting. She argues that, far from inhibiting feminist projects and goals, relativism can provide support for them. Her basic view is that relativism is (or, at least, can be) a *liberatory* view, in the sense that it aims (or, at least, can aim) at increasing social equality and decreasing social inequality. Thus, those who want to further feminist goals need not be worried about relativism, or about embracing the seemingly relativistic implications of their views.

McKenna explores the similarities and differences between feminist epistemologies and "pragmatic encroachment" views in epistemology. Pragmatic encroachers hold that whether one knows something can depend on what is at stake for one. Thus, for pragmatic encroachers, knowledge is, in some sense, socially situated. But how does this sort of social situatedness relate to the idea of situated knowledge in feminist epistemologies? McKenna argues that, while there are some similarities, there are also some important differences. First, the view defended by pragmatic encroachers is actually more radical. Second, the case for it is largely based on intuitions about cases. He concludes that it is therefore somewhat surprising that pragmatic encroachment is a "core topic" in

Introduction 5

contemporary epistemology, whereas feminist epistemology has, until recently, been relegated to the margins.

Much work in feminist philosophy of science focuses on the role of feminist values in science and on the question of whether introducing values into science opens the door to relativism. In previous work, Clough has argued that this question is based on a false dichotomy between political values and evidence. Political values can be supported by the evidence, and when this is so, introducing them into science need not undermine the objectivity of scientific theories. In her contribution to this volume she identifies conditions for objective, evidence-based deliberations about political values, with a focus on debates about the safety of childhood vaccinations. She argues that cultivating virtues such as charity and empathy is important here, because these virtues are necessary in order to recognize that those with different values to our own are genuine interlocutors and as interested in objective evidential deliberations as we are.

In her contribution, Kristina Rolin considers what she calls "epistemic responsibility relativism", which is the view that whether one's knowledge claims are responsible or not is relative to one's audience and its epistemic standards. One strategy for refuting this form of relativism belongs to the instrumentalist about epistemic rationality: there is a best set of epistemic standards, because there is a set that best serves our epistemic ends. Rolin argues that the instrumentalist has to accept that the criteria for choosing between one audience's epistemic standards and another audience's standards have moral implications. Thus, the norm of epistemic responsibility is a moral norm.

Part III brings together three chapters at the intersection of the philosophy of science, social epistemology and the "Strong Programme" in the "Sociology of Scientific Knowledge". The relationship between these fields has attracted interest amongst social epistemologists for some time. David Bloor, Paul Boghossian and Martin Kusch debate the challenge that Bloor's Strong Programme poses to philosophy. Although these three authors have criticized each other's positions in print before, this is the first time that they engage with each other more directly in the form of chapters and a reply.

Bloor argues in favour of "sociologism" in epistemology and ethics: knowledge and morality are social phenomena, and epistemology and ethics should therefore be replaced by social science. He is (more than) ready to embrace the resulting relativism. Bloor uses his reading of Durkheim to construct a relativist response to an argument against relativism from Crispin Wright, which he takes as emblematic of the contemporary philosophical view of relativism. He argues that Durkheim helps us see why Wright's argument is mistaken and therefore to see the problem with contemporary opposition to relativism.

Boghossian criticizes Bloor's sociologistic account of knowledge and morality. While many have taken Bloor (and his fellow travellers in

6 *Natalie Alana Ashton et al.*

the Strong Programme) to task for their perceived lack of respect for science, Boghossian takes the opposite view. He takes the core disagreement between him and Bloor to lie in Bloor's *scientism*. For Boghossian, Bloor is sceptical about irreducibly normative entities and truths because he is unable to find a place for them in a scientific picture of the world. Boghossian agrees that science can't find a place for irreducible normativity, but he concludes that science therefore cannot give us a complete picture of the world.

Kusch's chapter discusses the relationship between the Strong Programme and Boghossian's criticism of relativism. He defends three theses. First, Strong-Programme relativism is not an instance of Boghossian's standard "template" for relativism. Second, Strong-Programme relativism is therefore not directly threatened by arguments targeting this template position. And third, Strong-Programme relativism is nevertheless in the vicinity of this template, and it offers at least sketches of arguments for distinctive and original relativist theses.

Notes

1. For a detailed overview, see Goldman and Blanchard (2018). For a different take, see Kusch (2010).
2. For a general overview of relativism, see Baghramian and Carter (2019) and Kusch (ed.) (2020).
3. See, for example, Hales (2014).
4. See, for example, Rorty (1991).
5. See Stich (1991).
6. For more on the possible connections between epistemic relativism and reliabilism, see Carter and McKenna (forthcoming).
7. For an excellent overview of feminist epistemology and philosophy of science, see Anderson (2017).

References

Anderson, E. (2017), "Feminist Epistemology and Philosophy of Science," in *The Stanford Encyclopedia of Philosophy*, edited by E.N. Zalta, Spring 2017 edition, https://plato.stanford.edu/archives/spr2017/entries/feminism-epistemology/

Baghramian, M. and J.A. Carter. (2019), "Relativism," in *Stanford Encyclopedia of Philosophy*, edited by E.N. Zalta, Winter 2019 edition, https://plato.stanford.edu/archives/win2019/entries/relativism/

Carter, J.A. and R. McKenna. (forthcoming), "Relativism and Externalism," in *The Routledge Handbook of Philosophy of Relativism*, edited by M. Kusch, Abingdon, UK: Routledge.

Goldman, A. and T. Blanchard. (2018), "Social Epistemology," in *The Stanford Encyclopedia of Philosophy*, edited by E.N. Zalta, Summer 2018 edition, https://plato.stanford.edu/archives/sum2018/entries/epistemology-social/

Hales, S. (2014), "Motivations for Relativism as a Solution to Disagreements," *Philosophy* 89 (1): 63–82.

Kusch, M. (2010), "Social Epistemology," in *Routledge Companion to Epistemology*, edited by S. Bernecker and D. Pritchard, New York: Routledge, 873–884.

Rorty, R. (1991), *Objectivity, Relativism and Truth: Philosophical Papers*, Vol. 1, Cambridge: Cambridge University Press.

Stich, S. (1991), *The Fragmentation of Reason: Preface to a Pragmatic Theory of Cognitive Evaluation*, Harvard, MA: MIT Press.

Part I
Foundational Issues in Social Epistemology

2 Hinge Disagreement[1]

Annalisa Coliva and Michele Palmira

2.1. Introduction

Wittgenstein's remarks in *On Certainty* are at the roots of the ever-accelerating trend in contemporary epistemology which goes under the label of "hinge epistemology." Key to this trend is the acknowledgement of the philosophical significance of the idea that justification and knowledge of empirical propositions always take place within a system of assumptions, or hinges. Such hinges, Wittgenstein maintains, are the scaffolding of our thoughts (OC §211) and the foundations of our research and action (OC §§87–8) and of our doubt and enquiry (OC §151). For instance, for Wittgenstein, it is only by taking for granted that there are mind-independent physical objects that we can take our perceptual experiences, say as of a tree in front of us, as bearing on the question of what reality is like, that is, of whether there is in fact a tree in front of us. If we doubted that there were physical objects, we could no longer consider such experiences as being evidentially significant for that specific enquiry, since we could no longer take for granted that such experiences are formed in response to the presence of mind-independent physical objects. These experiences would then be compatible with alternative hypotheses, such that there are only collections of sense-data for instance. Thus, if we didn't accept a hinge like "There are physical objects," in order to be rational, we should also reinterpret all beliefs not as being about specific physical objects *qua* mind-independent entities but as being about collections of sense-data.

Wittgenstein had a very wide conception of hinges, including propositions such as "The Earth has existed for a very long time," "There are physical objects," "My name is N.N.," "Nobody has ever been on the Moon," etc. Irrespective of the differences in generality and plausibility exhibited by these hinges, it seems safe to contend that individuals can disagree about all of them. Consider the following exchanges:

(Earth)

MARY: The Earth has existed for a very long time.
JOHN: No, the Earth has come to exist with my birth.

(Moon)

LISA: Nobody has ever been on the Moon.
MARC: I disagree, twelve people have been on the Moon.

(Objects)

LUCAS: There are physical objects.
GEORG: There aren't any, Lucas.

(World)

JANE: There is an external world.
JUNE: No, Jane. There is no external world.

On the face of it, there is nothing wrong with describing such cases as instances of disagreement. Moreover, insofar as the disagreement at stake seems to be doxastic in kind, it seems legitimate to wear the epistemologist hat and ask how the involved parties should rationally respond to their disagreement.

However, these seemingly harmless claims are hard to square with the distinctive metaphysical-cum-epistemological profile of hinge propositions. Famously, Wittgenstein regarded hinges as neither true nor false (OC §§196–206); as neither justified nor unjustified (OC §§110, 130, 166); as neither known nor unknown (OC §121); and as neither rational nor irrational (OC §559).

Reading through the extensive contemporary literature on disagreement reveals that such a phenomenon has been variously defined in terms of:

a. a relation of interpersonal non-cotenability between the two doxastic attitudes held by the disagreeing parties, which would result in irrationality (see e.g. MacFarlane 2014; Worsnip 2019);
b. a counterfactual relation between the attitudes' accuracy conditions such that the fulfilment of one's attitude's accuracy conditions makes the other's attitude *ipso facto* inaccurate, where the notion of accuracy is ultimately understood in terms of truth (for full belief) or closeness to truth (for partial belief) (see e.g. MacFarlane 2014; Palmira 2017);
c. a relation of exclusion between the two attitudes, to be understood in terms of one proposition's truth strictly entailing the other proposition's falsity (see Marques 2014).

Since notions such as truth, rationality, and their cognates have variously been taken to constitute central ingredients of what disagreement is, it seems that that there cannot be disagreement over hinges, if they are neither true nor false, and neither justified and rational nor unjustified and irrational. Call this the *lost hinge disagreement problem*.

Hinge Disagreement 13

Moreover, the question of the rational resolution of disagreement does presuppose the existence of shared epistemic standards whereby to assess the rationality of retaining or revising our doxastic stances towards the contested proposition. Since hinge disputes are such that the parties do not share epistemic standards, it seems that cases such as (EARTH), (MOON), (OBJECTS), and (WORLD) couldn't exhibit the usual normative trappings of disagreement whereby we can rationally resolve our ordinary disputes. As observed by Robert Fogelin in "The Logic of Deep Disagreement" (1985, 6): "the possibility of a genuine argumentative exchange depends ... on the fact that together we accept many things." Consequently, disagreements over hinges "cannot be resolved through the use of argument, for they undercut the conditions essential to arguing." To illustrate the problem, consider (OBJECTS) and suppose that Lucas attempts to provide Georg with reasons in favour of the existence of ordinary midsize objects. Plausibly, Lucas might reason as follows: since it seems to him, and to us in general, that there are tables, chairs, plants, and the like, we should accept the existence of mind-independent midsize objects. Georg, however, couldn't be moved by such a line of reasoning, for he rejects that our sensory experiences are formed in response to mind-independent objects in the first place. Thus, Lucas and Georg's hinge disagreement is bound to be rationally inert. Call this the *problem of rational inertia*.

This chapter is devoted to exploring solutions to the lost hinge disagreement problem and the problem of rational inertia.

2.2. Solving the Lost Hinge Disagreement Problem

The lost hinge disagreement problem is philosophically significant for two different, albeit related, reasons. First, inasmuch as there is strong pressure to consider (EARTH), (MOON), (OBJECTS), and (WORLD) as *bona fide* disagreements, it seems preferable to endorse such an appearance of disagreement, as opposed to explaining it away. Second, as witnessed by the contemporary debate on truth relativism, lost disagreement problems are often mustered in favour of certain philosophical views. In a similar vein, the lost hinge disagreement problem might be taken to speak in favour of an anti-propositionalist interpretation of hinges *qua* rules, which are not subject to truth-conditional evaluation.[2] Roughly put, the argument, in the form of an inference to the best explanation, might go as follows: given that disagreement cannot take place between two rules, the hypothesis that hinges are rules best explains why the lost disagreement problem arises.

However, Wittgenstein's remarks are not univocal and some passages in *On Certainty* can be taken to suggest the view that hinges, while playing a rule-like role, are still propositions and are minimally truth-apt. If so, then they could be the content of propositional attitudes of

14 *Annalisa Coliva and Michele Palmira*

acceptance (more on this in a moment) and could be contents on which subjects could, at least conceivably, disagree.

Some of Wittgenstein's remarks might help us frame the discussion of hinges' truth:

1. Their truth "belongs to our frame of reference" (OC §83). That is, that we regard them "as certainly true also characterizes [our] interpretation of experience" (OC §145).
2. "The *truth* of our statements is the test of our *understanding* of these statements" (OC §80). "That is to say: if I make certain false statements, it becomes uncertain whether I understand them" (OC §81).
3. "The reason why the use of the expression 'true or false' has something misleading about it is that it is like saying 'it tallies with the facts or it doesn't', and the very thing that is in question is what 'tallying' is here" (OC §199).
4. "It is the truth only inasmuch as it is an unmoving foundation of [the] language-games" (OC §403).
5. Their truth is kept fixed by what rotates around them (OC §152), like our methods of empirical investigation (OC §§151, 318), and "the rest of our procedure of asserting" (OC §153).

Hinges make it possible for us to engage in our empirical enquiries and investigations and, for Wittgenstein, they also play a meaning-constitutive role and are therefore conditions of possibility of meaningful discourse. This, on closer inspection, reveals that the truth of hinges cannot be conceived in purely correspondence-theoretical or evidentialist terms (see Coliva 2018). To illustrate this point, let us take the correspondence-theoretical notion of truth first. It is not in virtue of the obtaining of a certain fact in the world that the proposition that there are physical objects turns out to be true: such a proposition is indeed true "only inasmuch as it is an unmoving foundation of [the] language-games" (OC §403) and not because it "tallies with the facts" (OC §199). Irrespective of whether or not hinges play a meaning-constitutive role, there is good reason to regard general hinges – such as "There is an external world," "There are physical objects" – as the conditions of possibility for the existence of representations, be they conceptual or non-conceptual, of what the world is like. To illustrate this point with the case of "There are physical objects": insofar as our perceptual experiences as of a tree in front of us afford us the means to latch onto a tree, they can do so only if the hinge "there are physical objects" stays put; for otherwise we would not be latching onto anything outside our minds and the very idea of there being *bona fide* representations of an external reality would be jeopardised. Now, a realist account of hinges' truth would rest on the existence of a correspondence relation between our representations of reality and reality itself; however, the very existence of such a relation cannot be established independently of a frame of reference that rests on hinges such as "There are physical objects." Thus, since the very explanation of truth in terms of correspondence is ultimately grounded on and explained by the truth of certain hinges, such as "There are physical objects," we cannot in turn explain the truth of such hinges in terms of correspondence.

As for evidentially-constrained accounts of truth (see e.g. Putnam 1981; Wright 1992), the problem is that they heavily rely on the idea that statements are true just in case they enjoy warrants exhibiting a distinctive epistemic pedigree – that is, that they cannot be defeated by improvements or enlargements of one's state of information (see Wright 1992, 42). Now, take a hinge such as "There are physical objects." Surely, if propositional at all, this proposition is empirical in kind. Thus, the kind of evidence in its favour has to be sensory. And yet, as is familiar from traditional Cartesian sceptical worries, that evidence would be compatible with its being produced in ways which do not depend on any causal interaction with physical objects. Hence, it seems that the evidence we have cannot justify, in and of itself, the belief in the existence of physical objects. An argument such as G. E. Moore's celebrated proof, far from producing a warrant to believe that there is an external world, would rather expose the kind of epistemic circularity involved in any such attempt. For the conclusion should already be taken for granted in order for the premises to be warranted in the first place.

Even if traditional realist and anti-realist conceptions of truth cannot be harnessed to make sense of what it is for hinge propositions to be true or false, we can vindicate the truth-aptness of hinges. For the failure of realist and anti-realist conceptions of hinges' truth should not lead us to a wholesale rejection of the idea that truth may be sensibly predicated of hinges in a way that obeys disquotational schemas. Furthermore, hinges can be embedded in conditionals, and thus be semantically assessed, or be embedded in meaningful negations, at least in further conditional statements. This would make the truth-predicate a device of disquotation and generalisation with no *sui generis* metaphysical nature. In a deflationary fashion (see Horwich 1998), then, all there is to be said about (hinges') truth is captured by instances of the equivalence schema:[3]

(ES) <p> is true if and only if p.

Thus,

(ES_{obj}) <There are physical objects> is true iff there are physical objects

together with platitudes about negation, conditionals (and possibly some more, see Lynch 2009; Wright 1992, 2013) would be all there is to predicating the truth of that proposition. The virtue of such an approach would be to maintain the very possibility of predicating truth for these

16 *Annalisa Coliva and Michele Palmira*

kinds of problematic propositions while eschewing the problems that beset any of its possible stronger renderings.

To forestall misunderstandings, though, we should hasten to emphasise that this explanation of the truth-aptness of hinge propositions does not – nor is it meant to – cover all cases that fall under Wittgenstein's broad conception of hinges. Surely, the statements at issue in (MOON) and (EARTH) are not conditions of possibility of representation and, plausibly, the statement at issue in (MOON) should not be counted as a hinge at all.[4] So, we shall henceforth sidestep these cases and focus on disagreements over general hinges, such as those found in (OBJECTS) and (WORLD). This restriction allows us to have the only part of the cake worth eating, that is, the general hinges which are most relevant to our epistemological concerns, and eat it too, to wit, to make room for their truth-aptness.

Vindicating the truth-aptness of hinge propositions is the first step towards solving the lost hinge disagreement problem. The second (and last) step consists in showing that the minimalist approach just sketched affords the means to recover a genuine notion of doxastic disagreement. It takes a bit of care to explain why (OBJECTS) and (WORLD) are cases of disagreement, since there is some debate as to whether our doxastic commitment towards hinges is to be spelled out in terms of the traditional notion of belief (see Kusch 2018; Neta 2019), or else whether we should appeal to other doxastic attitudes, such as "assumption" (Coliva 2015), "trust" (Wright 2004), or "(visceral) commitment"/"conviction" (Pritchard 2016, 2018).[5]

In light of both of Wittgenstein's own remarks about the role of hinges and the subsequent development of hinge epistemology, we had better not understand our doxastic commitment towards hinges in terms of belief. This can be seen irrespective of whether or not we adopt a purely functionalist or normativist approach to the type-individuation of belief. Suppose that the cognitive mechanisms of belief formation, revision, and retention are geared towards truth-tracking. This suggests that the function of belief, in our cognitive architecture, is to afford us a correct representation of what the world is like. However, entertaining hinge propositions such as "There are physical objects" would not fulfil the function of representing what the world is like, for hinges are to be seen as conditions of possibility of the existence of cognitive propositional attitudes about specific physical objects, geared towards truth-tracking. As for the normativist approach, its core contention is that belief is the cognitive attitude which is subject to a certain norm that individuates it. The relevant norm has been variously spelled out in terms of evidence, knowledge, epistemic justification, (correspondentist) truth, and the like. However, hinges are such that no evidence can be produced in their support, for all empirical evidence would presuppose them, and this should lead us to think that hinges cannot be epistemically justified (and therefore known) in the same way as the propositions we ordinarily believe; moreover, we have argued earlier that hinges' truth cannot be explained in correspondentist terms. Hence, it seems that none of the usual norms that have been variously taken to govern belief could be satisfied in the case of hinges. Therefore, if those norms are also meant to type-individuate belief, it seems that we should conclude that hinges cannot be believed.[6]

As has emerged previously, well-worked accounts of doxastic disagreement focus primarily on the phenomenon of disagreement in belief. Yet, insofar as attitudes such as assumption can be sensibly assessed for their (minimal) truth or falsity in virtue of their being cognitive – as opposed to conative – propositional attitudes, we can extend definitions of disagreement in belief that ultimately rely on the notion of truth (see e.g. Marques 2014; Palmira 2017) so as to make sense of disagreement in assumption.

We shall remain neutral on the question of what disagreement really is, and how it manifests itself across its doxastic varieties. For insofar as we accept that all varieties of doxastic disagreement are unified under the eminently plausible idea that an opposition in what two parties hold as true is integral to the very notion of *doxastic* disagreement, we can maintain that two parties assuming the truth and falsity of the same proposition respectively do disagree about it. This provides us with a neat solution to the lost hinge disagreement problem.

2.3. The Problem of Rational Inertia

As previously seen in §2.1, there is a legitimate epistemological aspiration to rationally resolve our disagreements. On the face of it, though, this aspiration is bound to be frustrated in the case of hinge disagreement. To illustrate, by assuming the hinge "There are physical objects" in (OBJECTS), Lucas *ipso facto* subscribes to a given system of epistemic evaluations and practices, namely a system in which we can rationally form, retain, and revise beliefs towards mind-independent objects, we can criticise or praise individuals for correctly or incorrectly forming such beliefs, and so on. By assuming a hinge incompatible with this system, Georg subscribes to a different system of epistemic evaluations and practices, one in which we can rationally form, retain, and revise beliefs bearing on sense-data only. On reflection, if Lucas had to incorporate the hinge "There are no physical objects" into his epistemic system, this would render his epistemic practices *eo ipso* irrational, for it would no longer make sense for him to form or retain beliefs about tables and chairs, nor could he be criticised for not believing that there's a tree in front of him in virtue of a perceptual experience as of a tree in front of him. The same would happen, *mutatis mutandis*, if Georg had to incorporate "There are physical objects" into his epistemic system. Thus, insofar as the very practice of rationally resolving a disagreement rests on the

18   *Annalisa Coliva and Michele Palmira*

given epistemic system we end up subscribing to in virtue of the set of hinges we assume, if the object of the disagreement is the truth or falsity of such a set of hinges, it follows that the parties would have to give up their own epistemic systems in order for them to be able to appreciate, or even have access to, whatever reasons the other party may produce in favour of their view. This, in a nutshell, is the problem of rational inertia.

On closer inspection, however, the problem of rational inertia runs even deeper than this. As is well-known, recent years have witnessed a surge of interest in the question of whether disagreement carries any distinctive epistemological significance. Focusing on so-called "peer disagreement," that is, disagreements between individuals who reasonably take each other to be equally well-positioned epistemically *vis-à-vis* a given issue, epistemologists have asked whether the discovery of such disagreements provides us with higher-order counterevidence, evidence on the epistemic pedigree of our doxastic attitudes bearing on the contested issue. And yet, it seems that peer hinge disagreement is simply impossible: insofar as our judgements of epistemic parity/superiority/inferiority are epistemic, and insofar as such judgements hold in virtue of the given set of hinges we assume, it follows that we cannot have reasons to regard someone assuming a different set of hinges as being our peer, superior, or inferior. That is to say, we cannot pronounce ourselves on the epistemic credentials of somebody accepting a different set of hinges from ours. For any evaluation of the epistemic credentials of an epistemic agent is relative to the epistemic practices we endorse against the background of a set of hinges. Thus, insofar as our opponent is committed to a different set of hinges, she cannot be epistemically evaluated or assessed, for she simply endorses an epistemic system, with its characteristic hinges, which is alternative to ours. Rather than an "epistemic peer" she would therefore be an "epistemic alien."

The foregoing shows that the problem of rational inertia is not only that we can't rationally resolve hinge disagreements, but it is also the problem that we are unable to establish the epistemic significance or insignificance of such disagreements by making judgements concerning the epistemic credentials of our opponents.

Drawing on two recent developments of hinge epistemology, we will focus on two different strategies to tackle the problem of rational inertia.

2.3.1. *The Problem of Rational Inertia and the Entitlement Version of Hinge Epistemology*

In a number of writings (e.g. Wright 2004, 2014), Crispin Wright has argued for the existence of non-evidential and unearned warrants, called *entitlements*, for those propositions which act as general background presuppositions of our cognitive projects. Putting into question such presuppositions, Wright argues, would make us stop regarding the project as significant and even doubt the very feasibility of carrying

Hinge Disagreement 19

it out. Moreover, there is no sufficient reason to take these presuppositions to be false, and every attempt to justify them would call for other presuppositions whose epistemic status is no more secure than the one of the initial presuppositions, thereby launching an infinite regress about their justification.

In a Wittgensteinian fashion, Wright maintains that hinges such as "There is an external world" and "My sense organs work mostly reliably" are the presuppositions thanks to which our sensory experiences can be taken to provide (defeasible) justification for our ordinary empirical beliefs about midsize objects in our environment. Wright agrees here with the Humean sceptic[7] that our experiences can do so only if those background presuppositions are themselves warranted. Yet, the Humean sceptic can be defeated since, even if we cannot earn warrants for such presuppositions through the collection of empirical evidence, nor can we reach such warrants through a priori reflection, there exist non-evidential warrants – entitlements – for trusting such presuppositions.

In a recent paper, Chris Ranalli (2018) harnesses the entitlement version of hinge epistemology to take up the problem of rational inertia by distinguishing three senses in which the problem of rational inertia can be taken up. Here they are (see also Lynch 2016):

Rational Resolvability: A and B's disagreement over p is rationally resolvable if and only if there is some doxastic attitude D that A and B can jointly take to p which is the (uniquely) rational attitude for A and B to have towards p.

Rational Response: A and B rationally respond to their disagreement over p if and only if there is some doxastic attitude D_A that A takes to p which is the (uniquely) rational attitude for A to take to p, and there is some doxastic attitude D_B that B takes to p which is the (uniquely) rational attitude for B to have to p.

Rational Persuasion: A rationally persuades B to adopt A's doxastic attitude D to p if and only if there is a set of premises accepted by A that A can appeal to in an argument that rationally ought to persuade B into adopting D towards p (and vice versa).

(Ranalli 2018, 3–4)

Against the backdrop of such a three-fold distinction, Ranalli argues for two claims. First, two parties entitled to incompatible hinges are bound to rationally respond to their disagreement by retaining their respective trust towards such hinges. Second, in cases where one party fails to trust a common hinge for reasons that are independent of apparent evidence, that party ought to trust that hinge as well. Here is such a case (Ranalli 2018, 27–28):

(INDUCTION DISAGREEMENT) A* and B* meet and become aware of their disagreement about the reliability of induction. A*

> trusts that induction is reliable (Q), while B* trusts that induction is unreliable (~Q). Moreover, A* hasn't viciously avoided inquiry into whether induction is reliable, and neither of them have evidence sufficient for believing that induction is unreliable. However, B *merely* trusts that ~Q, as she has so far avoided inquiry into whether Q, and has adopted trust that ~Q because of her pessimistic psychological tendencies, saying that 'induction is unreliable'. Nevertheless, both A* and B* believe many shared propositions on the basis of induction (e.g., the sun will rise tomorrow, the trees near our communities will not start flying, etc.), and ordinarily employ inductive methods in their reasoning. B* is just unaware of the fact that many of her beliefs and patterns of reasoning are based on or employ induction, while A* is aware of this fact. Indeed, A* and B* trust all of the same hinge propositions, except for Q.

Ranalli's idea is that ~Q is not a background presupposition of B*'s cognitive project. For B* frequently adopts inductive reasoning as a basis for her beliefs, and therefore has no sufficient reason to take Q to be false. For this reason, B* ought to revise her attitude and trust Q.

Summing up: the entitlement-based solution to the problem of rational inertia is that we can always rationally respond to hinge disagreements by retaining our entitlements to trust different hinges; we can sometimes rationally resolve such hinge disagreements. However, we can never rationally persuade the opponent to assume the set of hinges we assume, because the reasons we would produce in favour of our hinges would always presuppose them.

We are happy to organise our discussion around the three-fold distinction used by Ranalli and rethink the problem of rational inertia as pertaining to rational resolvability, rational responsiveness, and rational persuasion. Now, the entitlement-based approach to these three aspects of the problem of rational inertia is unsatisfactory, for various reasons. For one thing, it is a well-known complaint against Wright's entitlements that they are merely pragmatic, and not fully epistemic, in kind (see Coliva 2015; Jenkins 2007; Pedersen 2009; Pritchard 2007. C.f. Wright 2013). Insofar as we have stressed that the problem of rational inertia seems to call for a distinctively epistemic, as opposed to pragmatic, solution, we'd better not rely on a solution to the problem whose epistemic nature is, in fact, highly disputable.

Moreover, even granting that entitlements are genuine epistemic warrants, it is unclear whether such a strategy really makes room for the rational resolution of disagreement. Take for instance (INDUCTION DISAGREEMENT). We agree that (INDUCTION DISAGREEMENT) elicits the intuitive verdict that B* should in the end rationally commit herself to the hinge "Induction is reliable." However, this verdict can be easily explained by taking it to be issued by the rational requirement to be coherent. That is to say, the reason why it seems that B* should assume (or trust) that induction is reliable is that, by doing so, she would align her higher-order beliefs about how to form beliefs with her first-order beliefs. This explains why B* should assume that hinge without committing ourselves to the existence of entitlements. We therefore doubt that cases such as (INDUCTION DISAGREEMENT) speak in favour of the existence of Wright's entitlements.

Finally, we should register our dissatisfaction with the fact that the entitlement-based approach to the problem of rational inertia precludes a rational resolution via persuasion. As has emerged previously, the problem of rational inertia manifests itself in a variety of ways, chief amongst them the fact that there is no way to make sense of the possibility of offering reasons in favour of one's own stance, which can be acknowledged as such – even if ultimately discarded – by our opponent. By acknowledging that we cannot rationally resolve our hinge disagreements via persuasion, the entitlement-based approach gives it up. In the next section we pursue an approach which, we believe, can do better on this count than the entitlement strategy just reviewed.

2.3.2. Constitutivist Hinge Epistemology and the Problem of Rational Inertia

In this section, we will assess the prospects for a solution to the problem of rational inertia that harnesses some of the main tenets of the constitutivist version of hinge epistemology developed in Coliva (2015). Constitutivist hinge epistemology is best seen as a systematic attempt to defeat a certain kind of Humean sceptic. The target Humean sceptic holds the following two theses: firstly, we have evidential warrants for ordinary empirical propositions, such as "Here is a hand";[8] secondly, we cannot empirically or a priori warrant general propositions, such as "There is an external world," which are entailed by ordinary ones. It has to be stressed that, contrary to the Wittgensteinian version of hinge epistemology, constitutivist hinge epistemology recognises as hinges only very general propositions, such as (WORLD) and (OBJECTS), that are constitutive of entire domains of discourse (such as physical objects) or that are constitutive of universal practices of acquiring evidence.

A constitutivist agrees with a Humean sceptic that warrants for ordinary propositions are possible thanks to a system of hinges which, as such, can neither be a priori/empirically justified, nor can be rationally held in virtue of unearned warrants which entitle us to trust them. However, a constitutivist points out that epistemic rationality is grounded in our epistemic practices, which are shared by both (Humean) sceptics and non-sceptics. These practices – for example, forming, revising, retaining, and evaluating

22 *Annalisa Coliva and Michele Palmira*

our beliefs based on sensory experience – do make sense only if certain hinges, such as "There is an external world," "Our sense organs are by and large reliable," stay put. Thus, by being conditions of possibility of our epistemic practices, such hinges are constitutive of epistemic rationality itself. Hence, it turns out that we are actually *mandated by epistemic rationality itself* to assume "There is an external world." Importantly, a rational mandate is not an epistemic warrant – namely, an epistemic good that speaks to the truth of what it is meant to warrant.

Our epistemic practices can be illuminated by an analogy with games with constitutive rules. Just as constitutive rules individuate a game for what it is and make it possible for us to play it, and just as both rules and moves are part of any game, both hinges and perceptual justifications are part of the "game" of giving reasons for forming, retaining, and revising our ordinary empirical beliefs in light of the experience we acquire through our senses.

Now, insofar as it is possible for this "game" to take place only if we assume that our senses are reliable and that there is an external world, a Humean sceptic is an epistemic agent who ultimately wants to play such a "game" while, at the same time, rejecting the very rule that constitutively defines it.

The constitutivist version of hinge epistemology provides us with a novel framework for systematising the problem of rational inertia. In particular, a constitutivist and a Humean sceptic agree on the claim that epistemic rationality is grounded in our practices. A constitutivist maintains that assuming hinges is constitutive of epistemic rationality and that hinges are therefore rational even though they are unwarrantable. By contrast, a Humean sceptic precisely denies this claim: for her hinges are not constitutive of epistemic rationality. This, together with the additional negative claim that hinges are not (a priori or empirically warrantable), leads a Humean sceptic to conclude that hinges are not rational. Thus, a constitutivist and a Humean sceptic might be taken to disagree on how we should explicate the very concept of epistemic rationality. More precisely, a Humean sceptic subscribes to the following (see Coliva 2015; 129–130):

Narrow Rationality: It is epistemically rational to believe only evidentially warranted propositions.

By contrast, a constitutivist holds the following:

Extended Rationality: It is epistemically rational to believe evidentially warranted propositions and to assume those unwarrantable propositions that make the acquisition of perceptual warrants possible in the first place and are therefore constitutive of ordinary evidential warrants.

Hinge Disagreement 23

As a consequence, a sceptic holds that the concept of epistemic rationality should be RATIONALITY$_{NARROW}$, whereas a constitutivist maintains that the concept of epistemic rationality should be RATIONALITY$_{EXTENDED}$.

This, on the face of it, appears to be a *conceptual* – as opposed to a merely *descriptive* – disagreement. Now, conceptual disagreements come in different fashions. For instance, two parties may be said to disagree if one of them uses a concept C, such that some object *a* falls within its extension, while the other refuses to do so, thereby denying that for any object *a*, *a* falls under C.[9] Alternatively, parties may agree with respect to the constitutive inferences that individuate a concept C, while disagreeing about some of its non-constitutive inferences.[10] Finally, they may disagree about the constitutive inferences that individuate a given concept C, thus ending up having different, although possibly partly overlapping concepts. We submit that the latter form of conceptual disagreement is the one relevant to the debate between a Humean sceptic and a constitutivist. While they do overlap on some constitutive inferences – they both hold that if a specific empirical proposition is perceptually justified, believing it would be epistemically rational – they diverge on the inference that would licence the application of the concept EPISTEMIC RATIONALITY to hinges. This, however, is a constitutive inference of RATIONALITY$_{extended}$. Hence a Humean sceptic and a constitutivist entertain this latter kind of conceptual disagreement.

Having clarified the nature of the conceptual disagreement amongst a constitutivist and a Humean sceptic we are in a better position to take up the problem of rational inertia. The disagreement indeed bears on the question of whether or not it is epistemically rational to assume hinges – that is, whether or not the concept of epistemic rationality should be RATIONALITY$_{EXTENDED}$ – in order to make sense of our first-order epistemic practices. As we see it, considerations about which concept of rationality, i.e. RATIONALITY$_{EXTENDED}$ or RATIONALITY$_{NARROW}$, is the best one are going to be considerations whereby the disagreement can be *rationally* resolved in one way or another. The dialectical situation is the following. A constitutivist will maintain that RATIONALITY$_{EXTENDED}$ is better than RATIONALITY$_{NARROW}$ for the latter cannot coherently account for the rationality of the practice, which a Humean sceptic engages in, since that practice would rest, by her lights, on arbitrary hinges. In contrast, a constitutivist can coherently account for the rationality of the practice and of the hinges which make it possible, since, thanks to RATIONALITY$_{EXTENDED}$ those hinges are themselves rational, even though unwarrantable.

The foregoing strikes us as a perfectly legitimate way in which a disagreement about hinges could be amenable to a rational resolution – one which favours a constitutivist position over a sceptical one. Thus, it seems that a constitutivist version of hinge epistemology can offer a

24 Annalisa Coliva and Michele Palmira

solution to the problem of rational inertia understood as the problem of how rationally to resolve disagreements over hinges.[11]

To reiterate, the conceptual disagreement between a constitutivist and a sceptic can be rationally resolved: insofar as both parties to the disagreement aim to account for our first-order practices, we had better prefer an explanation of the rationality of the practices which rests on rationally mandated, as opposed to merely arbitrary, hinges. It of course remains to be seen whether these considerations can offer a solution to the problem of rational inertia understood as the problem of how *rationally to persuade* the opposite party in a hinge disagreement. That is to say, the question is whether it is possible for the constitutivist to rationally persuade a sceptic to acknowledge that hinges such as "There is an external world" are rational, and therefore that the concept of rationality should be explicated by RATIONALITY$_{\text{EXTENDED}}$ and not by RATIONALITY$_{\text{NARROW}}$.

To be clear, the issue is not whether a constitutivist succeeds in the mission of actually convincing a sceptic that the concept of rationality should be understood in the extended way. Rather, the best way of looking at the problem of rational inertia *qua* problem of rational persuasion consists in asking whether or not the considerations offered by the constitutivist in favour of resolving the conceptual disagreement in a given way are such that they can be acknowledged as such by a sceptic and not simply dismissed as question-begging or utterly incomprehensible.

Bear it in mind that, according to the constitutivist version of hinge epistemology, the rationality of our practices would be left unexplained if it was meant to rest merely on arbitrary assumptions. This is what, ultimately, should move us towards explicating the concept of rationality via RATIONALITY$_{\text{EXTENDED}}$ and not via RATIONALITY$_{\text{NARROW}}$. That is to say, RATIONALITY$_{\text{EXTENDED}}$ is to be accepted in virtue of its superiority *vis-à-vis* RATIONALITY$_{\text{NARROW}}$ *qua* explanation of the rationality of our ordinary epistemic practice.

On the face of it, this is neither a dogmatic pattern of reasoning, nor does it rely on the existence of a mysterious species of epistemic justification. Hence a Humean sceptic could not object to the constitutivist explanation by retorting that it is question-begging, nor can a sceptic protest that it trades upon mysterious and seemingly *ad hoc* and *sui generis* species of warrant. This suggests that a Humean sceptic should face this disagreement head on and directly challenge the constitutivist claim that explicating the concept of rationality via RATIONALITY$_{\text{EXTENDED}}$ is the only way to coherently explain the rationality of our ordinary epistemic practice. The very fact that the only way a sceptic can resist this pattern of reasoning is by directly engaging with it, as opposed to simply dismissing it as either prejudicial or *ad hoc*, shows that the disagreement is not rationally inert even in a dialectical sense. Let us repeat the definition of rational persuasion we have accepted above:

Rational Persuasion: A rationally persuades B to adopt A's doxastic attitude D to p if and only if there is a set of premises accepted by A that A can appeal to in an argument that rationally ought to persuade B to adopt D towards p (and vice versa).

Surely the constitutivist's claim that the rationality of our practices would be left unexplained if it was meant to rest merely on arbitrary assumptions can feature as a premise in an argument that rationally ought to persuade a Humean sceptic into explicating the concept of rationality via RATIONALITY$_{\text{EXTENDED}}$. This shows that a Humean sceptic and a constitutivist can engage in a dispute over hinges that was out of the purview of the entitlement-based approach to hinge disagreement.

We have been focusing on the hinge disagreement between a constitutivist and a Humean sceptic concerning the correct explication of the concept of epistemic rationality. We have maintained that such a disagreement is not rationally inert by arguing that the constitutivist position is superior to the sceptic's position. This said, we deem it instructive to conclude our examination of the problem of rational inertia by touching upon an alternative stance to Humean scepticism that still gives rise to a disagreement with the constitutivist approach to epistemic rationality.

The present challenge is the one an epistemic relativist would press by noticing that there may be different notions of epistemic rationality with their constitutive hinges. In response, it is important to keep in mind that here we are considering hinges of epistemic rationality understood as a notion determined by the kind of epistemic practices human beings engage in. That is, practices of forming and revising beliefs about midsize physical objects based on the deliverances of our perceptions. Creatures who were altogether different in their epistemic practices – in the sense of forming justifications by utilizing different methods and for different kinds of propositions (i.e. not about physical objects), thus showing a commitment to different hinges – would likely defy conceivability in detail for creatures like us and would show little, if anything, of relevance to an understanding of *our* epistemic situation. Hence, insofar as such a challenge is worth exploring, it would have to deal with creatures like us, who use their senses to acquire perceptual justifications, yet subscribe to different hinges. A good example would be the one of idealists or perhaps phenomenalists. Their view is that the objects of experience are sense data and that physical objects are collections of sense data, hence they do not subscribe to the hinge that there are physical objects taken as mind-independent entities. However, this view has problems in explaining the objectivity of perceptual content. For it can be shown that our perceptions do not simply represent sense data that are then bound together by our conceptual repertoire to represent objects such as chairs, tables and so on. Furthermore, our perceptions are as of mind-independent objects that have certain physical

26 Annalisa Coliva and Michele Palmira

properties, and which appear to have them even when our proximal stimuli are not uniform.[12] Thus, an idealist or a phenomenalist will have to account for the objectivity of perception while, at the same time, maintaining that the sense data we are immediately aware of are not caused by external objects. We hold out little hope that this project can be successfully carried out.[13]

2.4. Conclusion

We have examined two problems that supporters of hinge epistemology have to face: the lost hinge disagreement problem and the problem of rational inertia. We have argued that we can make sense of there being genuine doxastic disagreement amongst individuals holding apparently incompatible hinges in a limited but epistemologically significant number of cases, that is, the cases in which two individuals assume hinges that act as conditions of possibility of representations and can be regarded as minimally true in a deflationary sense.

Focusing on precisely those hinges that can give rise to genuine doxastic disagreements, we have approached the problem of rational inertia, starting from how the entitlement-based version of hinge epistemology takes up such a problem. This view is saddled with an initial worry: insofar as entitlements appear to be pragmatic in kind, we would only have a pragmatic reason to assume hinges such as "There is an external world." Thus, no *epistemic* inertia would in the end be overcome. Moreover, given the unearned nature of such entitlements, it would be rationally impossible to make our entitlement to "there is an external world" available to the sceptic who precisely suspends judgement about such a hinge. Therefore, we would not be able to engage in a rational dispute with such a sceptic, thereby making our disagreement with her rationally inert all the same.

We have then developed a new approach to the problem of rational inertia, which deploys the resources of the constitutivist version of hinge epistemology. The first advantage of this approach is that it enables us to precisely locate the disagreement between a hinge epistemologist and a sceptic: the object of their disagreement is the question of how we should explicate the concept of rationality, granted that our ordinary epistemic practices are epistemically rational. The second advantage of the constitutivist approach is that the pattern of resolution of this conceptual disagreement is grounded in purely explanatory considerations: without appealing to the mysterious notion of "entitlement," and without dogmatic premises, a constitutivist maintains that the concept of rationality should be extended. Without this extension we would not be able to explain the overall rationality of our first-order practices. Thus the disagreement between a constitutivist and a sceptic is not rationally inert: first, a constitutivist offers a reason why we should take her explication of the concept of rationality to be superior to the sceptic's; and second, a sceptic cannot simply dismiss the constitutivist's stance as merely dogmatic or *ad hoc*, but must engage with the constitutivist pattern of reasoning head on and show where it fails.

Finally, in our view, the absence of potentially off-putting relativistic implications of this constitutivist way of dealing with the problem of rational inertia is to be seen as an additional motivation in favour of this approach to hinge disagreement.

Notes

1. Annalisa Coliva is mainly responsible for §§2.2 and 2.3.2 and Michele Palmira for §§2.1, and 2.3.1. The rest of the chapter has been written together.
2. Moyal-Sharrock (2005) has defended the anti-propositionalist reading of Wittgenstein's hinges. For a critical discussion, see Coliva (2010, Chapters 2 and 5).
3. Angle brackets are used to mention propositions.
4. Or, more mildly, it would count as a hinge only insofar as, until around 1969, it went *de facto* unchallenged, due to the unavailability of scientific and technological findings that would have made it possible to call it into question. The kinds of hinge we will be focusing on are the ones that cannot be challenged *de jure*. That is, without thereby renouncing an entire area of discourse and basic methods of enquiry. In the case of (MOON), moreover, the disagreement between opposite parties can now be resolved by appealing to empirical and testimonial evidence. This signals the fact that "Nobody has ever been on the Moon" is no longer a hinge for us, but an ordinary empirical proposition.
5. Of course, assumption, trust, and conviction (or visceral commitment) are different doxastic attitudes. While it is not our aim here to explore the differences between such attitudes, we do think that, ultimately, we had better take assumption to be the relevant type of doxastic attitude to be entertained towards hinges. For assumption does better than visceral conviction/commitment and trust in avoiding the risk of becoming a non-propositional and non-cognitive kind of attitude.
6. We are thus regimenting the use of "belief," which in ordinary language is extremely multifarious, going from holding P true with a justification, to merely having faith in something or even someone.
7. This is the kind of sceptic Wright focuses on. Key to this position is the idea that justification for ordinary empirical beliefs is not immediate and is possible only inasmuch as, besides a certain course of experience, the collateral assumption that there is an external world is warranted.
8. This is due to the fact that Coliva (2015) puts forward a moderate account of perceptual justification, according to which, in order to be perceptually justified to believe that P, it is enough to have a certain course of experience with a representational content that P, together with the assumption that there is an external world, absent defeaters. Hence, by a Humean sceptic's lights, we could have such a justification for ordinary empirical belies like "Here is a tree," yet none for the assumption that there is an external world that makes the acquisition of justification for those beliefs possible in the first place.
9. Stroud (2019) mentions the case of Oscar Wilde, who agreed that a given text was profane and disgusting but refused to call is "blasphemous" on the grounds that BLASPHEMOUS was not part of his conceptual repertoire.

28 *Annalisa Coliva and Michele Palmira*

Another case in point may be the one of a subject who thinks that some Germans are cruel (e.g. Hitler) while denying that Germans are boche, for she refuses to make use of that concept (since, by definition, it would entail that all Germans are cruel).

10. We are assuming here a molecularist account of concepts *à la* Dummett and Peacocke. Accordingly, concepts are individuated by some constitutive inferences. Molecularism stands opposed to both atomism *à la* Fodor and to holism *à la* Quine or Brandom. For a discussion of all these options, see Coliva (2006). An example would be a case in which two subjects agree on focal cases of red, while disagreeing on some at the fringe.
11. The same would hold in the case of (INDUCTION DISAGREEMENT).
12. These are known as perceptual constancies. For a discussion of their relevance to the objectivity of perceptual content, see Burge (2010).
13. For a more extensive treatment of this kind of relativism, see Coliva (2015, Chapter 4, §4) and Coliva (2019a). For a discussion of relativism and various kinds of hinge epistemology, see Coliva (2019b).

References

Burge, T. (2010), *Origins of Objectivity*, Oxford: Oxford University Press.

Coliva, A. (2006), *I Concetti: Teorie ed Esercizi*, Roma: Carocci.

———. (2010), *Moore and Wittgenstein: Scepticism, Certainty and Common Sense*, London: Palgrave Macmillan.

———. (2015), *Extended Rationality: A Hinge Epistemology*, London: Palgrave Macmillan.

———. (2018), "What Anti-Realism about Hinges Could Possibly Be?," in *Metaepistemology: Realism and Anti-Realism*, edited by C. Kyriacou and R. McKenna, London: Palgrave MacMillan, 267–288.

———. (2019a), "Hinges, Radical Skepticism, Relativism and Alethic Pluralism," in *Non Evidentialist Epistemology*, edited by L. Moretti and N. Pedersen, Leiden: Brill.

———. (2019b), "Relativism and Hinge Epistemology," in *Routledge Handbook of Philosophy of Relativism*, edited by M. Kusch, London and New York: Routledge.

Fogelin, R. (1985), "The Logic of Deep Disagreements," *Informal Logic* 7: 1–8.

Horwich, P. (1998), *Truth*, Oxford: Clarendon Press.

Jenkins, C. (2007), "Entitlement and Rationality," *Synthese* 157 (1): 25–45.

Kusch, M. (2018), "Disagreement, Certainties, Relativism," *Topoi*, doi: 10.1007/s11245-018-9567-z.

Lynch, M. (2009), *Truth as One and Many*, Oxford: Oxford University Press.

———. (2016), "After the Spade Turns: Disagreement, First Principles and Epistemic Contractarianism," *International Journal for the Study of Skepticism* 6: 248–259.

MacFarlane, J. (2014), *Assessment Sensitivity: Relative Truth and Its Applications*, Oxford: Oxford University Press.

Marques, T. (2014), "Doxastic Disagreement," *Erkenntnis* 79 (S1): 121–142.

Moyal-Sharrock, D. (2005), *Understanding Wittgenstein's On Certainty*, London: Palgrave Macmillan.

Neta, R. (2019), "An Evidentialist Account of Hinges," *Synthese*, doi: 10.1007/s11229-018-02061-0.

Palmira, M. (2017), "How to Be a Pluralist about Disagreement," in *Epistemic Pluralism*, edited by A. Coliva and N.J.L.L. Pedersen, London: Palgrave Macmillan, 285–316.

Pedersen, N.J. (2009), "Entitlement, Value, and Rationality," *Synthese* 171 (3): 443–457.

Pritchard, D. (2007), "Wittgenstein's On Certainty and Contemporary Anti-Scepticism," in *Readings of Wittgenstein's On Certainty*, edited by D. Moyal-Sharrock and W.H. Brenner, Basingstoke: Palgrave Macmillan, 189–224.

———. (2016), *Epistemic Angst*, Princeton, NJ: Princeton University Press

———. (2018), "Disagreement, of Belief and Otherwise," in *Voicing Dissent*, edited by C. Johnson, London: Routledge, 22–39.

Putnam, H. (1981), *Reason, Truth and History*, Cambridge: Cambridge University Press.

Ranalli, C. (2018), "Deep Disagreement and Hinge Epistemology," *Synthese*, doi: 10.1007/s11229-018-01956-2.

Stroud, S. (2019), "Conceptual Disagreement," *American Philosophical Quarterly* 56 (1): 15–28.

Wittgenstein, L. (1969), *On Certainty*, Oxford: Blackwell.

Worsnip, A. (2019), "Disagreement as Interpersonal Incoherence," *Res Philosophica* 96 (2): 245–268.

Wright, C. (1992), *Truth and Objectivity*, Cambridge, MA: Harvard University Press.

———. (2004), "Warrant for Nothing (and Foundations for Free)?," *Proceedings of Aristotelian Society, Supplementary Volume* 78 (1): 167–212.

———. (2013), "A Plurality of Pluralisms," in *Truth and Pluralism. Current Debates*, edited by N.J.L.L. Pedersen and C. Wright, Oxford: Oxford University Press, 123–153.

———. (2014), "On Epistemic Entitlement II: Welfare State Epistemology," in *Scepticism and Perceptual Justification*, edited by D. Dodd and E. Zardini, Oxford: Oxford University Press, 213–247.

3 Norms of Inquiry in the Theory of Justified Belief[1]

Sanford C. Goldberg

3.1. A Practice-Based Challenge to Orthodox Epistemology

Epistemic practices – the set of practices through which we pursue knowledge and justified belief – can vary widely by community and by historical epoch. This opens up the prospect of a route to epistemic relativism, wherein what counts as good epistemic practice is relative to the community one is in.

Such forms of relativism have traditionally been regarded as unpalatable within epistemological orthodoxy. Epistemology is in the business of evaluating belief (or credence) in terms of the subject's twin goals of acquiring true belief and avoiding error. The tradition – henceforth 'orthodox epistemology' – seeks to identify the types of factors that are relevant to such an evaluation. By the lights of orthodoxy, these include such things as the subject's evidence or reasons, as well as the reliability profile – or more generally the modal profile – of the type of processes she used in forming and sustaining her belief. More recently, some have proposed to expand this domain to include such things as the attributor's interests in the context of attribution (*attributor contextualism*) or to facts pertaining to S's practical situation, e.g. stakes (*pragmatic encroachment* views). But all of these views repudiate the suggestion that *a community's epistemic standards themselves* will be among the factors relevant to epistemic evaluation. This is true even for contextualists and pragmatic encroachers. While such theorists allow that variation in attributor interests or in a subject's practical situation produce variation in the standards a subject must meet if she is to count as knowing, articulating the standards themselves is seen as the exclusive remit of epistemological theorizing itself. In this the orthodox view is that community standards can have nothing to do with epistemology, at most they fall in the purview of anthropology, sociology, or history.

Recent work in epistemology has seen one important exception to this exclusion of community standards in epistemic evaluation. According to this exception, there is – or at any rate there can be – more than

Norms of Inquiry in the Theory of Justified Belief   31

one legitimate standard of rationality (or justification). In the contemporary literature in epistemology, this sort of position is perhaps most familiar in connection with the doctrine of *permissivism*. Permissivism itself is best understood as the denial of *uniqueness*, a view according to which for any body of evidence E and proposition that p, there is a single uniquely rational attitude to have towards p. Those who deny uniqueness, and so who think that epistemic standards are permissive, often appeal to variations in community standards, usually in combination with some minimal coherence requirements, as setting the range of legitimacy.[2] For this very reason, permissivism poses a threat to the orthodox consensus regarding the irrelevance of community standards to epistemic evaluation.

I will not be appealing to permissivism in the argument to follow. Instead, my interests lie instead with pursuing another, less appreciated line of argument for a (mildly) relativist conclusion. In addition to having no need for permissivism itself, the argument I will be developing has two additional selling points. First, the version of relativism that results is compatible with the idea that epistemology *and epistemology alone* is in charge of specifying epistemic standards. The relevance of the social is not in specifying the epistemic yardstick itself, but rather in specifying what I will be calling norms of inquiry. These clearly vary by community, and it will be my contention that intercommunity variation in such norms can affect epistemic evaluation. And this is the second selling point of the proposal on offer: the argument I will be developing aims to show how social norms – in particular, norms of inquiry (at least some of which I will construe as social norms) – bear on epistemic evaluation but in a way that should appeal even to those whose basic sympathies are to orthodoxy.

3.2. The Epistemic Significance of Norms of Inquiry

The theory of justified belief can be regarded as the theory responsible for articulating the standards for epistemically proper belief. Views abound: evidentialism, reliabilism, dogmatism, traditional internalist foundationalism, coherentism, etc. While I will try to remain neutral among the various options, I will be insisting that whatever the standards of epistemically proper belief are, they are *objective* in the sense that they do not depend on any particular person's (or group of people's) opinions as to what those standards are.

Theorists who work within orthodox epistemology typically distinguish the theory of justified belief from what we might call norms of inquiry more generally: the set of standards and procedures that govern how one ought to inquire, including but not limited to the evidence one ought to have in one's possession, the sources one ought to consult, the

32 Sanford C. Goldberg

tests one ought to perform, the procedures one ought to follow, and so forth.[3] In this respect, epistemology proper, as conceived in this orthodox tradition, only cares to evaluate the state of belief (or credence) itself, not the process of inquiry through which one came to be in this state. To be sure, not all orthodox epistemology is committed to what Alvin Goldman called "time-slice" epistemology: epistemic externalists, for example, are interested in the causal pedigree of a belief (including the cognitive process through which it was formed and sustained). Even so, orthodox epistemology is committed to a highly restricted view of the materials relevant to epistemic assessment: they restrict their attention to the cognitive processes operating in the epistemic subject in the immediate interval leading up to the formation and sustainment of the belief itself.[4] Since the norms pertaining to how to conduct inquiry go beyond this, even externalists will insist that such norms are simply irrelevant to epistemic assessment.

I find this narrow epistemic focus rather curious. It is not that I have anything against the sort of evaluation that orthodox epistemology recommends *per se*. Rather, I find it curious that epistemology should restrict its attention *exclusively* to this – with the corollary being that nothing else can ever be of any epistemic significance whatsoever. To appreciate the curiosity, consider a case in which S is currently in possession of good evidence for p, but where S failed to satisfy the prevailing norms of inquiry (relevant to the question whether p). We might wonder what effect, if any, S's failure has on the epistemic evaluation of her belief. Anyone who endorses the corollary above is committed to thinking that S's failure to satisfy the prevailing norms of inquiry can have no epistemic significance whatsoever on the epistemic evaluation of her belief that p. To be sure, orthodox epistemologists need not deny that S might be subject to *some* form of censure for failing to have satisfied the norms of inquiry. Perhaps S was professionally deficient, or deficient as an expert or as a scientist, or ethically deficient, or. ... But whatever the nature of this censure, it can have no relevance to epistemic evaluation itself.[5]

Prima facie, this should strike us as curious. After all, the norms of inquiry bear on our attempts to acquire true belief (while avoiding error), and epistemology aims to assess, for a given belief, how well we did in this regard. In this light, it should seem curious that the fact that one failed to follow the norms of inquiry has *no possible effect* on the epistemic evaluation of one's resulting belief. This sense of curiosity can be reinforced by reflecting on the role that the norms of inquiry play in rationalizing our epistemic reliance on others. We rely on others for a good deal of what we know, and we often do so precisely because of their recognized profession or expertise in a given domain. When this is so, we presume that they are conforming to whatever norms of inquiry prevail in the relevant profession or expert community. This presumption underwrites a core part of the rationale for the division of intellectual labor itself. The thought that an expert can fail to conform

Norms of Inquiry in the Theory of Justified Belief 33

to relevant norms of expertise in connection with her belief that p, and yet suffer no epistemic demerit for that belief, can strike us as peculiar.

How might an orthodox epistemologist respond to my allegation that orthodox views have this curious result? One response would be to deny the allegation itself. After all, orthodox epistemology will evaluate the expert's belief in terms of her evidence; failing to follow the norms of inquiry will have an effect on the evidence she has, so this will be reflected in the corresponding justifiedness verdict. Our orthodox epistemologist might go further, attempting to offer an explanation of the value of norms of inquiry as follows: when the norms of inquiry are sound, conforming to them will result in better epistemic outcomes than failing to do so, since in the former case one will have more (and presumably better) evidence on the matter at hand.

Such a view is good as far as it goes, but it does not go far enough. If non-experts' expectation[6] that the experts themselves[7] live up to the relevant norms of inquiry does not bear at all on the epistemic evaluation of experts' beliefs, what role can the norms of inquiry themselves be seen as playing in shaping the practices in which we rely on experts and professionals? Here it seems to me that the best our proponent of orthodox epistemology can do is to describe two indirect types of relevance, one in connection with a non-expert's reliance on experts, the other in connection with would-be experts interacting with one another. I will take these up in order.

Take a case in which a non-expert S wants to know whether p, where this is something S recognizes to fall within a given expert domain. On the orthodox account of the norms of inquiry, these norms can be used by the non-expert as she attempts to discern who the experts are. S might try to assess whether a given candidate is an actual expert by trying to discern how well the individual satisfies the norms in question. This will put some practical pressure on would-be experts to live up to the norms of their expertise: insofar as a would-be expert manifestly does not live up to those norms, this increases the chance that she will not be taken to be an expert. Here, the norms of inquiry do not really bear on the would-be expert's beliefs *per se*, though their existence might put practical pressure on her, and in this way might inspire her to aim to satisfy the norms (so as to be reasonably taken by others to be an expert).[8]

Next consider how the norms of inquiry (or of expertise) figure in to how would-be experts interact with one another. Insofar as a community of experts has norms that govern how they ought to inquire, we might think of the members as forming a self-governing epistemic community. Perhaps the members will regularly check up on one another (all of them tending to their common epistemic garden);[9] or perhaps some in the community will be ascribed the role of epistemic policing, making sure that the others live up to community standards. In either case, so long as a given member encounters some other member(s) who will ensure

34 Sanford C. Goldberg

that the norms are being satisfied, all goes well. When one member of the expert community encounters another who is failing to satisfy the norms, the former can then take action in an attempt to motivate compliance. Insofar as the noncompliant is *told* of her non-compliance, she has a potential defeater for those beliefs whose formation violated the relevant norms.[10] This would be a way in which the norms of inquiry themselves have a potential (indirect) bearing on the epistemic evaluation of the beliefs of the noncompliant. Alternatively, a second sort of action that might be taken against the noncompliant would be to shun him or her from the community itself. If the shunning were manifest even to those outside the community, this would decrease the chance that the noncompliant would be relied upon as an expert. Here, while the norms of inquiry have no bearing on the epistemic evaluation of the noncompliant's beliefs, the threat of shunning might serve as yet another practical motivation to conform to those norms.

I think that both of these practices – those in connection with non-expert reliance on experts, and those in connection with expert–expert exchanges – can and do play some role in reinforcing norm compliance among the experts themselves. But as an account of how the norms of inquiry relate to the theory of justified belief, the picture remains incomplete. It leaves too much to chance and so yields incorrect verdicts of justifiedness in a range of cases. One illustration will serve to make the point. (I will make the point in terms of evidence, but the same point can be made using whatever materials one takes to be relevant to justification.) Suppose that EX1 is an expert whose total evidence at time t_1 is E. Suppose that, by the lights of orthodox epistemology, this evidence suffices at t_1 to justify EX1's belief that p. But suppose that EX1 did not satisfy all of the norms of inquiry, so that there is further evidence he should have had. Suppose too that had EX1 gotten this evidence, his belief that p would not have been justified.[11] And finally suppose that EX1 does not encounter any other expert who makes EX1 aware of this fact. Orthodox epistemology is then committed to the verdict that EX1's belief that p is justified at t_1 (since this is supported by his total evidence at t_1). But this seems wrong; at the very least, at t_1 EX1's belief that p does not have the sort of epistemic credentials that those who rely on EX1 as an expert would be entitled to expect.[12]

In fact, we can make things seem even worse for orthodox epistemology in this regard. Suppose that EX2 is another expert who, like EX1, has E as her total evidence at t_1, and who also on this basis believes that p at t_1. (So by hypothesis EX2's belief that p is justified at t_1.) Suppose that EX3 is another expert in this domain who knows that EX2 does not have all of the evidence she ought to have, and so at t_2 EX3 tells EX2 of the existence of such counterevidence. Then at t_3 (immediately after t_2) EX2's belief that p is not justified. Yet because EX1 did not encounter

Norms of Inquiry in the Theory of Justified Belief 35

EX3, EX1's belief that p continues to be justified. And so it seems that orthodox epistemology will render these two verdicts:

At t_3 EX1's belief that p is justified;
At t_3 EX2's belief that p is not justified.

But I submit that when it comes to whether p, at t_3 EX1 is no more to be relied on than is EX2. This impression is not gainsaid by the fact that EX2 happened to encounter another expert, EX3, who told her of the further evidence she should have. In short, orthodox epistemology's use of 'justified belief' does not track those expert beliefs which are to be relied upon.

The lesson I want to draw from this is a general one: orthodox epistemology dismisses the relevance of the norms of inquiry to the theory of justified belief only at the cost of a notion of justified belief that doesn't do one of the jobs we should want it to do – namely, indicate which expert beliefs are those to be relied on. If I am right about this, then, at least when it comes to expert and professional communities, the norms of inquiry are more intimately related to the theory of justified belief than orthodox epistemology recognizes. Precisely how to see the relationship between them is the topic of the next two sections.

3.3. How Not to Incorporate the Norms of Inquiry Into the Theory of Justified Belief

For those who are unhappy with orthodox epistemology's wholesale dismissal of the relevance of norms of inquiry to the theory of justified belief, how might we propose to see the two as related? In this section, I consider and reject an alternative answer to this question. According to this view, *necessarily, if S violates one or more relevant norms of inquiry in the process that eventuates in her belief that p, then the belief that p is epistemically unjustified.*[13]

I reject such a view, for two reasons. First, it is hard to see how one might motivate the targeted view save by endorsing a broadly deontological approach to epistemic justification.[14] According to epistemic deontologism, justification is a matter of satisfying all of the relevant rules – alternatively, fulfilling all of one's epistemic duties – in connection with belief-formation. Unfortunately, deontologism regarding epistemic justification is a view with a seriously troubled history.

My second (more substantial) objection to the targeted view is that it makes false predictions of unjustifiedness. One circumstance in which it will do so is when a community's norms of inquiry are themselves epistemically suspect. Consider a community whose members take it as proper to consult bird entrails (and as improper to fail to consult such entrails) when attempting to divine the weather. And suppose further that there

36 Sanford C. Goldberg

are community-wide rules for the interpretation of the entrails. Such an attitude informs their views as to how inquiry ought to proceed: they praise those who so consult (and who do so in conformity with the rules), and they condemn those who do not. Imagine that Sam is an emerging scientific meteorologist in this community whose weather predictions, though not based on the consultation of bird entrails, are highly reliable. I submit that the mere fact that he fails to satisfy the norms of inquiry of his community does not, *ipso facto*, render his weather predictions unjustified.

It might be thought that the targeted view can avoid this result if it restricts norms of inquiry to those that are epistemically legitimate (e.g. reliability-enhancing). But this is not so: it will make false predictions of justifiedness even in some cases in which the norms themselves are epistemically legitimate. Suppose Martha is on a research team in which it is a norm of inquiry for each member to perform by herself a time-consuming literature search every two months, with the aim of determining whether there are any new developments bearing on the team's research program, in which case one is to report it at the bimonthly team meeting. Martha regularly does this. But one month a highly reliable friend tells her that there have been no new developments that month. Since it is burdensome to do the literature search, and since she has excellent reason to trust her friend, she decides to take her friend's word for it; on this basis she comes to believe that there have been no new developments this month. In fact, her friend's testimony was knowledgeable. In that case it is plausible to think that Martha's belief (that there have been no new developments this month) is justified, despite her having violated the norm to do the literature search herself.

I have been arguing against the view according to which, *necessarily, if S violates one or more relevant norms of inquiry in the process that eventuates in her belief that p, then S's belief that p is epistemically unjustified.* If I am correct about this, then in effect the mere fact of having violated a relevant norm of inquiry does not render one's belief unjustified. Combining this result with our result from Section 3.2, we might summarize the discussions by saying that violations of relevant norms of inquiry can, but need not, result in the loss of justification. The remaining question is: under what conditions do they do so?

3.4. The Doctrine of Epistemic Strict Liability

I propose to approach this question by assuming that evidence is the material that determines justifiedness, and that the standard for evidential justification is both objective and invariant.[15] On the assumption that evidence is what determines the justificatory status of belief, we have an explanation for why the mere failure to satisfy the norms of inquiry, by itself, does not constitute unjustifiedness: the claim that there has been such a failure is not a claim about one's evidence, so,

Norms of Inquiry in the Theory of Justified Belief   37

since evidence is what determines (degree of) justifiedness, the claim that there has been such a failure is not a claim about the (degree of) justifiedness of one's belief. What is more, we have a way to approach the question of justifiedness itself: we can do so by seeing how one's failure to satisfy the norms of inquiry affects one's evidential situation. That is, for any case in which one failed to satisfy relevant norms of inquiry, we need to determine (i) what evidence one would have acquired had one satisfied the relevant norms, and (ii) how the evidence one would have acquired would bear on the justifiedness of one's belief that p.

With this as background, I am in a position to account for the relationship between the norms of inquiry and the theory of justified belief. I do so in terms of the notion of *epistemic strict liability*, which is spelled out in terms of the following two claims:

Epistemic Strict Liability

Failure to satisfy relevant norms of inquiry in relation to one's belief that p places one in a context of *epistemic strict liability* with respect to one's belief that p.

Liability Downgrade

If one is in a context of epistemic strict liability with respect to one's belief that p, then one's belief that p is unjustified when (a) one would have had further evidence relevant to one's belief that p if one would have satisfied the norms of inquiry, and (b) one's belief that p would not have been justified if one had had that evidence (holding all else, including the rest of one's evidence, fixed).

The account I wish to defend consists of the conjunction of EPISTEMIC STRICT LIABILITY and LIABILITY DOWNGRADE, together with the further assumption that these are the *only* two claims connecting the norms of inquiry to the theory of justified belief. In what follows I will spell out and defend this account.

To begin, the account itself delivers what I regard as proper verdicts across a range of cases. For one thing, it does *not* imply that failing to satisfy the norms of inquiry, by itself, has any downgrading effect on the justificatory status of one's belief. On the contrary, the account implies that whether one's failure to satisfy the norms of inquiry results in an epistemic downgrade is a function of the evidence one would have had if one had satisfied those norms.

In addition, insofar as EPISTEMIC STRICT LIABILITY and LIABILITY DOWNGRADE are the only two claims connecting the norms of inquiry to the theory of justified belief, there will be no way for evidence one should have had to *enhance* the justifiedness of one's belief. Suppose for example that, relative to one's belief that p (formed on the basis of evidence E), one ought to have had additional evidence E+, but that

38 *Sanford C. Goldberg*

E+ would only have enhanced the degree of justification of one's belief that p. Even so, one doesn't benefit from this: neither EPISTEMIC STRICT LIABILITY nor LIABILITY DOWNGRADE provide for a liability *enhancement*, and these are the only two claims connecting the norms of inquiry to the theory of justified belief. This is a happy result, since, while it is plausible to think that your failing to have evidence you should have had can hurt the epistemic standing of your belief, it is not plausible to think that your failing to have evidence you should have had can enhance the epistemic standing of your belief.[16]

Still, it is one thing to say that this account delivers happy verdicts; it is another to provide independent grounds for endorsing the account itself. (Lacking such grounds, the account itself might be accused of being tailor-made to accommodate the data – hardly an achievement.) But I believe that the account on offer can be independently motivated by appeal to the normativity of knowledge and justification. Since this was the theme of my most recent book (Goldberg 2018), here my remarks will be brief.

Knowledge is a normative standing in at least two senses, one evaluative and one prescriptive. Knowledge is a normative standing in the *evaluative* sense in that it involves satisfying standards for proper belief-formation.[17] Arguably, these standards are the subject-matter of the theory of epistemic justification. Knowledge is a normative standing in the *prescriptive* sense in that it involves conforming to legitimate (normative) expectations others are entitled to have of us as epistemic subjects. (These expectations are grounded in our nature as social beings, whose sociality includes the practices by which we acquire, evaluate, preserve, and transmit information.) Corresponding to the claim asserting others' legitimate expectations of us is a claim asserting the requirement on us as epistemic subjects to conform to these expectations.

Both the theory of justified belief and the norms of inquiry are, or give rise to, a species of these expectations. We can get at the content of these expectations, as well as appreciate our entitlement to them, in terms of our fundamental aims as believers. As William James noted, there are two: when we form beliefs, we aim to believe what is true and to avoid error. In this respect, our engagements with others give rise to expectations as to how others manage their corpus of beliefs: when we engage with others, we expect them to have beliefs befitting those aims. This is so whether our engagements are practical – as when we engage in coordinated and cooperative behavior with others, where the truth or falsity of others' beliefs can affect the success of our coordinated efforts – or theoretical – as when we rely on one another for information about the world, where the truth or falsity of others' beliefs typically affect what they attest to, and so affect how they (try to) shape our beliefs. In these terms, the theory of justified belief can be seen as capturing the expectations we have of other epistemic subjects merely in virtue of their status as epistemic subjects (and so as potential interlocutors and cooperators).

Norms of Inquiry in the Theory of Justified Belief 39

And the norms of inquiry can be seen as the expectations grounded in the various social practices we engage in as we seek to acquire and distribute knowledge – including the practices of professions whose status depends on their specialized knowledge, as well as the practices of experts in any domain in which expertise is a socially-recognized phenomenon.[18]

With this as my background, I am now in a position to defend the account above in terms of the normativity of knowledge and justification, so understood. Here we have three claims to defend: EPISTEMIC STRICT LIABILITY; LIABILITY DOWNGRADE; and the claim that these two principles are the *only* two claims connecting the norms of inquiry to the theory of justified belief. According to EPISTEMIC STRICT LIABILITY, failure to satisfy relevant norms of inquiry in relation to one's belief that p places one in a context of epistemic strict liability with respect to one's belief that p. Such contexts are ones in which LIABILITY DOWNGRADE holds: one's belief that p is unjustified when (a) one would have had further evidence relevant to one's belief that p if one would one have satisfied the (expectations corresponding to the) norms of inquiry, and (b) one's belief that p would not have been justified if one had had that evidence (holding all else fixed). Taken together, these two principles capture the idea that if, in the course of forming or sustaining one's belief that p, one violates one or more of the relevant expectations constituting (or corresponding to) the norms of inquiry, one is answerable (for the justification of one's belief) to the evidence one would have had if one had conformed.

This picture can be defended as follows. The standards of epistemic justification are the standards for epistemically proper belief, where this is a matter of the expectations that others are entitled to have of one as an epistemic subject. Since these standards are the standards of epistemology, they can only take into account the type of materials that make for a belief's epistemic goodness. Here I have been assuming that these materials consist exclusively of evidence. To say that one's belief that p is justified, then, is to imply that one's evidence – the total evidence currently in one's possession – is sufficient to render one's belief proper from the epistemic point of view. Helping ourselves to (one) a notion of evidential support and (two) a standard (threshold) above which one's evidential support for p is sufficient to justify one's belief that p, we can then say the following: one's belief that p is justified just in the case that one's total evidence adequately supports the belief that p, *and* there is no further evidence which one should have had and which (if one had it) would prevent one's expanded total evidence from adequately supporting the belief that p. This, I submit, can be motivated by appeal to the claim that it captures what we are entitled to expect of one another in the way of (evidence-based) belief. In this manner 'justified belief' captures a normative standing a belief enjoys when it is the sort of belief on which others can rely.

40 *Sanford C. Goldberg*

One claim remains to be defended: the claim that EPISTEMIC STRICT LIABILITY and LIABILITY DOWNGRADE are the *only* two claims connecting the norms of inquiry to the theory of justified belief. Orthodox epistemology endorses an account of epistemic assessment in which the relevant epistemic materials are those in the subject's possession at the time of assessment. If we assume (as I have been) that the only materials consist of evidence, then this account holds that epistemic assessment is a matter of assessing an individual's beliefs in terms of the evidence in her possession at the time of assessment. If we help ourselves to (one) a notion of evidential support and (two) a standard (threshold) above which one's evidential support for p is sufficient to justify one's belief that p, the picture put forward by orthodox epistemology is this: one's total evidence is sufficient to render one's belief proper from the epistemic point of view so long as one's total evidence meets the threshold for justification.

I have embraced this approach, with one caveat: there are cases in which there is evidence one should have had – evidence which one would have had if one had conformed to all relevant norms of inquiry – and this additional evidence can defeat one's justification in a case in which the evidence in one's possession is otherwise adequate. I have defended this divergence from the orthodox approach above by appeal to the normativity of knowledge and justification. Insofar as one endorses a *further* divergence from orthodox epistemology, the burden is on one to justify one's proposal. Absent such a justification, we ought to assume that the divergence I've defended is the only divergence from orthodox epistemology. This is (weak) support for the idea that EPISTEMIC STRICT LIABILITY and LIABILITY DOWNGRADE are the *only* two claims connecting the norms of inquiry to the theory of justified belief.

But we can say more. It seems that any further deviation from orthodoxy will be hard to justify. For one thing, we have already seen a reason to resist any attempt to defend a view in which there can be *enhancements* in one's epistemic position in contexts of epistemic strict liability. For another, insofar as we think of knowledge and justification as normative statuses, it is hard to see how else we might affect the justificatory status of one's belief, save in the ways mentioned above (and for the reasons given). While none of these considerations are knock-down proof that our two principles are the only relevant ones, they do offer reasons to think that they are. In this chapter I will have to be satisfied with that.

3.5. A Mild Relativism

The time has come, finally, to characterize the (mild) relativistic implications of the picture on offer. I begin by distinguishing three types of case. *Type 1*: S forms the belief that p on the basis of her total evidence E. E provides adequate support for p, so that (at least by the lights of orthodox

Norms of Inquiry in the Theory of Justified Belief   41

epistemology) S's belief that p is justified. In addition, there are no relevant norms of inquiry which S failed to satisfy in connection with her belief that p. I will describe this sort of case as of the 'happy ordinary' type. (It is *happy* in that the ultimate verdict is one of 'justified belief,' and it is *ordinary* in that this type of case involves no unsatisfied norms of inquiry.) *Type 2*: This is just like Type 1, except that there *are* relevant norms of inquiry which S failed to satisfy in connection with her belief that p. Happily, had S satisfied them, she would have acquired additional evidence which, when added to E (resulting in E+), would have had no negative impact on S's belief that p. Cases like this I will describe as scenarios of the 'happy missing evidence' type. (They are of the *missing evidence* type since there is evidence which S should have had but doesn't, owing to her failure to have satisfied all relevant norms of inquiry.) *Type 3*: This is like Type 2, except that the additional evidence would have defeated the justification enjoyed by S's belief that p. Cases like this I will describe as scenarios of the 'unhappy missing evidence' type. (They are *unhappy* in that the ultimate verdict is one of 'unjustified belief.')

To make the case for relativism, it suffices to note that there can be a subject who, depending on which norms of inquiry are in play, is either in a Type 1 case or a Type 3 case – with the result that whether her belief is justified depends on, and in this sense is relative to, which set of norms is in play. To this end, suppose that Sanchez, with her evidence E and belief that p, is in a scenario of the ordinary happy type. So Sanchez's belief that p, based on E, is justified. Now imagine that Sanchez has a doppelganger – call her Sanchez* – who is in a community with norms of inquiry other than those in Sanchez's community. And suppose that Sanchez* fails to fulfill some of the norms of inquiry relevant to her belief that p, with the result that she is in a scenario of the unhappy missing evidence type. So Sanchez*'s belief that p, based (like Sanchez's) on E, is *un*justified. But by hypothesis the only difference between Sanchez and Sanchez* are the norms of inquiry that are relevant to them. We might then say that if Sanchez were in Sanchez*'s community (and were subject to the norms of inquiry to which Sanchez* is subject), then, leaving everything else as is, Sanchez's belief that p would be unjustified. In sum, Sanchez's belief that p is justified relative to the norms of inquiry to which she is subject in *her* community, but not relative to the norms of inquiry to which she would be subject if she were in *Sanchez*'s* community. It seems that we have a route to a kind of relativism about justification that proceeds through the relevant norms of inquiry.

The foregoing assumes that Sanchez and Sanchez* are in precisely the same evidential situation, both possessing E, despite the fact that they have different norms of inquiry that bear on them. Is this plausible? One might worry that insofar as there are different norms of inquiry in play, they will be aware of this fact, in which case they will *not* be

42 Sanford C. Goldberg

in the same evidential situation. To this I have two replies, one more concessive, one less concessive.

My more concessive reply is to grant my objector's allegation of a difference in their evidential situation, but to argue that this does not undermine my conclusion. Suppose I believe that p on the basis of E. Now add to E my evidence for thinking that there are relevant norms of inquiry that I have not satisfied. Even so, if I have no evidence to think that my failure to have satisfied these norms puts the justification of my belief that p into jeopardy, then adding this additional evidence to E will have no epistemic effect on my belief that p. If this is so, then we can stipulate (as part of the thought experiment) that, while Sanchez and Sanchez* differ in that they are each aware of the (different) norms of inquiry that bear on themselves, even so, neither of them has any evidence to think that their failure to fulfill those norms puts the justification of their respective beliefs that p in jeopardy. In such a scenario, we still have a relativistic conclusion: that part of their belief corpus that affects the justification of their beliefs is the same, yet their justificatory status is not, owing to the fact that there are different norms in play.

Against this concessive reply, it might be argued that one who believes that there are norms of inquiry one hasn't satisfied *ipso facto* has a reason to think that there is further relevant evidence out there, and so has a reason to worry that such evidence might put the justification of one's belief that p in jeopardy. In response, it is worth noting that my case depends on the mere *possibility* of a case of the sort I've described. Thus it seems that it is my opponent, rather than me, who is in a dialectically precarious position on this score.

This brings me to my less concessive reply. My argument can be made so long as it is possible to imagine a subject who is in an unhappy missing evidence scenario – Type 3 – but who is unaware of the fact that there is a relevant norm of inquiry she failed to fulfill. I submit that this is indeed possible. As finite creatures we are not always aware of all of the norms to which we are subject. ("Ignorance of the law is no excuse.") Norms of inquiry are no exception. To imagine a concrete case, take a professional who is highly responsible and who is generally aware of all of the professional norms of inquiry that bear on her but who, through no fault of her own, non-culpably fails to be aware of one such norm. The fact that she is non-culpably unaware of the professional norm of inquiry does not mean that she is not subject to the norm, though it may offer her some sort of excuse from not having satisfied it. But even if she is blameless in her violation of the norm, she is still subject to the epistemic effects of the violation. And insofar as this is imaginable,[19] the sort of case needed by my argument is possible, and the conclusion stands.

I conclude, then, that a case for a mild kind of relativism can be made by appeal to the normativity of knowledge and justification. I regard this relativism as mild for several reasons. First, it is consistent with the idea

Norms of Inquiry in the Theory of Justified Belief 43

that the standards of justification are objective: these standards do not depend on what any particular person thinks the standards are. Second, it is consistent with the idea that the standards of justification are truth-conducive: satisfying these standards objectively increases the chances that one's belief is true (in comparison with cases in which the standards are not satisfied). Third, the resulting relativism is consistent with the idea that the standards are thoroughly epistemic in nature, and that it is the remit of epistemology *and epistemology alone* to characterize them: in the case I've considered, it is only evidence that bears on the justificatory status of one's beliefs. Fourth, the resulting relativism is consistent with the idea that the standards are invariant: there is a single threshold of adequacy for justification, and one's belief is justified so long as the relevant evidence meets that threshold. Finally, there are reasons to think that what I will call *differential relativistic verdicts* themselves – verdicts asserting that a given subject S's belief that p is justified with respect to (the norms of inquiry in) community C1 but not justified with respect to (the norms of inquiry in) community C2 – will be highly uncommon. Such differential relativistic verdicts arise only when several distinct conditions are met: C1 and C2 must be such that they differ in the norms of inquiry they impose on their members, where these differences are relevant to the belief that p; each of the norms of inquiry satisfies the (reliability) constraints on legitimacy (for which see earlier); following the norms of inquiry of C1 would result in S's acquiring evidence in C1 that is different from the evidence she would acquire in C2 were she to follow the norms of C2; and this difference of evidence must make a difference, so that the addition of the evidence S would acquire in C1 to the evidence S already has would have differential effects on the justification of S's belief than would the addition of the evidence S would acquire in C2 were *it* added to the evidence S already has. While these conditions can be jointly satisfied, this will be rare.

Still, it is easy to appreciate how there can be such cases. Imagine a detective, Smith, who is a member of a detective agency whose detectives are expected to send all of the materials that require scientific analysis (genetic materials, fingerprint identification, etc.) to the Acme company for analysis as a double-check for the in-house analysis they initially do themselves. And imagine Jones who is a detective at another detective agency whose detectives are only expected to analyze all of *their* materials in-house (there is no double-checking policy there). Since Acme uses different techniques than those used by the in-house teams in the two detective agencies, it can happen that, on occasion, Acme's method delivers different results. (Acme's method is a bit more reliable even, as it is much more expensive to perform.) Now suppose that both Smith and Jones believe that the blood found at the crime scene belongs to The Joker, and that they both do so on the basis of having analyzed the blood in their respective detective agencies. At this point both have

44 Sanford C. Goldberg

precisely the same (adequate) evidence in support of the hypothesis that the blood is The Joker's (namely, the results from the same type of in-house analysis). But Smith neglects to send in the blood to Acme for further analysis, and if he had, he would have gotten a different verdict on the blood sample. Then we have a case in which both Smith and Jones have the same evidence for their belief that the blood is the Joker's, but only Jones' belief is justified. We can say the same thing by saying that the belief is justified relative to the norms of inquiry of Jones' agency, but not relative to the norms of inquiry of Smith's agency. This is a case in which the previously mentioned conditions are all met.

3.6. Conclusion

In this chapter I have tried to bring out the basis for a mild form of epistemic relativism by appeal to the relationship between the norms of inquiry and the theory of justified belief. I defended this relationship in terms of the normativity of knowledge and justification. What is noteworthy about my argument is that it reaches its (mild) relativistic conclusion in a way that avoids assuming that the very standards of rationality are themselves culturally variable.

Notes

1. With thanks to the members of the audience at Martin Kusch's "Relativism" conference at the University of Vienna, 23–25 May 2019. Special thinks to Martin Kusch, Natalie Alana Ashton, and Alessandra Tanesini for their extensive comments on an earlier version.
2. See, for example, Schoenfield (forthcoming, 2014).
3. Typically, but not always: there are versions of virtue epistemology (e.g. Zagzebski 1996) and feminist epistemology (e.g. Longino 2001) that have long acknowledged the role of the norms of inquiry in epistemic assessment; and arguably – though this is nowhere made explicit – there is a role within a Drestke-style *relevant alternatives* approach to knowledge for considerations pertaining to the norms of inquiry, as these might determine which alternatives need to be ruled out. (With thanks to Alessandra Tanesini and Max Kölbel.)
4. In this respect, I am not part of orthodoxy: see Goldberg (2010).
5. For an expression of this view, see Feldman (2004).
6. Our expectation here is a normative one, not a predictive one.
7. In what follows I will be speaking of experts, not professionals, but what I have to say about the former goes, *mutatis mutandis*, for the latter.
8. Compare to Paul Faulkner's (2011) and Peter Graham's (2015, forthcoming) suggestion how the existence of social norms might encourage people to exhibit greater reliability in their statements.
9. This metaphor was suggested to me by Lisa Miracchi, in conversation.
10. For a recent treatment of defeaters in epistemology, see Brown (2018). For an earlier discussion of normative defeat, see Lackey (1999).

11. It might be wondered how EX1's total evidence E can justify his belief that p despite the fact that he did not satisfy the relevant norms of inquiry. But we can imagine that EX1 was non-culpably ignorant of this fact, and that E justifies the belief that p.
12. The entitlement here is a normative one, reflecting EX1's status as an expert in a domain in which expertise is recognized.
13. To a first approximation, we will understand a violation of a norm of inquiry as 'relevant' just in case S wouldn't have formed the belief that p if she hadn't violated that norm.
14. For a recent defense of a modified version of such a view, see Peels (2017, Appendix).
15. The account to follow can be formulated, albeit perhaps with added bells and whistles, using any of the main accounts in orthodox epistemology. For discussion, see Goldberg (2018).
16. I defend this claim at length in Goldberg (2017).
17. For recent work on this (albeit from a different theoretical orientation within epistemology than the one endorsed here), see Miracchi (2015a, 2015b).
18. It also includes the social practices that arise between people in virtue of their relationships to one another (friendship, neighbors, etc.). See Goldberg (2018).
19. See Goldberg (2018), where I discuss several cases of this sort. I call them cases of the "blameless *should have known* variety."

Literature

Brown, J. (2018), *Fallibilism*, Oxford: Oxford University Press.

Faulkner, P. (2011), *Knowledge on Trust*, Oxford: Oxford University Press.

Feldman, R. (2004), "The Ethics of Belief," in *Evidentialism*, edited by E. Conee and R. Feldman, Oxford: Oxford University Press, 66–195.

Goldberg, S. (2010), *Relying on Others: An Essay in Epistemology*, Oxford: Oxford University Press.

———. (2017), "The Asymmetry Thesis and the Doctrine of Normative Defeat," *American Philosophical Quarterly* 54: 339–351.

———. (2018), *To the Best of Our Knowledge: Social Expectations and Epistemic Normativity*, Oxford: Oxford University Press.

Graham, P. (2015), "Epistemic Normativity and Social Norms," in *Epistemic Evaluation: Purposeful Epistemology*, edited by D. Henderson and J. Greco, Oxford: Oxford University Press, 247–273.

———. (forthcoming), "The Function of Assertion and Social Norms," in *The Oxford Handbook of Assertion*, edited by S. Goldberg, Oxford: Oxford University Press.

Lackey, J. (1999), "Testimonial Knowledge and Transmission," *Philosophical Quarterly* 49: 471–490.

Longino, H. (2001), *The Fate of Knowledge*, Princeton: Princeton University Press.

Miracchi, L. (2015a), "Competence to Know," *Philosophical Studies* 172: 29–56.

———. (2015b), "Knowledge Is All You Need," *Philosophical Issues* 25: 353–378.

Peels, R. (2017), *Responsible Belief*, Oxford: Oxford University Press.

46 Sanford C. Goldberg

Schoenfield, M. (2014), "Permission to Believe: Why Permissivism Is True and What It Tells us about Irrelevant Influences on Belief," *Nous* 48: 193–218.

———. (forthcoming), "Permissivism and the Value of Rationality: A Challenge to the Uniqueness Thesis," *Philosophy and Phenomenological Research*.

Zagzebski, L. (1996), *Virtues of the Mind*, Cambridge: Cambridge University Press.

4 Relativism
The Most Ecumenical View?

Alexandra Plakias

4.1. Introduction

In contemporary analytic philosophy, relativism often gets a bad rap: it's something we retreat to, rather than aspire to. Relativism is seen as the view we adopt as a consequence of the failure to realize our realist ambitions, and an important reason for this perception is the assumption that everyday normative talk and practice is, at bottom, realist. Therefore, to adopt a relativist analysis is to adopt a revisionary account of our moral and epistemic practices. Relativists themselves have been surprisingly concessionary – apologetic, even – on this point. And while recent years have seen a resurgence of interest in relativism about aesthetic discourse (particularly, predicates of personal taste), moral and epistemic relativism have not enjoyed the same image rehabilitation. In this chapter, I argue that relativists have been too quick to concede the dialectical advantage to realists. In particular, I argue against the presumption that ordinary normative discourse is uniformly realist. To the extent that it is, I suggest that the main feature of realism we can read off ordinary practice – namely, objectivity – can be vindicated on a relativist analysis. Since relativism can explain and accommodate both objective *and* non-objective normative facts, I argue that it in fact enjoys an advantage over realist accounts when it comes to vindicating ordinary discourse.

This chapter investigates the role of empirical evidence in the debate over relativism and argues that such evidence can do two things: first, refute the anti-relativist presumption so prevalent in the literature, and second, provide the basis for a pro-relativist argument. I argue that making the case for relativism requires broadening the current focus on experimental research to include qualitative methods and ethnographic research, and I discuss some examples. Throughout the chapter, I discuss both moral and epistemic relativism. That's because the two domains have much in common: research done by experimental philosophers and psychologists studying our moral intuitions can illuminate questions affecting the plausibility of epistemic relativism, and ethnographic work done on our epistemic concepts provides a potentially

48   *Alexandra Plakias*

useful model for research in empirical moral psychology. Thus, not only do I outline a kind of relativist analysis that can be applied to either domain; I show how each domain can benefit from empirical work done in the other.

4.2. Objectivity, Realism, Relativism

A common objection to relativism is that it's revisionary of ordinary talk and thought. For example, Boghossian (2006, 19) writes, "the relativist's project must be seen to be a reforming project, designed to convince us that we should abandon the absolutist discourse we currently have." The idea that our ordinary discourse is at odds with relativism is a common theme among moral realists, in particular. Thus Brink (1989, 23) claims,

> We begin as (tacit) cognitivists and realists about ethics ... we are led to some form of antirealism (if we are) only because we come to regard the moral realist's commitments as untenable.... Moral realism should be our metaethical starting point, and we should give it up only if it does involve unacceptable metaphysical and epistemological commitments.

Dreier (himself a relativist) concedes that, "relative morality may be less than common sense can hope for ... [it is] at odds with common sense moral thinking" (2006, 241).

  As these comments suggest, many theorists (both realist and antirealist) begin with a presupposition in favor of methodological conservatism. That is, in theorizing about normative discourses such as ethics and epistemology, we favor views that capture the central commitments of ordinary thought and talk – we accommodate the central tenets of folk theory where possible. Smith (1994, 11) describes metaethics as aiming, first, to "identify features that are manifest in ordinary moral practice" and then to "make sense of a practice having these features." The relativist arguably makes sense of the practice having non-absolutist features, but their explanation involves attributing a kind of error or confusion to ordinary practitioners. The realist, on the other hand, makes sense of the practice in a way that vindicates its practitioners. For this reason, realism is thought to enjoy a dialectical advantage: the realist need only defend against objections, while the relativist requires substantial argument and motivation for her view. Dancy (1998, 233) summarizes the situation quite nicely: "The phenomenology of moral experience is the first and perhaps the only argument for realism, remaining thoughts being used for defence/offence." At first glance, "only" might seem hyperbolically strong given the many advantages claimed by realism. For example, in addition to the supposed objectivity of moral judgment, realists can account for the so-called inescapability of moral demands; the ability

Relativism 49

to make pronouncements on other cultures and eras; the phenomenon of moral progress; and the nature of moral disagreement. However, when we examine the reason for thinking that any of these phenomena *should* be captured, it seems that the answer often appeals to an intuition (supposedly) held, not by philosophers, but by ordinary users and speakers.

The particular intuition I'm interested in here involves objectivity. *The Objectivity Assumption* is the idea that normative claims are, in ordinary discourse and practice, taken to be objective. Before investigating this assumption, we need to ask what we mean by 'objectivity' here. The term itself can be used in a variety of ways to convey commitments from the metaphysical to the epistemological. For our purposes, there are two interpretations worth noting. The first is what I'll call the *mind-independence* conception of 'objectivity': a claim is objective just in case it is made true (or false) by a mind-independent fact – a fact that doesn't involve the attitudes, beliefs, or mental states of any agent(s). Facts about trees and electrons are objective in this sense: electrons existed and had their current properties before and independent of our beliefs that they existed and had any such properties. One sort of litmus test for mind-independent objectivity is the 'global error' test: could we be globally wrong about the fact in question? If so, it is (at least) a candidate for this type of objectivity.

We can contrast this with the *convergence conception* of objectivity. On this understanding, a fact is objective in case it's one that any rational agent would agree upon if given time to deliberate and all the relevant facts and non-doxastic inputs (such as the relevant imaginative capacities). This conception of objectivity is espoused by realists like Smith, who observes, "We seem to think that … by engaging in moral conversation and argument, we can discover what these objective moral facts … are. The term 'objective' here simply signifies the possibility of a convergence in moral views" (1994, 6).

Subsequently, I'll argue that there are empirical reasons to favor the convergence conception of objectivity. But there are also a priori reasons. Rosen (1994) has argued that 'mind-independence' doesn't confer a status that's particularly philosophically robust or interesting: there's no really significant difference between the set of facts that's mind-independent and those that are mind-dependent. (Or perhaps: there are differences, but they don't track the mind-independence *per se*.) In contrast, if we understand objectivity in terms of convergence, we can see that the objective facts do have a special property: they command the assent/recognition of rational agents. To say that a fact is objective is to say that it makes a claim on all agents occupying a certain epistemic position. A second reason to prefer the convergence conception is that it's more metaphysically modest: whereas the mind-independence conception requires us to commit to the existence of a domain of mind-

50   Alexandra Plakias

independent facts (to underwrite the truth of the claims in question), the convergence conception requires only ordinary psychological facts about agents and their dispositions to believe or feel. It's worth noting, too, that the convergence conception doesn't necessarily rule out the existence of mind-independent facts – it could be that the reason agents converge on certain beliefs or attitudes is because they recognize or are otherwise guided by those facts. But this explanation isn't required. With a convergence conception in hand, we can remain agnostic about the existence of mind-independent moral, epistemic, or aesthetic facts while retaining our commitment to objectivity.

However, another appealing feature of the convergence conception – and one we'll make use of in what follows – is that it doesn't require us to commit to objectivity a priori, nor does it require us to assume that the domain in question is *uniformly* objective. Objectivity might be a feature of moral or epistemic discourse; it might not. And it might be a feature present in some areas of that discourse but not others. That's because we might find that there's convergence on some claims but not on others. We'll start by looking at the question: what exactly *are* our intuitions about objectivity? Is the objectivity assumption borne out by empirical investigation? I begin with some evidence from metaethics, because that's where the most experimental work has been done.

Before we go on to examine the evidence (or lack thereof) for the objectivity assumption, it's worth pausing to say a bit more about how I'll understand 'realism' and 'relativism'. Both realists and relativists agree that the target claims are truth apt and that (at least) some claims are true; where they disagree is on what underwrites the truth of these claims. In particular, we can understand relativism as the view that the truth of claims in the discourse can only be evaluated with reference to a framework or standard, and that there is no single correct framework, but rather a multiplicity of frameworks, with no way of choosing between them. In the moral case, this amounts to the view that moral claims can only be evaluated with reference to a moral code or standard, and that there is no single correct moral code or standard. In the epistemic case, it can be understood as the view that we can only evaluate claims about justification or knowledge with reference to some epistemic standard or another, and there is no single such standard. In any case, the upshot is that there are no absolute facts about justification, knowledge, rightness, or wrongness; all such facts must be understood as relative to a certain framework.

Realism can then be understood as agreeing with the relativist that there are truths in the relevant domain but as maintaining that these truths are underwritten by framework-independent facts. That is, claims are true or false independent of any particular framework; we do not need to specify any kind of 'location' or standard in order to evaluate the justificatory status of a belief, whether an agent has knowledge, or whether an act is wrong.

Relativism   51

One way of understanding what's at issue in the objectivity assumption is the extent to which relativism requires us to understand ordinary users as being in error. It's true that most users do not explicitly relativize judgments of rightness and wrongness: we talk about things being justified or not; known or not; wrong or right. But this linguistic observation doesn't show that people don't understand such claims to be *implicitly* relativized. After all, we don't always (or even often) say, "it's raining here today, at the moment." We can't read off the content of our judgments from their linguistic expressions. Instead, to investigate the objectivity assumption, we'll have to look at the judgments themselves. In the next section, I'll look at some of the data bearing on this issue. While the topic of this volume is epistemic relativism, some of the most relevant experimental work on folk conceptions of objectivity can be found in the metaethics literature, so we'll begin there. One of the methodological claims of this chapter is that, when it comes to investigating folk intuitions about objectivity, experimental moral psychology can be instructive. But as we'll see later in the chapter, experimental methods aren't the only way to empirically investigate relativism, and here moral relativists can learn a lesson from cross-cultural epistemology. More about that later – first, let's look at what experimental data tells us about ordinary conceptions of objectivity.

4.3. Objectivity Examined

While the empirical study of 'common sense' or folk moral discourse is relatively new, what evidence there is points to the fact that folk moral discourse is not wholly objective – but nor is it entirely non-objective. Some of the strongest evidence for the objectivity of the moral domain can be found in the literature on the moral/conventional distinction, which treats the ability to distinguish objective moral norms from contingent social norms as partly constitutive of moral competence. Even in childhood, subjects appear to treat moral obligations as unconditional, whereas the obligation to comply with conventional norms is contingent on the existence of a rule or an authority figure's backing of the norm (Turiel 1983). That is, conventional norms can be overturned – if the teacher says it's okay to chew gum in class, chewing gum isn't wrong – but moral norms cannot. No one can cancel the rule against hitting and thereby make it the case that it's okay to hit others, because hitting is *morally* wrong. This pattern of distinguishing moral and conventional violations along the dimensions of contingency/non-contingency and seriousness (moral violations are more serious than conventional violations) has been discovered in study after study and so appears quite robust. Furthermore, psychopaths show reduced capacity for drawing the moral/conventional distinction (Blair 1995).[1] And unlike the studies I'll discuss subsequently, the ability to draw the distinction is measured by people's performance and not by what they

52 *Alexandra Plakias*

themselves believe about morality. So, one might be impressed by these studies even if one were inclined to think that folk *beliefs* about metaethics were metaethically irrelevant. If these findings are correct, we may not need to rest morality's claim to objectivity solely on a conceptual claim; it may turn out to be part of the nature of moral judgment as much as it is part of the concept of morality.

But there are good reasons to think that these studies don't give the whole story. Virtually all the work on the moral/conventional distinction has used moral transgressions that involve one individual inflicting unprovoked violent harm on another (this description, while accurate, may make the vignettes sound more dramatic than they are – the stories often involve things like hitting someone). Thus, there is little evidence that the distinction extends to other, non-harm-based types of moral violation. And studies that examine a broad range of violations find that the judgments we make about moral violations depend on the type of act involved.

For example, the psychologists Geoffrey Goodwin and John Darley (2008) set out to see whether subjects would treat ethical statements as objective and how this might differ from the way they would treat statements of scientific fact, social convention, and taste. The experimenters gave subjects a range of statements in all three areas (for example, "Anonymously donating a percentage of one's income to charity is a morally good action"; "Scientific research on embryonic human stem cells that are the product of in vitro fertilization is morally permissible") and asked them to rate their agreement with each statement as well as to indicate whether they thought it was a true statement, a false statement, or an opinion or attitude. In the second phase, subjects were told that another person strongly disagreed with them and asked whether they thought one of the two parties must be mistaken, or whether it is possible that neither party is mistaken. Overall, subjects treat ethical statements as more objective than statements of convention or taste but less objective than statements of fact. The more interesting result, however, is the degree of variation *within* the category of ethical statements: subjects tended to strongly agree with claims about the wrongness of robbing a bank or opening gunfire on a crowd and were likely to judge these claims to express 'true statements,' but, while the strength of agreement with claims concerning the permissibility (or lack thereof) of abortion, euthanasia, and stem cell research were similar, subjects proved extremely reluctant to describe these latter claims as expressing 'true statements,' choosing instead to categorize them as opinions or attitudes. For example, 68% of subjects said it was a true statement that it's wrong to open fire on a crowd, but very few subjects said it was a true statement that abortion is permissible – 92% categorized this judgment as an opinion or attitude and maintained that in the event someone were to disagree with them about the judgment, neither party need be mistaken.

Relativism 53

And yet subjects tended to *agree* equally strongly with both claims. This indicates that whether subjects regarded a statement as expressing an 'opinion or attitude' or an objective fact is heavily influenced not just by the *domain* (aesthetic, ethical, factual) but also by the specific *content* of the statement. A subsequent study (Goodwin and Darley 2012) confirms that judgments of objectivity vary depending on the type of moral violation; Wright et al. (2013) show that while individuals differ in which acts they classify as moral, variations in judgments of objectivity persist even when subjects are allowed to group transgressions themselves, demonstrating that the effect is not explained by the hypothesis that subjects simply don't see abortion as *morally* wrong. Rather, subjects see both shooting into a crowd and abortion as moral issues and maintain that the wrongness of one is more objective than the permissibility of the other.

These data are not conclusive. But they undercut the realists' claim to enjoy a presumption in their favor on the grounds that the ordinary view of morality is objectivist. The experiments that have been done so far suggest three things: first, that according to 'ordinary' moral discourse, moral claims are neither uniformly objective nor uniformly non-objective; second, that individuals disagree over where to draw the boundary around the moral domain; third, to the extent that there is an ordinary notion of objectivity, it is best understood as convergentist, rather than mind-independent, since convergentism explains the ordinary treatment of morality as variable with respect to objectivity.

What, if anything, do these experiments tell us about epistemic objectivity? To date, most experimental research into epistemic intuitions has focused on two areas: cross-cultural variation in intuitions about classical philosophical thought experiments and intuitions about the role of contextual features in knowledge attributions. In both categories, we find mixed results. Early work by Weinberg et al. (2001; see also Nichols et al. 2003) identified cross-cultural differences in intuitions about both 'Trutemp' and Gettier cases, with East Asian subjects being more likely (than Western subjects) to attribute knowledge in Gettier cases and less likely to attribute knowledge in Trutemp cases. However, subsequent studies have failed to replicate these results, leaving the results in doubt.

More recent research into cross-cultural intuitions has looked at the effect of error salience on knowledge attribution. Waterman et al. (2018) found that while presenting subjects with scenarios that raised skeptical possibilities (such as abnormal lighting conditions) to salience lowered subjects' willingness to attribute knowledge to the actors in those scenarios, the magnitude of this effect varied across cultures. The authors argue that this finding complicates the debate over *epistemic universalism* – "the idea that epistemic intuitions are culturally universal" (2018, 187) – by suggesting that "folk epistemic intuitions might display interesting patterns of cultural difference even when there are

54 Alexandra Plakias

widespread cultural similarities to the folk epistemic intuitions themselves" (2018, 210). That is, even though all subjects responded to the mention of skeptical considerations by reducing their willingness to attribute knowledge, the effect of this mention was stronger in some cultures than in others. The authors explain this variation in terms of differing effects on subjects' 'subjective certainty' – in some cultures, mentioning skeptical considerations had a greater effect on subjects' certainty than in others. So while the elements of the epistemic intuition (knowledge, certainty, belief) seem cross-culturally shared, as do the basic relationships between them (highlighting possibilities of error decreases knowledge attributions), the way these relationships play out is also culturally determined (in ways not yet fully explored or understood).

While all of these results are interesting, they bear only *indirectly* on the question of epistemic objectivity; unlike the metaethical experiments described previously, they don't tell us what the 'folk' themselves think about the status of their epistemic intuitions, only what those intuitions consist of. Still, we can draw some conclusions, as well as some methodological lessons. First, the fact that intuitions do vary cross-culturally (an issue we'll return to later) is *prima facie* evidence for epistemic relativism. Different cultures might have different standards for attributing knowledge. They might also (if the experiments showing variation in Gettier intuitions, for example, were to be replicated) have different concepts of knowledge itself – a point we'll return to later. But these findings aren't evidence against the objectivity assumption, since they don't tell us whether the folk view epistemic judgments are objective or relative, are the sorts of things that hold true across all cultures or only locally.

At the moment, then, the empirical evidence is inconclusive: while preliminary results from metaethics suggest that the objectivity assumption is false, folk intuitions about epistemic objectivity are unclear; more investigation into the question of whether people treat epistemic judgments as uniformly objective or not is needed. In the absence of such evidence, we can note a few things. First, some moral realists have argued that moral and epistemic normativity must stand or fall together (see e.g. Cuneo 2007). So, if there is evidence for a convergence conception of objectivity and against the objectivity assumption, in metaethics, this might be evidence for similar conclusions in the epistemic domain. Second, the fact that we don't have evidence for or against an objectivity assumption in the epistemic domain argues against letting the assumption constrain our theorizing here. In the absence of such evidence, we might prefer an account on which it's an open question whether epistemic claims are objective or not. That is, we should not make it a requirement on true epistemic claims that they be *objectively* true, both because our intuitions about epistemic normativity might turn out to contain an element of relativism and because we might discover that epistemic concepts are themselves relative. Therefore, the way we identify the

Relativism 55

standards underwriting the truth of epistemic claims should allow that they might vary with culture (or some other feature). In the remainder of this chapter, I'll do two things: first, I'll argue that a significant advantage of relativism is that it allows for this agnosticism; second, I'll argue that there is empirical reason to think we will want to make use of this advantage.

4.4. Degrees of Objectivity

As a first approximation, we can think of relativism as the view that things are right and wrong only relative to a standard or judge.[2] In contemporary literature, this is often formulated as the view that claims take truth-values only when assessed against an individual, a culture, or a moral framework – but not absolutely. For the relativist, expressions will include a parameter whose value is determined by context and which helps determine the truth-value of that expression. The exact contribution context makes varies from view to view: in some views, it is the context of utterance that determines the value; in others, it is the context of assessment. Or it could be some combination of the two. The important point, for present purposes, is to note that in a relativist view, expressions contain an extra parameter, one that is absent from non-relativist analyses of those expressions.

In some views (e.g. Harman 1975; Dreier 1990), the parameter in question stands for a set of standards or a (moral) code, usually that subscribed to by the speaker's culture or group. But there are problems with this approach. The first is that it has trouble accommodating iconoclasm – a particularly pronounced problem for moral relativists, but one that should worry epistemic relativists as well. We want to be able to critique our social practices from within. But consider the problem of individuals who hold dissenting views – 19th century abolitionists, anti-apartheid activists in 20th century South Africa, or defenders of the scientific method against the teachings of the church. According to cultural relativism, the views expressed by these speakers are assessed against the predominant moral and epistemic norms and therefore turn out to be false. A second problem for cultural relativism is the difficulty of accurately characterizing the norms of a group or culture. Cultural relativism relies on the assumption that cultures are homogeneous and amenable to generalization, and several philosophers have argued that this is an oversimplification (e.g. Moody-Adams 2002). Cultures contain a plurality of views and beliefs, making it difficult to identify a predominant moral outlook. Moreover, many individuals identify with more than one culture – or none at all.

The type of view I'll be discussing is one on which, instead, the parameter picks out an agent or agents whose beliefs or attitudes will determine the truth-value of the claim under consideration. There are various

56 Alexandra Plakias

specifications of this kind of relativism, and I won't go into all of them here. But for clarity's sake, it will be advantageous to work through a specific view rather than speak in generalities. So, as an example, I'll use a kind of relativism developed by Egan (2012), sometimes called 'self-locating relativism.' Much of what follows will be applicable to other types of relativism that make the truth of moral claims relative to an agent's attitudes or beliefs; these types of relativist views have an advantage over non-relativist alternatives insofar as they are able to account for variation in objectivity within the moral domain.

This type of relativism builds on Lewis' (1989) dispositional theory of value. According to Lewis, when an agent judges that X is good, they are self-attributing the property, *being disposed to have a certain response R to act X in circumstances C*. In a dispositional view, moral claims (like value claims more generally) are claims about *us*; more specifically, they're claims about the responses we're disposed to have to certain acts or features. The view also shares some features with Smith's (1994) realism, since both Smith and Egan analyze rightness in terms of the desires that idealized agents would have. But there are two important differences: first, Smith analyzes moral claims as claims about possible worlds; and second, Smith requires convergence among ideally rational agents regarding those desires in order for morality to have a subject matter. That's because, for Smith, what we are talking about when we talk about morality just is the desires we'd converge upon were we fully rational.[3] Egan drops this requirement – what's morally right for me depends on the desires, not of all idealized agents, but of an idealized version of myself – which guarantees that morality has a subject matter whether or not convergence obtains.

Notice that any possible worlds proposition can be transformed into a centered-worlds proposition; in most cases, this will in no way affect the truth value that proposition gets assigned at a possible world. Any possible worlds proposition that is true in the actual world *simpliciter* will be true in any centered world within the actual world. Call these 'boring centered worlds propositions' – possible worlds propositions that *can* be analyzed as centered worlds proposition, but whose truth value is not altered by adopting either the former (coarse-grained) analysis or the latter (finer-grained) analysis.

This may seem like a trivial observation, but appreciating this point is a crucial first step towards seeing why this view is able to handle the puzzle discussed above without forcing us into either metaethical pluralism or incoherence. In a self-locating relativist view, we can accommodate the observation that some facts are objective and others are relative. We can accommodate intuitions that some disagreements (about abortion, euthanasia, or whether a speaker knows the truth of some claim despite not being able to rule out a certain skeptical possibility) are faultless, as well as the intuition that any reasonable person

Relativism   57

would agree that torturing babies is just *wrong*, and that knowledge just *is* factive. And we can remain agnostic about the extent of relativism versus objectivity – this account leaves the question of which normative judgments we will or would converge upon open and amenable to empirical investigation. (This is similar to Jackson's (1998, 117) discussion of 'mature folk morality' – in his view, whether there is an objective moral subject matter depends on the truths on which we would converge at something like 'the end of inquiry;' if there is no such convergence, relativism is true. But one might respond, from our current standpoint both outcomes are possible, so we ought not adopt a theory that rules out either possibility a priori.) We can deny that objectivity is required for the domain in question to have a subject matter, without ruling it out a priori.

Let me illustrate how. Suppose that for some achievement ϕ, everyone's informed, rational self would endorse standards on which ϕ-ing counts as achieving knowledge. (For example, ϕ might be true belief accomplished via a reliable exercise of intellectual virtue; the standards being endorsed would be standards according to which this achieving of this type of belief counts as knowledge.) Then everyone would be correct to self-attribute the property of being someone whose informed, rational self counts ϕ as knowledge. Now suppose A and B disagree over whether ϕ counts as knowledge. A is correctly self-attributing the property, B is mistakenly denying that he has the property; we have a case *not just* where two people are disagreeing and it happens that one is mistaken, but where if *any* two people disagree over whether ϕ is knowledge, one of them must be mistaken. So we have something that is behaving just like an objective fact; 'ϕ-ing is knowledge' is true, regardless of who says it. In other words, it's a boring proposition. Even those who are impressed by the extent of diversity should grant the possibility that there are facts like this; perhaps torturing babies for fun is something that, just by virtue of being human and having the kind of psychology we do, no one's ideally rational self would approve of; perhaps given our psychology, no one would endorse standards according to which an incorrect lucky guess counts as knowledge. In these cases, the truth-value of the proposition remains constant regardless of which agent(s) we fill in the parameter with. As a result, if any two people disagree over the truth of the proposition, one of them is mistaken. To reiterate: this is starting to resemble objectivity.

In other cases, agents' attitudes towards the proposition might differ, and these differences might remain after idealization. Here, it's entirely possible to end up with cases of faultless disagreement, with one party correctly self-attributing a property and the other party denying they have that property. We get variation in truth-value, depending on which agent is plugged in to the individual parameter. In the case of properties like this, we *can* have disagreements where one party is at fault –

58 *Alexandra Plakias*

perhaps they haven't thought fully about the issue, or there is some incoherence in their beliefs, or a factual error – but insofar as faultless disagreements are possible, they won't behave like disagreements over objective facts.

4.5. Relativism and Ethnography: Past and Future

The preceding arguments describe a way of modeling epistemic discourse, modeled on moral relativism, that allows for a domain containing both relative and objective facts. Earlier in the chapter, we saw that the existence of relative facts does not, contrary to what realists claim, go against ordinary practice and belief; indeed, allowing for a domain that varies with respect to objectivity may be our best strategy if the aim is to characterize ordinary practice. But intuitions about objectivity itself are just one prong of the debate over realism. The other involves establishing, not only that our intuitions about epistemic (and moral) discourse allow for relativity, but that such relativity is actual. In other words, the arguments so far have shown that, *if* it turns out that there's fundamental variability in moral and epistemic norms and standards, this discovery isn't at odds with ordinary intuitions or practice. But what we haven't yet shown is that such variability exists. In this section, I'll discuss some strategies for doing so, thereby strengthening the second prong of the relativist's argument.

Recent empirical work on both moral and epistemic variation has centered around experiments involving subjects' intuitions about hypothetical cases. Previously, we looked at how people responded to learning about hypothetical moral disagreements, which tells us something about the extent of folk objectivity. But those experiments also involved subjects' assessment of the wrongness of various actions, which tells us something about the extent to which subjects hold divergent intuitions about actions like abortion, euthanasia, and so on. In addition to these experiments, there is a significant body of experimental research involving intuitions about moral dilemmas such as trolley problems. Here we see less variation, and certain themes emerge: distinctions such as doing vs allowing, and personal vs impersonal harms, seem to be widespread if not universal, suggesting some widely shared moral frameworks. Early experimental work in this tradition has been criticized for focusing too heavily on so-called 'WEIRD' subjects – that is, individuals who, regardless of their cultural background, are Westernized, Educated, Industrialized, Rich, and Democratic (Henrich et al. 2010). This is partly a result of experimental philosophy and psychology's tendency to draw their subjects from pools of university students, who are a self-selecting, WEIRD group (a similar critique has been leveled against developmental psychology – see e.g. Nielsen et al. 2017). If we're interested in diversity, the experimental literature may not be the best place to look.

Admittedly, this is changing. The philosophers Stephen Stich and Edouard Machery, along with the anthropologist Clark Barrett, have spearheaded a large-scale effort to survey intuitions from cultures across the globe (the "Geography of Philosophy" project), including a number of small-scale societies, thereby ameliorating concerns about WEIRD results. Broadening the subject pool of experimental philosophy is therefore one way to investigate the extent of cross-cultural epistemic diversity. But it's not the only way.

Moral relativism and anthropology have a long (and perhaps vexed?) history. The terms are often linked, such that anthropology is sometimes taken to be committed to a kind of relativism. While it is well beyond the scope of this chapter to comment on that assumption, it is interesting for our purposes to note that, throughout the 20th century, philosophers identifying as moral relativists turned to the methods of anthropology to investigate the existence of fundamental moral disagreements. For example, Richard Brandt's work with the Hopi was motivated by his observation that,

> We have ... a question affecting the truth of ethical relativism which, conceivably, anthropology can help us settle. Does ethnological evidence support the view that 'qualified persons' can disagree in ethical attitude?[4] ... Some kinds of anthropological material will not help us – in particular, bare information about intercultural differences in ethical opinion or attitude.
>
> (1954, 238)

Brandt's last line here reveals the motivation for a move from experimental to ethnographic investigations; from quantitative to qualitative methods: to establish that standards genuinely vary, in the way the relativist claims, it's not enough to establish that different groups have different intuitions. Rather, we need to know that these intuitions represent genuine, deep differences, rather than different auxiliary beliefs (say, about a related matter of fact). Certainly, experimental data is useful too: it can tell us where to focus our efforts, and it can provide *prima facie* evidence against claims about uniformity (as it did in Section 4.3). But to really establish genuine difference, a more in-depth investigation may be necessary.

Brandt undertook his own investigation among the Hopi, observing and interviewing them about their moral views; his contemporary, John Ladd, engaged in a similar project with the Navajo. The results of their work have proven to be less than influential. Brandt himself claimed to identify a disagreement between the Hopi and other Americans in their attitudes towards the treatment of animals: he reports that children would capture birds and treat them as toys, tying them up and batting them around until they died, and that no one objected

60 *Alexandra Plakias*

to this practice (1954, 213–215). Leaving aside the fact that, for Americans familiar with factory farming, the claim that we are more compassionate and protective towards animals is dubious at best, one might wonder whether this solitary difference is sufficient to ground a genuine relativism.

Ladd's work with the Navajo was not much more game-changing; a contemporary reviewer (Morgenbesser 1958, 790) reports finding them, "at least as reported by Mr. Ladd, a rather dull lot," who want no more than to "avoid obviously dangerous things like adultery and witchcraft, and to engage in the dull and safe life of amassing property and having a good reputation." The review goes on to compare them to "other-directed Victorians" – hardly the type of wild cultural divergences that historical relativists such as Herodotus based their claims upon.

Leaving aside the substance of Ladd's findings, we can make a couple of interesting observations about his methods. First, Ladd is explicitly not concerned with what his informants *do*. Nor is he concerned with what they say when they're actually involved in moral debate (1957, 23). Instead, people's moral beliefs are best identified via what they say in their reflective moments (25). Secondly, and relatedly, Ladd prefers to focus on an informant he considers to be an 'intellectual' member of society, someone who is more prone to reflection and explanation of moral beliefs. There's much to criticize about Ladd's methods: his choice to identify moral beliefs with professed, reflective thought rather than action; the fact that he bases his characterization of an entire culture on interviews with just a few members. However, both Ladd and Brandt offer us the beginnings of an alternative – albeit a very imperfect one – to the current approach taken by experimental philosophers. In almost every respect, their methods are opposite: while Brandt and Ladd engage in interviews with fewer individuals and observations, and focus on reflection, experimental philosophers aim to gather data from large subject pools, and base their conclusion on relatively quick intuitive responses. (This latter aspect is a response to armchair philosophy's perceived reliance on appeals to intuition, though whether the two mean the same thing by 'intuition' is itself a topic for debate – see e.g. the essays in DePaul and Ramsey 1998, as well as Sosa 2007.)

The point here is not that one of these methods is inherently superior to the other, but that they are likely to access different types of data. And philosophers themselves are undecided as to which of these – relatively quick intuitive processes, or considered reflective beliefs – we should identify with the relevant criteria underwriting the truth of normative claims. Is it subjects' moral and epistemic intuitions, or is it the standards they endorse under consideration? Perhaps these ideally coincide, but do they actually? This question itself demands gathering both types of data and comparing them.

This is just one reason for empirically-minded philosophers to broaden their methodological repertoire. Andow (2016) argues that experimental

Relativism   61

philosophers would be well-served by adding qualitative research to their investigations; while, admittedly, few philosophers are likely to uproot themselves and conduct fieldwork, we might follow Machery and Stich's lead, listening to and collaborating with geographically and culturally diverse colleagues.

I want to now look at one illustration of the use of ethnographic methods to investigate epistemic diversity, specifically. Hallen and Sodipo (1986) set out to investigate the inter-translatability – or lack thereof – between Yoruba and contemporary Western epistemic concepts. The two philosophers interviewed Yoruba about their conceptions of (the rough equivalent of) knowledge and belief, focusing their investigation on conversations with individuals considered to be teachers and experts, the *onisegun*. They explain, "We chose them for several reasons," including the fact that "the onisegun represent and exercise a level of understanding and analysis of Yoruba life and thought that is more critically sophisticated than that of the ordinary person" (1986, 10). They are often "asked to give advice and counsel," and form a society that

> acts as the institutional guardian of the knowledge that is at the heart of the profession. It judges every member in terms of his competence and character.... It determines whether an individual has demonstrated that he is sufficiently responsible to advance, to be entrusted with greater knowledge and powers.
>
> (1986, 13)

In sum, the onisegun are chosen because of their expertise in the production and transmission of knowledge.

Hallen and Sodipo describe their method: "data was collected in the context of guided, cross-cultural, discussions rather than in question and answer sessions." In these sessions, "the onisegun introduce numerous concrete examples ... they ... provide action-oriented illustrations of ... the criteria of these two concepts" of knowledge (1986, 10). The authors compare their method to the traditional philosophical project of conceptual analysis, calling it a kind of 'collaborative analysis' (1986, 124), the goal of which is to work with their informants to determine the conditions for attributing certain epistemic achievements to agents and thereby arrive at an understanding of Yoruba epistemology.

So far, the version of relativism under consideration in this chapter has been the idea that standards for achievements like 'knowledge' and 'justification' (and 'right' and 'wrong') vary cross-culturally. Hallen and Sodipo go further: their claim is that propositional attitudes themselves are not universal. We do not have to follow them quite this far to appreciate their argument that the criteria governing the application of epistemic concepts resembling 'know' and 'believe' are cross-culturally variable. Their discussion focuses on two Yoruba concepts: 'mo' and 'gbagbo.'

62   Alexandra Plakias

Through their discussions with the onisegun, Hallen and Sodipo arrive at two conditions a person must satisfy in order to 'mo': one must have seen or otherwise directly perceived the thing, and one must comprehend what one is seeing and judge that one has done so. The term 'gbagbo,' by contrast, is used in cases where one has not seen/witnessed/experienced the thing oneself, but rather has heard about it from someone else – for example, in cases involving testimony, oral tradition, and formal education.

The authors' point is that neither of these terms map neatly onto the English categories of belief or knowledge. They note that 'mo' is closely linked to visual perception and observation; 'gbagbo' is used only in the absence of witnessing something and (the authors suggest) is perhaps best understood as "agreeing to accept what someone says" (1986, 83), rather than belief, though they insist that this translation is imperfect. Interestingly, the authors note that the link between first-person observation and greater certitude contravenes the Western stereotype of 'traditional' cultures elevating oral traditions and teachings as sources of knowledge:

> How ironic, then, that the model of African thought systems produced by English-language culture should typify them as systems that treat second-hand information (oral tradition, book knowledge, etc.) as though it were true, as though it were knowledge! This is precisely what the Yoruba epistemological system ... outspokenly and adamantly refuses to do! But the English-language epistemological system does – grossly. Therefore, in the end, it fits its own model for traditional thought better than Yoruba ever can!
>
> (1986, 81)

Cross-cultural ethnographic work is instructive both substantively and methodologically. From a substantive perspective, work like Hallen and Sodipo's offers evidence of cross-cultural variation in epistemic standards and concepts. From a methodological perspective, it's significant in that it addresses and evades a number of critiques leveled against contemporary work in experimental philosophy: the authors do not rely on surveys, so their results are not simply aggregations of quick, intuitive judgments. And because the authors chose to conduct in-depth interviews with members of Yoruba society considered experts in knowledge-gathering and transmission, they are not gathering untutored or unconsidered judgments. Rather, they're amassing considered, reflective judgments about what counts as knowledge, asking follow-up questions and engaging in conversation to allow them to understand the meaning of those judgments. Indeed, one might argue that this sounds a lot like philosophy itself. If that's true, perhaps what we need are not *radically* new methods, but greater engagement with other viewpoints, perspectives, and cultures.

4.6. Conclusion

This chapter has attempted to outline an empirical argument for moral and epistemic relativism. The strategy is multi-pronged: first, the relativist must push back on realist accusations of revisionism. I've shown how experimental work in moral psychology can be useful here. Furthermore, because relativism can accommodate both objective-seeming and relative facts, the relativist's view is actually more promising when it comes to capturing our ordinary intuitions and the existence of diversity; unlike the realist, the relativist isn't hostage to predictions about a convergence in moral views nor the existence of mind-independent facts. Should such things emerge, the relativist can accommodate them, but should they fail to, the relativist is ready to allow for something less than full-blown objectivity. Finally, the relativist should look beyond experimental methods and return to ethnographic and qualitative methods to make the case for genuine epistemic diversity. Far from something to be feared, or a philosopher's bizarre invention, relativism may offer our best hope of accepting and reflecting the world as we find it.

Notes

1. Interestingly, when it comes to the question of contingency, psychopaths don't treat the moral norms as equally contingent as the social norms – rather, they treat the social norms as though they were moral norms, judging that they are not contingent. See Aharoni et al. (2012) for discussion.
2. Some of the views I mention here are also sometimes referred to as 'contextualism.' There's a fair amount of intramural debate concerning the right formulation of relativism, as well as a proliferation of terminology. Since I'm mainly concerned with relativism as it contrasts with realism, error theory, and expressivism, I'll be using relativism in the broad sense. I go on to say more about the type of relativist view I mean to be suggesting. Taxonomy is not my focus here; pointing to the various features that are important for my purposes will, I hope, make matters clear enough.
3. In fact, it's a subset of these desires: those that are for something of the right substantive kind (see e.g. 1994, 183–184). But the important point, for present purposes, is that Smith analyzes moral talk in such a way that it is about desires we'd converge upon.
4. By 'qualified persons,' Brandt means roughly what we mean by 'ideally rational agent' – he is interested in cases of disagreement that are not explicable by appeal to epistemic shortcomings or ignorance on the part of the disputants.

References

Aharoni, E., W. Sinnott-Armstrong and K. Kiehl. (2012), "Can Psychopathic Offenders Discern Moral Wrongs? A New Look at the Moral/Conventional Distinction," *Journal of Abnormal Psychology* 121 (2): 484–497.

Andow, J. (2016), "Qualitative Tools and Experimental Philosophy," *Philosophical Psychology* 29 (8): 1128–1141.

64 Alexandra Plakias

Blair, R.J.R. (1995), "A Cognitive Developmental Approach to Morality: Investigating the Psychopath," *Cognition* 57: 1–29.

Boghossian, P. (2006), "What Is Relativism?," in *Truth and Relativism*, edited by P. Greenough and M.P. Lynch, Oxford: Clarendon Press, 13–37.

Brandt, R. (1954), *Hopi Ethics*, Chicago: University of Chicago Press.

Brink, D.O. (1989), *Moral Realism and the Foundations of Ethics*, Cambridge: Cambridge University Press.

Cuneo, T. (2007), *The Normative Web: An Argument for Moral Realism*, Oxford: Oxford University Press.

Dancy, J. (1998), "Two Conceptions of Moral Realism," in *Ethical Theory 1: The Question of Objectivity*, edited by James Rachels, Oxford: Oxford University Press.

DePaul, M. and W. Ramsey (eds.). (1998), *Rethinking Intuition: The Psychology of Intuition and its Role in Philosophical Inquiry*, Lanham, MD: Rowman & Littlefield.

Dreier, J. (1990), "Internalism and Speaker Relativism," *Ethics* 101 (1): 6–26.

———. (2006). "Moral Relativism and Moral Nihilism," in *Oxford Handbook of Ethical Theory*, edited by David Copp, Oxford: Oxford University Press, 240–264.

Egan, A. (2012), "Relativist Dispositional Theories of Value," *The Southern Journal of Philosophy* 50 (4): 557–582.

Goodwin, G. and J. Darley. (2008), "The Psychology of Meta-Ethics: Exploring Objectivism," *Cognition* 106: 1339–1366.

———. (2012), "Why Are Some Moral Beliefs Perceived to be More Objective Than Others?," *Journal of Experimental Social Psychology* 48 (1): 250–256.

Hallen, B. and J.O. Sodipo. (1986), *Knowledge, Belief, and Witchcraft: Analytic Experiments in African Philosophy*, Stanford: Stanford University Press.

Harman, G. (1975), "Moral Relativism Defended," *The Philosophical Review* 84 (1): 3–22.

Henrich, J., S.J. Heine and A. Norenzayan. (2010), "The Weirdest People in the World?," *Behavioral and Brain Sciences* 33 (2–3): 61–83.

Jackson, F. (1998), *From Metaphysics to Ethics: A Defence of Conceptual Analysis*, Oxford: Oxford University Press.

Ladd, J. (1957), *The Structure of a Moral Code: A Philosophical Analysis of Ethical Discourse Applied to the Ethics of the Navaho Indians*, Cambridge, MA: Harvard University Press.

Lewis, D. (1989), "Dispositional Theories of Value," *Proceedings of the Aristotelian Society* 63: 113–137.

Moody-Adams, M. (2002), *Fieldwork in Familiar Places*, Cambridge, MA: Harvard University Press.

Morgenbesser, S. (1958), "Reviewed Work: The Structure of a Moral Code: A Philosophical Analysis of Ethical Discourse Applied to the Ethics of the Navaho Indians by John Ladd," *The Journal of Philosophy* 55 (18): 785–790.

Nichols, S., S. Stich and J. Weinberg. (2003), "Metaskepticism: Meditations in Ethnoepistemology," in *The Skeptics*, edited by S. Luper, Burlington, VT: Ashgate, 227–247.

Nielsen, M., D. Haun, J. Kärtner and C. Legare. (2017), "The Persistent Sampling Bias in Developmental Psychology: A Call to Action," *Journal of Experimental Child Psychology* 162: 31–38.

Rosen, G. (1994), "Objectivity and Modern Idealism: What Is the Question?," in *Philosophy in Mind*, edited by J. O'Leary-Hawthorne and M. Michael, Dordrecht: Kluwer Academic Publishers, 277–319.

Smith, M. (1994), *The Moral Problem*, Oxford: Blackwell.

Sosa, E. (2007), "Experimental Philosophy and Philosophical Intuition," *Philosophical Studies* 132 (1): 99–107.

Turiel, E. (1983), *The Development of Social Knowledge: Morality and Convention*, Cambridge: Cambridge University Press.

Waterman, J.P., C. Gonnerman, K. Yan and J. Alexander. (2018), "Knowledge, Certainty, and Skepticism: A Cross-Cultural Study," in *Epistemology for the Rest of the World*, edited by S. Stich, M. Mizumoto and E. McCready, Oxford: Oxford University Press, 187–214.

Weinberg, J., S. Nichols and S. Stich. (2001), "Normativity and Epistemic Intuitions," *Philosophical Topics* 29 (1–2): 429–460.

Wright, J. et al. (2013), "The Meta-Ethical Grounding of Our Moral Beliefs: Evidence for Meta-Ethical Pluralism," *Philosophical Psychology*: 1–26.

5   Naturalism, Psychologism, Relativism

Hilary Kornblith

5.1. Introduction

The late nineteenth and early twentieth centuries saw a great debate in the German-speaking philosophical world on the status of psychologism and its relation to relativism and naturalism.[1] Parties to the debate were not always entirely clear about just what was meant by these terms, but central to the debate were issues concerning the relationship between philosophy and the emerging discipline of experimental psychology. Champions of psychologism promoted a view in which logic and an account of proper reasoning would be founded on principles of psychology, while opponents sought to secure the autonomy of philosophy, and with it, an autonomous view of both logic and proper reasoning. The vigorous and often rancorous debate of that period largely petered out in the years following the First World War. Experimental psychologists, whose academic home had been in philosophy departments prior to the war, moved, or were moved, out, thereby assuring, if not the autonomy of philosophy, the autonomy of philosophy departments. It is not so much that the issues which had been debated were rationally resolved. Rather, the attentions of the disputants largely moved elsewhere.

The concerns of that period, however, are once again a focus of much attention, debate, and, in some cases, real rancor as well. The late twentieth and early twenty-first centuries have seen discussions of naturalism, the relationship between philosophy and psychology, and issues about the autonomy of philosophy return to the center of philosophical attention. Questions about the status of "armchair philosophy" and "experimental philosophy" have been the subject of numerous conferences, collections of papers, and monographs.[2] While it is certainly too early to claim that any of these issues has been resolved, it is, perhaps, a good time to take stock of the current status of these debates, to clarify just what the available positions seem to be, and what is to be said for and against them.

In this chapter, I provide one small piece of this very large picture. My focus here will be on naturalistic epistemology, and the perspective it

Naturalism, Psychologism, Relativism   67

offers on these issues. And since even among naturalistic philosophers there is not complete agreement on these matters, it will be more accurate to say that I will offer one naturalistic perspective on the relationship between philosophy and psychology, on the relationship between psychology and the principles of proper reasoning, and on the upshot of these matters for relativism. I believe that, as a result of the very substantial advances which have been made in experimental psychology, we are now in a position to make progress on the matters which were much debated one hundred years ago. And I believe that these advances give us reason to support a refined version of both psychologism and relativism about evidential relations.

5.2. Doxastic Justification Is Fundamental

Let me begin with a discussion of Alvin Goldman's reliabilism and the dramatic reorientation it brought about in late twentieth-century analytic epistemology.[3,4] Goldman argued that a belief is justified just in case it is reliably produced, and this account was rightly seen as a dramatic break with much of the prevailing epistemology of the time in virtue of its externalist account of justification. In Goldman's view, it is the mere fact that a belief is reliably produced which makes it justified; a believer need not know, or justifiably believe, or even believe that his or her belief is reliably produced in order for that belief to be justified. The externalist character of Goldman's account has been much discussed, and deservedly so.[5] It did, indeed, present an importantly different kind of account of justified belief from the vast majority of work being done at the time.[6] But I would like to focus on a different feature of Goldman's account, and this will require introducing the distinction between propositional justification and doxastic justification.[7]

Roughly, a claim is propositionally justified for a person if that person is in possession of good reasons to believe that proposition. The claim needn't be believed by the person in order for it to be propositionally justified for that person. If the claim is believed, it needn't be believed for the reasons which justify it. A claim is doxastically justified for a person, on the other hand, if it is believed on the basis of the good reasons which make it propositionally justified.[8]

Following the publication of Edmund Gettier's famous paper "Is Justified True Belief Knowledge?" in 1963, analytic epistemologists set about the task of trying to figure out what might be added to justified, true belief to provide both necessary and sufficient conditions for knowledge. The distinction between propositional and doxastic justification would not be made for another fifteen years, but during this interim period, it is quite clear that when epistemologists spoke of "justified belief," the notion of justified belief they were working with was the

68   Hilary Kornblith

notion of propositionally justified belief. Once the distinction was introduced, and it became clear that not only propositional justification, but doxastic justification as well was a necessary condition for knowledge, the typical response to this realization was to add a clause to one's account of knowledge requiring that a belief be based on the reasons which make it propositionally justified if it is to count as knowledge.[9] Propositional justification was thus viewed as the more fundamental of the two notions; doxastic justification was defined in terms of it.

One of the really striking features of Goldman's "What is Justified Belief?," the paper which introduced Goldman's reliabilism, is that, when Goldman addressed his title question, his attention was focused on doxastic justification rather than propositional justification. Goldman did not even mention the distinction between these two notions[10] until three paragraphs before the end of the paper, at which point he gave an account of propositional justification in terms of doxastic justification. Doxastic justification was thus viewed as the more fundamental notion, thereby reversing the order of explanation found in other writers.

While this issue about the order of explanation might have seemed like a minor point, I believe that it was of the first importance. The idea that propositional justification is the more fundamental notion is an entirely natural one. Authors who favored this view regarded the principles of evidence as a priori knowable: these principles included the laws of logic and the principles of probability theory. The facts about logic and probability theory are entirely independent of the contingent features of human psychology, in this view, and thus, the principles of evidence are independent of psychology as well. Whether the proposition that p supports the proposition that q has nothing to do with the way our minds might work. Facts about evidential support are facts about the relations among propositions.

In reversing the order of explanation and viewing doxastic justification as the more fundamental notion, Goldman introduced a psychological element into the account of evidential support. A belief is doxastically justified if it is formed in the right sort of way: on Goldman's view, if it is reliably produced. A claim is propositionally justified for an individual just in case that individual has available psychological processes which would allow for the reliable production of belief in that proposition.[11] While this account does not preclude the possibility that these psychological processes might track logical and probabilistic principles, there is no requirement that they must. What makes a proposition a good reason to believe another proposition has to do with whether there are available psychological processes which will reliably take one from belief in the first proposition to belief in the second. The account of good reason, or of evidential principles, or of the laws of evidence, is thereby psychologized.

As it turns out, this account of evidential relations will not closely track logical and probabilistic laws. Work on human inference, beginning with the extraordinarily fruitful and illuminating work of Tversky and Kahneman, showed that the ways in which we actually reason do not approximate the a priori principles of logic and probability which served to define good reasoning according to those epistemologists who viewed propositional justification as fundamental.[12] One might, of course, respond to this discovery by simply declaring that human beings are often irrational, and that our beliefs are thus typically unjustified, but toughing it out in this way is not without its costs. Given that doxastic justification is a necessary condition for knowledge, such a view would entail that there is, at best, precious little knowledge available to us. Such a broad skepticism sits badly with our pretheoretical intuitions about knowledge and constitutes a substantial cost for most traditional epistemologists. More importantly, from my own perspective, such a view loses touch with the very phenomenon of human knowledge which prompted our philosophical interest in the topic in the first place. We human beings, and other animals too, surely know a great deal about the everyday world around us; there is no other way to make sense of our ability to function in the world as successfully as we do. In addition, the obvious successes of the sciences in the last few hundred years gives vivid testimony to our ability to gain substantial knowledge that goes far beyond everyday matters. Insisting that none of this amounts to true knowledge because it is arrived at in ways which fail to conform to a priori approved principles of reasoning saves the traditional philosophical view about the standards for knowledge by mere linguistic stipulation, and a highly idiosyncratic stipulation at that. Such a notion of knowledge has nothing whatever to do with the intellectual achievements we value so highly or the more mundane intellectual achievements on which our daily lives depend.

5.3. A Psychologized View of Evidential Relations

Let me elaborate on the implications of this view for the relationship between psychology and philosophy. First, the version of psychologism which this view underwrites does not in any way support the view that the truths of logic are dependent on features of human, or any other, psychology. Indeed, I have assumed here that the truths of logic are entirely independent of psychology: what makes the Law of the Excluded Middle true, and what makes Modus Ponens a valid deductive rule, have nothing whatever to do with how anyone's mind works. They are true in virtue of mind-independent facts about logical relations. Thus the version of psychologism I favor does not support psychologism about logic.

Second, however, the proposed view does support a psychologistic account of evidential relations,[13] and in this it contrasts with the great majority of work in analytic epistemology throughout its history. Let

70 Hilary Kornblith

us briefly examine a number of traditional accounts of evidential relations in the past century in order to make this point clear.

Consider Hempel's groundbreaking work (1965) on the logic of confirmation. As Hempel explained, the goal of his work was to discover "general objective criteria determining (A) whether, and – if possible – even (B) to what degree, a hypothesis H may be said to be corroborated by a given body of evidence E" (1965, 6). Hempel was careful to distinguish his approach from others which, as he saw it, involved "a confusion of logical and psychological issues" (1965, 6). Questions of corroboration, or confirmation, or, as Goldman and many epistemologists would put it, justification, are matters of logic for Hempel, and logic, both deductive and inductive, is viewed as entirely independent of psychology. The logic of confirmation which Hempel sought would provide an account of the logical relations between a body of evidence E and a hypothesis H which make it the case that E supports H. This quest for a logic of confirmation gave rise to an extremely active program of research in formal epistemology, including objective and subjective Bayesian approaches, as well as work in decision theoretic epistemology. Evidential relations are logical relations, and although achieving an understanding of evidential relations is, to be sure, no easy matter, such an achievement is attained by way of a priori investigation.

The view that evidential relations are a priori knowable is not limited to formal epistemologists. Internalists about justification, both foundationalists and coherentists, have consistently viewed evidential relations as knowable by a priori means. Thus, whether we look to the foundationalist views of Bertrand Russell (1912) in *The Problems of Philosophy* or Roderick Chisholm's (1966, 1977, 1989) account in *The Theory of Knowledge*, evidential relations must, of necessity, be a priori knowable in order to play the role which such principles do within a foundationalist epistemology. Were evidential relations knowable only a posteriori, foundationalist requirements on justified belief would lead to total skepticism.

Nor is this point limited to foundationalism. Consider, for example, Laurence BonJour's (1985) coherentist account of justification in *The Structure of Empirical Knowledge*. BonJour took great pains to show that a coherentist view leaves room for a priori knowledge,[14] and in his detailed working out of his view on such knowledge in *In Defense of Pure Reason*, he illustrates this claim by arguing that an inductive principle is a priori knowable (1998, 187–216). As BonJour famously argued, the claim that evidential relations are only a posteriori knowable would lead to "intellectual suicide," a total rejection of the possibility of knowledge (1998, 5). But clearly, the psychologism I favor, which makes evidential relations contingent on empirical matters of a would-be knower's psychology, is incompatible with these views. A psychologistic

Naturalism, Psychologism, Relativism   71

account of evidential relations marks a radical departure from the vast majority of epistemological views from Aristotle to the present day.

Thus, suppose that some individual, call him Amos, is in possession of a body of evidence E, and E entails a certain hypothesis H. In traditional views, logical relations are evidential relations, and the fact that E entails H thereby makes it the case that Amos possesses conclusive evidence that H is true. On a psychologistic account of evidential relations, however, the fact that E entails H does not in any way assure that Amos has adequate evidence, let alone conclusive evidence, that H. The evidential facts depend on features of Amos's psychology. In order to know whether Amos has adequate evidence that H, we need to know whether Amos is in possession of reliable psychological processes that would allow him to derive H from E. If the logical connections here are complicated, and if Amos's logical abilities are not up to the task of recognizing these connections, then the psychologistic account I propose does not allow that Amos has adequate evidence for H. E is only evidence for H if one is in possession of psychological processes that allow one to reliably make the transition from E to H.

This is not to say that traditional accounts require us to say that if Amos believes that H in the circumstances described, he justifiably believes that H. Traditional accounts must say that Amos is propositionally justified in believing H, but this is compatible with allowing that Amos may believe H for reasons which fail to track the very facts which make him propositionally justified: he may believe H for bad reasons or no reasons at all, and in such circumstances, although he would be propositionally justified in believing H, he would not be doxastically justified in his belief, and his belief would thus fail to constitute knowledge. Both the psychologistic account of evidential relations and more traditional accounts thus agree that in such circumstances Amos fails to be doxastically justified. Where they disagree is in their claims about propositional justification. Traditional accounts hold, and the psychologistic account denies, that Amos is automatically propositionally justified in believing that H if he has evidence which entails it.

By the same token, the psychologistic account will allow that an agent may be propositionally justified in believing a hypothesis on the basis of evidence which bears no a priori certifiable connection to it. If Betty is in possession of evidence E which has no a priori bearing on H, but she has reliable psychological processes available to her which allow her to conclude that H on the basis of E, then the psychologistic account of evidential relations allows that she is propositionally justified in believing that H. Should she come to believe H on the basis of E by way of the application of such processes to her evidential base, her resulting belief is thereby doxastically justified as well. In the absence of any a priori certifiable relation between E and H, however, traditional accounts will

72 Hilary Kornblith

have it that Betty is not propositionally justified in believing H, and thus cannot be doxastically justified in believing H on such a basis.

The psychologistic account of evidential relations thus departs in a very substantial way from traditional accounts of propositional justification, which in turn has important implications for what we are in a position to know. As should be clear, this has implications for relativism as well.

5.4. Individual Variation

Traditional apriorist accounts of evidential relations are agent- and time-independent. Whether E is evidence for H is a matter of logic alone, and so if E is, in fact, evidence for H, it is evidence for H for all agents and at all times. Similarly, if E fails to provide evidence for H, then E is not evidence for H for any agent at any time. We thus need not speak of evidential relations for an agent at a time, since the reference to both agent and time is otiose.[15]

Matters are altogether different when we psychologize evidential relations. In the proposed view, if a given agent has available psychological processes which allow her to reliably conclude that H on the basis of E, then E is evidence for H for that agent; another agent who lacks such processes is in a position where E fails to provide evidence for H. Evidential relations must thus be relativized to agents, and, because processes available to an agent at one time may fail to be available to that agent at another time, they must be relativized to times as well.

It is important not to exaggerate the extent to which we should expect evidential relations to vary across agents. The simple fact that one agent, on learning that p, may rightly conclude that q, while another agent, on learning the very same fact that p, may be in no position to reasonably conclude that q, does not in any way suggest that matters of evidential relations need to be viewed as relativized to agents. If the first agent also believes that *if p, then q*, while the second agent does not, and if both agents have available psychological processes which track modus ponens, there is no basis for relativism here. It is, to be sure, a fact of life that different agents, when exposed to the same (new) evidence will reach different conclusions. How much of this should be attributed to simple irrationality or extraneous factors interfering with the smooth operation of inferential processes, how much to variations in background information, and how much to differences in available inferential processes is a complex empirical question. What is clear, however, is that we cannot take every such case as evidence of differences in available inferential processes.[16]

More than this, empirical work on human inference has shown a remarkable amount of uniformity across individuals.[17] Nor should this be surprising. We are all members of the same species, and we should no more expect tremendous variability in our basic cognitive equipment than we should expect tremendous variability in the basic structure of human anatomy across individuals. But while this does a good deal of work in tamping down worries that the kind of relativism about evidential relations proposed here will lead to some sort of "anything goes" view in which evidential relations vary wildly across individuals,[18] evolutionary and other empirical considerations will certainly not undermine the case for relativism.

Although the fact that we are all members of the same species serves to explain the commonalities in basic human anatomy, this is not to say, of course, that individual human beings are anatomically as interchangeable as individual electrons. We should expect no less variation in basic cognitive abilities and available inferential processes. There are, in addition, grounds for thinking that available inferential processes may vary with training[19] and with culture,[20] even if we should not expect that such changes are quickly or easily produced. And finally, we should expect large differences in cognitive equipment and inferential processes across species, since the informational demands which their environments make on different species, given their biological needs, vary widely.

In short, the psychologized account of evidential relations proposed here leads to a view of such relations which must be relativized both to individuals and to times, but the amount of variation that this leaves room for is highly constrained. Those who worry that relativism about evidential relations will lead to a view on which anything goes should thus find their worries at least partially allayed. Those who seek an account of evidential relations which is entirely agent-independent, however, will be quite right to recognize that the view proposed here will not allow for such independence. When evidential relations are psychologized in the manner suggested, a highly constrained relativism is the inevitable result.

5.5. Universality and Availability

Thus far, I have argued for two important claims about the nature of evidential relations. First, we must reject the traditional account of such relations, which makes them a matter of logic and probability theory and thus susceptible to a priori investigation. Our psychological processes do not track such a priori principles of inference, or even approximate them, and since doxastic justification, and with it the very possibility of knowledge, require just such tracking of evidential relationships, we must either give up the traditional account of evidential relations as a priori knowable or endorse a very radical skepticism. The skeptical conclusion is, in my view, completely untenable, and so I reject the account of evidential relations which makes them a priori knowable.

74 *Hilary Kornblith*

Second, I have argued that we are thereby led to a psychologized view of evidential relations, and this psychologism brings in its train a circumscribed relativism about evidence as well, making evidential relations relative to both agents and times.

Each of these claims runs counter to traditional views about evidential relations, but even those who would follow me on the first of these two points may wish to draw the line at accepting the second. The two claims, it may be argued, are far more independent of one another than I have made out. Even if the psychological evidence about human inference forces anyone who would reject skepticism to give up a view of evidential relations which makes them a priori knowable, this is wholly compatible with a view of such relations which is not itself psychologized, and which does not force us to regard such relations as relativized either to agents or to times.[21]

In order to best articulate this concern, it will be useful to go back to a feature of the traditional account of evidential relations which makes them a matter of logical and probabilistic relationships. Consider a case in which Frieda and Günter each have evidence E for hypothesis H, where E entails H. The fact that E entails H, in the traditional view, makes E conclusive evidence for H. We can now suppose that Frieda, who is a sophisticated reasoner, immediately concludes that H is true on discovering E. Günter, on the other hand, is not immediately moved to draw any conclusions from E; more than this, on carefully focusing his attention on E and its logical implications, he fails to recognize that H follows from E. On traditional accounts, although Frieda and Günter are both propositionally justified in believing H, only Frieda is doxastically justified in so believing. Both have conclusive evidence that H is true, but only Frieda is moved by her evidence. The notion of evidence is not psychologized, and thus what counts as evidence is independent of psychological facts about Frieda, or Günter, or any other would-be knowers. Evidential relations, in this view, need not be relativized to agents or to times.

Now Goldman's way of defining propositional justification in terms of doxastic justification does force us, as I've been urging, to psychologize the notion of evidence, and therefore to relativize evidential relations to both agents and times. But it is not clear that we need to follow Goldman in taking this tack. Just as the apriorist may offer a view of evidence which detaches it from the psychological capacities of individual agents, those who are sympathetic with Goldman's reliabilism may do the same.

Consider a simple example. Let us suppose that in normal environments, anyone who infers the presence of fire from the presence of smoke will be forming their beliefs in a reliable manner, since it is a fact about normal environments that smoke is rarely found without fire. We may now imagine two different epistemic agents, perhaps of

Naturalism, Psychologism, Relativism 75

different species, one of which has an innate tendency to infer the presence of fire from the presence of smoke without the need for any additional premises. The other, adapted to different environments, has no such inferential tendency: although this creature is perfectly capable of recognizing both smoke and fire, the presence of smoke, in the absence of any additional supporting evidence, does not prompt any belief about fire.

Because Goldman defines propositional justification in terms of doxastic justification, and thereby psychologizes the notion of evidence, he will say that the first of these creatures is both propositionally and doxastically justified in believing that fire is present on those occasions when it sees smoke. But the second creature, who lacks the inferential tendency connecting beliefs about smoke with beliefs about fire, not only fails to be doxastically justified in believing that fire is present on seeing smoke; this creature also fails to be propositionally justified in such a belief. Given this creature's inferential tendencies, Goldman is forced to say that the presence of smoke is not evidence of fire *for it*.

Reliabilists, however, need not follow Goldman in defining propositional justification in terms of doxastic justification. In keeping with reliabilism, one may offer an account of propositional justification in terms of reliability. To take our example, the reliabilist may say that because smoke is a reliable indicator of fire, smoke is evidence of fire. Just as Günter, given his lack of logical sophistication, is unable to respond to the logical connection between E and H and is thereby insensitive to the evidence he has, our second creature is unable to respond to the nomic connection between smoke and fire and is thereby insensitive to the available evidence. In conceptualizing matters in this way, we may retain Goldman's reliabilism and reject the apriorist conception of evidence, yet retain a notion of evidence which is apsychological, thereby obviating the need to relativize our conception of evidence to agents and times. Evidence, in this view, is a matter of certain nomic regularities in the world, and different creatures may be well- or ill-positioned to respond to the evidential facts.

What reason is there to favor either of these conceptions of evidential relations over the other? We are faced with a choice between a conception of evidence which relativizes evidential relations to the psychological capacities of epistemic agents and a more traditional conception of such relations which makes them independent of psychological capacities. In the first of these views, the very conception of evidential relations builds in their cognitive availability: for Goldman, and in the view I have been arguing for, a piece of evidence can only be evidence for an hypothesis for a given agent if that agent has the cognitive capacity to respond appropriately to it. In the latter view, however, facts about evidential relations are independent of such capacities; an agent may have evidence for a hypothesis without in any way being able to take account of it.

76   Hilary Kornblith

It is worth pointing out that historically, a central motivation for the view that evidential relations are a priori knowable had precisely to do with their cognitive availability. Internalist views about justification require that evidential relations between propositions be a priori knowable if they are to do their justificatory work. At the same time, these views were also committed to the claim that, in an important sense, the very fact of a priori knowability made an understanding of these relations available to all would-be knowers. Admittedly, some agents are not as successful in practice as others in recognizing the logical implications of their beliefs, as the case of Frieda and Günter clearly illustrates. All the same, for traditional theorists of knowledge, there is a world of difference between failing to recognize some a priori connection between propositions, on the one hand, and lacking some bit of empirical information, on the other. A priori knowability, in this view, is just a matter of epistemic availability, even if, as in Günter's case, there is also a straightforward sense in which he is unable to afford himself of such access.

What this means is that traditional apriorist views about evidential relations were committed to two substantive claims: that such relations are universal and thus agent-independent; and that they are essentially epistemically available. These views could build in the epistemic availability of evidential relations without compromising their agent-independence precisely because the apriority of such relations was held to assure their universal availability in principle, even if not in practice.

There is no need to comment on the tenability of this claim about the in principle availability of a priori truths, for both of the views we are now considering make evidential relations a posteriori. My point is simply that in apriorist views of evidential relations, one could both build in a requirement that such relations be cognitively available and, at the same time, make them universal and so reject any claim of agent-relativity. Once one gives up the view that evidential relations are a priori knowable, however, one is forced to make a difficult choice: either give up the claim of universality or give up the requirement of availability. Either way of proceeding has its counterintuitive consequences.

The view advocated here involves giving up universality. In this view, E may be evidence for H for one agent and yet fail to be evidence for H for another. There can be little doubt that many will find such a view highly counterintuitive. One may fail to recognize that E is evidence for H or respond to E as evidence for H, some will say, but that doesn't make it the case that E is not evidence for H. Differential responsiveness to E should not be accounted for by suggesting that it is evidence for H for those who respond one way, while it is not evidence for H for those who fail to take it into account. Indeed, it will be plausibly claimed, if E is a reliable indicator of H, those who fail to treat it as such are failing to take account of something epistemically important, and they are thus criticizable for that failure. The claim that whether

E is evidence for *H* is independent of an agent's responsiveness to *E* serves to explain why we find agents blameworthy should they fail to take *E* into account in such circumstances, and why we judge their epistemic performance as defective: they have failed to respond appropriately to their evidence.[22] But this is just to say that we should not give up on universality.

At the same time, it must be acknowledged that giving up on availability is not without its costs either. Conceptions of justified belief, or of rational belief, or of ideal reasoning, should not be conflated with the notion of omniscience. We don't, at least in the typical case, hold that an agent's belief is unjustified simply because they are unaware of some relevant bit of information.[23] Indeed, if we did, the notion of justified belief would simply collapse into true belief. But once we see evidential relations as knowable only a posteriori, ignorance of evidential relations looks no more culpable than failure to be in possession of other relevant empirical information. In such a view, therefore, it is only the requirement that evidential relations be cognitively available that allows us to have a conception of justified belief which is distinct from that of true belief. And this makes it hard to see how it can be legitimate to dispense with the requirement of availability. Moreover, if we do hold on to the requirement of availability, our account of evidential relations will be both psychologistic and relativistic.

I do not believe that these two ways of viewing evidential relations are equally defensible. But before I give my defense of the psychologistic and relativistic account of evidential relations, it will be important to clarify the notion of availability. So let us turn to an examination of that notion.

5.6. More on Availability

Both traditional apriorist views of evidential relations and the psychologized account of such relations which I favor honor a requirement that evidential relations be cognitively available. At the same time, the manner in which these two views conceive of such availability differs in important ways.

In apriorist views, if *E* is evidence for *H*, we are in a position to know that *E* is evidence for *H* precisely because that claim is a priori knowable. To say that we are in a position to know it comes to no more than this: no additional evidence is needed beyond what we already have in order to be able to know that *E* is evidence for *H*. And, of course, no additional evidence is needed to know this because, given its a priori knowability, no evidence at all is needed to know this claim. It is in this sense that, in the traditional view, evidential relations are universally available: all epistemic agents are in a position to know, without any additional evidence, the evidential relations among all propositions.

78 *Hilary Kornblith*

But this is not, of course, the sense in which the view I am defending sees evidential relations as available. Let us go back to Goldman's account of propositional justification. A belief is propositionally justified for an agent, according to Goldman, just in case that agent has available reliable psychological processes which would allow for the production of that belief without the need for any additional evidence. What makes E evidence for H for an agent, in this view, is that the agent has available reliable psychological processes which will allow for the production of belief in H given E as input. This is an externalist view about justification, and so the agent need not know that such a process is available to him or her, nor need the agent know, or be in a position to know, that E is evidence for H. But it is the psychological availability of the process connecting E and H that makes E evidence for H for an agent. And it is for this reason that evidential relations are not only psychologized in this view, but relativized as well. One agent may have available reliable psychological processes which another agent lacks.

5.7. Rejecting Universality

With this clarification of the notion of availability in hand, let us return to the question of whether we should give up the requirement of universality, or, instead, the requirement of availability.

It is universally agreed that the fact that a body of evidence E propositionally justifies H doesn't make me propositionally justified in believing H unless I have evidence E. If you have that evidence, and I don't, then you are propositionally justified in believing H and I am not. The mere existence of evidence is not sufficient to make a person propositionally justified; that evidence must have been taken in, in some sense. Unless it has become cognitively available to me, it does not affect what I am propositionally justified in believing.

Apriorist accounts of evidential relations need make no such special requirement on the relation between E and H precisely because the fact of its a priori knowability is thought to make it accessible to all knowers. But once we allow that evidential relations are knowable only a posteriori, the requirement of availability becomes no less significant for evidential relations than for evidence itself. Just as I cannot be faulted for failing to respond to evidence I don't have, I cannot be faulted for failing to respond to evidential relations which are not cognitively available to me. The requirement of cognitive availability, on apriorist accounts, amounts to a requirement that epistemic agents be in a position to gain a bit of propositional knowledge without obtaining any new evidence: they must be in a position to know that E is evidence for H. In the externalist view I favor, however, cognitive availability of evidential relations is less demanding: it requires only that one have available a reliable psychological process that takes E as input and

Naturalism, Psychologism, Relativism 79

produces H as output. But if one lacks even this – if the evidential relation between E and H is no more available to one than bits of evidence one is unaware of – then it can have no effect on what one is propositionally justified in believing. And this is just to say that, for such a person, E fails to count as evidence for H. E is evidence for H only for those for who have available the relevant psychological processes. And this, of course, is just psychologism, and with it, relativism, about evidential relations.

We do certainly hold people responsible, at times, for failing to see the connections among their beliefs. If I believe that *if p, then q,* and I also believe that p, it seems that I am blameworthy in my conduct as an epistemic agent if I do not believe that q as well;[24] under these conditions, I would be guilty of some sort of epistemic failure. But cases like this can be accounted for even by those who would see evidential relations as relative to the psychological capacities of agents. This example is a convincing case of epistemic failure precisely because it seems that all normal epistemic agents will have available a psychological process which allows them to make such a simple transition. Failure to make use of a reliable psychological process which is available to one is, indeed, blameworthy, and it does constitute an epistemic failing.

Matters are quite different, however, if one fails to conclude that q on the basis of one's knowledge that p, when the connection between p and q is knowable only empirically, and one has neither evidence of such a connection nor an available psychological process which is responsive to that connection. Here, one's epistemic behavior is not criticizable nor does it constitute any sort of epistemic failing. But this is just what one would expect if one holds that evidential relations are relative to available psychological processes.

The view that evidential relations must be both psychologized and relativized thus accounts for everything that the apsychological and unrelativized view accounts for, without falling prey to its problems. These difficulties are avoided, in traditional views, only because evidential relations are held to be a priori knowable. Once we give up the view that such relations are a priori knowable, however, we can no longer reasonably insist that evidential relations are uniform across all agents and all times.

5.8. Conclusion

I have argued for a view which is fundamentally at odds with most of the work not only in analytic epistemology of the last century, but most of the work in epistemology throughout the history of philosophy. Evidential relations, in the view that I have defended, are not knowable a priori. More than this, whether E is evidence for H is not an agent-independent fact. Evidential relations are relativized to the psychology of would-be knowers, and thus not only to agents, but to times.

80 *Hilary Kornblith*

Much of the resistance to both psychologism and relativism, throughout philosophy's history, can be traced to a worry that any such view will pose a threat to objectivity. If E can be evidence for H for you but not for me, the worry goes, then there is no objective fact about what we ought to believe, and there is no objective basis for resolving any dispute between us. Such a view, it seems, licenses each individual to believe whatever he or she takes the evidence to show. Anything goes! But the view defended here leads to no such conclusion. E may be evidence of H for you but not for me, in the view I have defended, but whether it is evidence for either one of us will depend on whether we have available reliable psychological processes which will take us from belief in E to belief in H. There is an objective fact about which processes are reliable. Merely believing that E is evidence for H does not make it so in the view defended here. Objectivity is not thereby threatened by this view.

The resolvability of the dispute, however, is compromised in the view I defend. If your total body of belief consists of the set E, and mine does as well, it may be that you believe one thing on that basis, and I another: you may believe that H, while I do not. More than this, I may believe that H is unjustified. We may both be right, in my view: that is, you may be justified, both propositionally and doxastically, in believing H, while I am justified, both propositionally and doxastically, in believing that I lack adequate evidence for believing H. As long as we have different psychological processes available to us, such a situation may arise. And this, to be sure, can create difficulties for the rational resolution of disputes.

Descartes, of course, did not think that such a situation could arise, and epistemologies which follow Descartes in seeing evidential relations as automatically epistemically available to all will follow him in such a conclusion. Descartes's view, however, that the light of reason allows us all equal access to the same evidential relations is one which we have very good empirical reason now to reject. There is no reason any more to think that the very same reliable psychological processes are available to all believers. Even if there is likely to be a good deal of overlap between the reliable psychological processes available to most pairs of believers – especially if they are members of the same species – this is a far cry from the Cartesian view that there are no differences to be found here at all. And once we acknowledge this, we must also acknowledge that not every dispute need be resolvable by rational means. This does not leave each individual agent isolated with their own inviolable body of beliefs, thereby making attempts at rational resolution utterly pointless, but neither can there be any assurances that such attempts at rational resolution will be successful. This is not, alas, the best of all possible worlds, even from an epistemological point of view. But neither is it the epistemological nightmare that opponents of relativism and psychologism seem to fear.

Notes

1. Martin Kusch (1995) gives an exceptionally illuminating account of the dynamics of this debate. My remarks in this paragraph are very much indebted to Kusch's work.
2. See, for example, Bishop and Trout (2004), DeCaro and MacArthur (2004), DeCaro and MacArthur (2010), DePaul and Ramsey (1998), Fischer and Collins (2015), Haug (2014), Knobe and Nichols (2008), Leiter(2004), Machery and O'Neill (2014), Maddy (2007), Putnam (2016), Stein (1996), Stich (1990), Wagner and Warner (1993), and Williamson (2008).
3. This section summarizes ideas I presented in greater detail in Kornblith (2017).
4. See Goldman (1992, 1986).
5. See, for example, BonJour (1985, Ch. 3), Conee and Feldman (2004), Stroud (2000), and Williams (2016).
6. Other important contributors to the rise of externalism were William Alston, David Armstrong, and Fred Dretske. See, for example, Alston (1976), Armstrong (1973), and Dretske (2000), which collects many of Dretske's pioneering papers from the same period.
7. This distinction was first introduced by Roderick Firth (1978).
8. There are a number of refinements which might be added to these definitions, and not everyone – myself included – will think that cashing this out in terms of "good reasons" is ultimately the best way to conceptualize this distinction. But these details need not detain us here, and these rough definitions should allow for an adequate grasp of the distinction.
9. Typical here is the discussion of well-foundedness in Conee and Feldman (2004). The discussion of well-foundedness is located at 92–3.
10. Goldman uses different terminology, speaking instead of ex ante justification and ex post justification.
11. See Goldman (1992, 124).
12. For a selection of papers, both by Tversky and Kahneman themselves and others working in that tradition, see Kahneman et al. (1982) and Gilovich et al. (2002). See also Kahneman (2011). For an important early review of the literature, see Nisbett and Ross (1980).
13. Ram Neta's (2017) discussion of this issue is especially illuminating.
14. See BonJour (1985, Appendix A, 191–211).
15. A qualification is needed here. In some traditional views, a body of evidence E counts in favor of a hypothesis H only relative to a background B. This reference to background, however, should not be understood, in these views, as a way of smuggling in any kind of relativization to agents or times. Rather, the relationship among E, H, and B is agent- and time-independent. Because these views, no less than those which do not relativize to background, view-relevant evidential relations as matters of logic, it would be extremely misleading to present these views as ones which relativize evidential relations to agents and times simply because different agents may hold different background beliefs, or because a single agent may hold different background beliefs at different times.
16. Elliott Sober (1978) makes this point.
17. See, for example, the works cited in note 12 above.
18. Note too, of course, that the proposed view relativizes evidential relations to available *reliable* processes, and the reliability constraint will do a great deal of work in responding to worries that the sort of relativism proposed here leads to a view on which just anything goes.
19. See, for example, Holland et al. (1986).

82 Hilary Kornblith

20. For an interesting, though certainly not uncontroversial, examination of this issue, see Nisbett (2003).
21. This very point was urged upon me by both Anna-Sara Malmgren and Lisa Miracchi when I presented "Doxastic Justification is Fundamental" at a conference at The College of William and Mary in honor of the thirtieth anniversary of the publication of Alvin Goldman's *Epistemology and Cognition*. At the time, I did not fully appreciate the point they were getting at, but I have been thinking about it ever since, and this section of the current chapter is an attempt both to articulate their concern and to respond to it.
22. Some will wish to divorce the notion of justification from the issues of praise and blame. Even those who favor such an approach, however, may still regard agents who are, for whatever reason, psychologically unresponsive to E even when it is a reliable indicator of H as failing to respond appropriately to their evidence. And this just amounts to a commitment to universality. Thanks to Robin McKenna for bringing this issue to my attention.
23. Of course, if the reason the agent is unaware of the relevant information has to do with some sort of culpable ignorance on the agent's part, this may bear on the epistemic status of the belief. But not all ignorance is culpable ignorance. I will ignore this complication in what follows.
24. Or, alternatively, give up either my belief that *p* or my belief that *if p, then q*. I will leave out this qualification in what follows.

References

Alston, W. (1976), "Two Types of Foundationalism," *Journal of Philosophy* 73 (7): 165–185.
Armstrong, D.M. (1973), *Belief, Truth and Knowledge*, Cambridge: Cambridge University Press.
Bishop, M. and J.D. Trout. (2004), *Epistemology and the Psychology of Human Judgment*, Oxford: Oxford University Press.
BonJour, L. (1985), *The Structure of Empirical Knowledge*, Cambridge, MA: Harvard University Press.
———. (1998), *In Defense of Pure Reason*, Cambridge, MA: Cambridge University Press.
Chisholm, R. (1989), *Theory of Knowledge*, 3rd edition, Upper Saddle River, NJ: Prentice-Hall.
Conee, E. and R. Feldman. (2004), "Internalism Defended," reprinted in their *Evidentialism: Essays in Epistemology*, Oxford: Oxford University Press, 53–82.
DeCaro, M. and D. MacArthur (eds.). (2004), *Naturalism in Question*, Cambridge, MA: Harvard University Press.
———. (2010), *Naturalism and Normativity*, New York: Columbia University Press.
DePaul, M. and W. Ramsey (eds.). (1998), *Rethinking Intuition: The Psychology of Intuition and its Role in Philosophical Inquiry*, Lanham, MD: Rowman & Littlefield.
Dretske, F. (2000), *Perception, Knowledge and Belief: Selected Essays*, Cambridge: Cambridge University Press.
Firth, R. (1978), "Are Epistemic Concepts Reducible to Ethical Concepts?," in *Values and Morals: Essays in Honor of William Frankena, Charles Stevenson, and Richard Brandt*, edited by A. Goldman and J. Kim, Dordrecht: Reidel, 215–229.

Naturalism, Psychologism, Relativism   83

Fischer, E. and J. Collins (eds.). (2015), *Experimental Philosophy, Rationalism and Naturalism: Rethinking Philosophical Method*, Abingdon: Routledge.

Gettier, E.L. (1963), "Is Justified True Belief Knowledge?," *Analysis* 23 (6): 121–123.

Gilovich, T., D. Griffin and D. Kahneman (eds.). (2002), *Heuristics and Biases: The Psychology of Intuitive Judgment*, Cambridge: Cambridge University Press.

Goldman, A. (1986), *Epistemology and Cognition*, Cambridge, MA: Harvard University Press.

———. (1992), "What Is Justified Belief?," reprinted in his *Liaisons: Philosophy Meets the Cognitive and Social Sciences*, Cambridge, MA: MIT Press, 105–126.

Haug, M. (ed.). (2014), *The Armchair or the Laboratory?*, Abingdon: Routledge.

Hempel, C.G. (1965), *Aspects of Scientific Explanation and other Essays in the Philosophy of Science*, New York: The Free Press.

Holland, J., K. Holyoak, R. Nisbett and P. Thagard. (1986), *Induction: Processes of Inference, Learning, and Discovery*, Cambridge, MA: MIT Press.

Kahneman, D. (2011), *Thinking, Fast and Slow*, New York: Farrar, Straus and Giroux.

Kahneman, D., P. Slovic and A. Tversky (eds.). (1982), *Judgment under Uncertainty: Heuristics and Biases*, Cambridge, MA: Cambridge University Press.

Knobe, J. and S. Nichols (eds.). (2008), *Experimental Philosophy*, Oxford: Oxford University Press.

Kornblith, H. (2017), "Doxastic Justification is Fundamental," *Philosophical Topics* 45 (1): 63–80.

Kusch, M. (1995), *Psychologism: A Case Study in the Sociology of Philosophical Knowledge*, London: Routledge.

Leiter, B. (ed.). (2004), *The Future for Philosophy*, Oxford: Oxford University Press.

Machery, E. and E. O'Neill (eds.). (2014), *Current Controversies in Experimental Philosophy*, Abingdon: Routledge.

Maddy, P. (2007), *Second Philosophy: A Naturalistic Method*, Oxford: Oxford University Press.

Neta, R. (2017), "Two Legacies of Goldman's Epistemology," *Philosophical Topics* 45 (1): 121–136.

Nisbett, R. (2003), *The Geography of Thought: How Asians and Westerners Think Differently ... and Why*, New York: Free Press.

Nisbett, R. and L. Ross. (1980), *Human Inference: Strategies and Shortcomings of Social Judgment*, New York: Prentice-Hall.

Putnam, H. (2016), *Naturalism, Realism, and Normativity*, Cambridge: Harvard University Press.

Russell, B. (1912), *The Problems of Philosophy*, London: Home University Library.

Sober, E. (1978), "Psychologism," *Journal for the Theory of Social Behavior* 8 (2): 165–191.

Stein, E. (1996), *Without Good Reason: The Rationality Debate in Philosophy and Cognitive Science*, Oxford: Oxford University Press.

Stich, S. (1990), *The Fragmentation of Reason: Preface to a Pragmatic Theory of Cognitive Evaluation*, Cambridge, MA: MIT Press.

Stroud, B. (2000), "Understanding Human Knowledge in General," reprinted in his *Understanding Human Knowledge: Philosophical Essays*, Oxford: Oxford University Press, 99–121.

84 *Hilary Kornblith*

Wagner, S. and R. Warner (eds.). (1993), *Naturalism: A Critical Appraisal*, South Bend, IN: University of Notre Dame Press.

Williams, M. (2016), "Internalism, Reliabilism, and Deontology," in *Goldman and His Critics*, edited by B. McLaughlin and H. Kornblith, Oxford: Blackwell, 3–18.

Williamson, T. (2008), *The Philosophy of Philosophy*, Oxford: Blackwell.

Part II
Feminist Epistemology and Social Epistemology

6 Relativism in Feminist Epistemologies[1]

Natalie Alana Ashton

6.1. Introduction

Many popular critics of feminist epistemology, and of feminist theorising more generally, assume that it involves some form of relativism. Objective reason, it is claimed, doesn't "care about your feelings", or about gender, race, and social justice (Kimball 1990; Shapiro 2019). And so, whenever social factors like these play a role in theorising, that theorising must be tainted by relativism. On the other hand, many political and social theorists and activists criticise anti-feminist and anti-social justice figures like Trump and Jordan Peterson for the same reason: they accuse them of "post-truth politics", which is bound up with, or even caused by, post-modernism and associated "anything goes" style relativism (Dennett 2000; Kakutani 2018). The relationship between relativism and different social and political views seems to be a tangled one then. This chapter is an attempt at beginning to untangle the knot.

I will frame my discussion around the following central question: are feminist projects and goals best served by relativism or by absolutism? This question is intended as a way to bring the debate about the relationship between feminist epistemology and relativism to life without presupposing that feminist goals are shared by everyone. It should be possible to critically engage with the chapter regardless of what one's political beliefs and goals are. This question is *not* intended as the first step in a simplistic form of pragmatism, where one's political goals straightforwardly dictate which epistemic theories one endorses. The relationship between political goals and theory choice is more nuanced than this, as should become clear in this chapter.

I won't be able to offer a conclusive answer to the central question in this chapter, but I will do a considerable amount of groundwork. I'll evaluate four existing views to determine both what they *say* and what they *show* about the relationship that our central question focuses on – and there will often be differences between what they say and what they show. My overall argument will be that feminist projects can, at least sometimes, be served by relativism, and that the claim they can be

88 *Natalie Alana Ashton*

served by anti-relativism is under-supported. But to begin with, I will clarify some key terms and positions which will be essential to understanding this debate.

6.2. Terms and Positions

Much of the confusion in this debate comes from the misunderstanding of different terms, and the resulting misapplication of them to views to which they don't rightfully apply. To counter this, I will begin my discussion by running through what might seem like some very basic terms.

6.2.1. 'Liberatory' and 'Regressive'

The first terms I need to define are *liberatory* and *regressive*. I'll use these to highlight the social consequences or aims of different epistemic positions. I will use the term *liberatory* to denote views which aim towards social equality and away from social inequality and oppression. Most of the authors I discuss focus predominantly on gender inequality, as though it can be isolated from other forms of inequality and oppression.[2] It can't; without understanding how other forms of oppression and privilege (such as those based on race, class, ability, sexuality, and so on) intersect with gender oppression, we don't really understand gender oppression at all – as will become clear in Section 6.6. So I intend the term 'liberatory' to encompass (existing and potential) epistemic positions which pay attention to various kinds of oppression.

I will use the term *regressive* to mean any epistemic positions which don't tend towards equality. This includes views which have the creation and maintenance of oppression as (explicit or implicit) goals, but also views which have these as an unintended consequence. I think it's reasonable to describe any view which doesn't seek to dismantle oppression as an obstacle to progress given that we currently inhabit a world which contains considerable inequality – those who disagree can feel free to mentally substitute their own preferred term in place of 'regressive' if they wish.

6.2.2. 'Relativism'

The other basic terms that I need to define are *relativism*, *objectivity*, and *absolutism*, which are used to describe an aspect of the picture of justification that a particular view depends on. These terms are used in various domains (e.g. moral, scientific, aesthetic) and have slightly different meanings in each. In this chapter I will only talk about the *epistemic* domain, so I won't specify the domain each time. From now on, when I say, for example, 'absolutism', I am talking about epistemic absolutism.

Relativism in Feminist Epistemologies 89

When I describe a view as *relativist*, I mean that it satisfies the following three criteria for epistemic relativism:

Dependence: A belief has an epistemic status (as justified or unjustified) only relative to an epistemic system or practice.
Plurality: There are, have been, or could be, more than one such epistemic system or practice.
Non-Neutrality: There is no neutral way of evaluating different systems or practices.

(Kusch 2016, 33–34)

The first two criteria aren't too controversial within feminist epistemology, and most of the debate surrounding relativism turns on the last one. Because of this, it's worth taking some time to distinguish non-neutrality from a superficially similar claim about justification, which it is sometimes confused with. This other claim is often called "equality" (Kusch 2016, 35) or "equal validity" (Boghossian 2006, 2).

Non-neutrality says that there's no *neutral* way to evaluate different systems or practices, and so all evaluations of systems and practices must be non-neutral or system-dependent. Equal validity says that all systems and practices are equally good. These might seem to be similar. They both appear to say that we can't, or shouldn't bother trying to, rank systems; in one case because evaluations are impossible, in the other because the outcome will be a universal draw. But they are different.

Looking more closely, non-neutrality doesn't say that rankings aren't possible but rather that *neutral* rankings aren't possible. System-dependent rankings are compatible with non-neutrality. Equal validity doesn't say that rankings aren't possible either – in fact it *is* a ranking. It ranks all systems as equal. However, it seems to be a ranking which isn't system-dependent. And this is where the crucial difference arises: equal validity contradicts the first component of relativism (dependence) which says that justification is system-dependent, whilst non-neutrality (which only allows for system-dependent rankings) doesn't. Versions of relativism which include a commitment to equal validity will be doomed to incoherence from the outset, and so any charitable investigation into whether a view (such as a form of feminist epistemology) is relativist or not will be sure to focus on relativism as a commitment to dependence, plurality, and *non-neutrality*.

6.2.3. *'Objectivity' and 'Absolutism'*

Relativism's opposite is sometimes taken to be objectivity and at other times absolutism – and to confuse matters further, different people use these terms in different, sometimes overlapping, ways. Except when quoting (or otherwise clearly using the terminology of) other authors, I

90 Natalie Alana Ashton

will use these terms as follows; *objectivity* is the idea that justification is independent of social and individual factors, whereas *absolutism* is the idea that standards for justification apply universally, regardless of time, place, etc. Whenever it's necessary to refer to these ideas collectively – or otherwise to refer to relativism's opposite without specifying one of these ideas in particular – I will use *anti-relativism* as a general umbrella term.[3]

Now that I've defined these terms, I can map out a matrix of four different positions that one might hold in this debate, depending on the social consequences of the view (i.e. liberatory or regressive) and the picture of justification it depends on (i.e. relativist or anti-relativist). This table represents this matrix and indicates in which section of the chapter each portion of the matrix will be discussed.

	Liberatory	*Regressive*
Anti-relativist	(Section 6.6)	(Section 6.4)
Relativism	(Section 6.3)	(Section 6.5)

In Section 6.3 I'll use Helen Longino's 'contextual empiricism' to illustrate *liberatory relativism*. I'll use Sandra Harding's criticism of 'weak objectivity' to illustrate *regressive anti-relativism* in Section 6.4 and her arguments against relativism as a framework to discuss *regressive relativism* in Section 6.5. In Section 6.6, I'll use Meera Nanda's discussion of 'modern science' as a way to explore *liberatory anti-relativism*.

My discussion of these arguments and views will be critical – with the exception of the criticism of weak objectivity in Section 6.4, I don't think that any of these arguments show what their author intends them to. Instead, I think that all of them lend support to the view that relativism is liberatory, or to the complementary view that anti-relativism is regressive, or to both. I'll revisit the matrix and consider what we should take from this in the conclusion.

6.3. Relativism as Liberatory

In this section, I'm going to discuss Helen Longino's 'contextual empiricism' (1994, 1997) as the view which I think most clearly demonstrates liberatory relativism. Longino doesn't apply this label to herself – she understands her own view as a liberatory *contextualism*, which she classifies as a third way between relativism and absolutism – but her view does have the three defining features of relativism, as I will demonstrate.

Longino's contextual empiricism starts from the premise that values play an important role in science and always have. In particular, she points out that values – such as the traditional theoretical virtues like simplicity and homogeneity – are needed to choose between different empirically adequate theories. Next, she highlights the scientific advances that have been made by feminist researchers deploying alternative theoretical

Relativism in Feminist Epistemologies   91

virtues, like novelty and heterogeneity, which suggest that more than one set of theoretical values is legitimate[4] (1994, 1997).

This view is liberatory because, as Longino explains, the virtues she highlights help to meet the feminist *cognitive goal* of revealing the mechanisms and institutions of women's oppression (1997, 27), which in turn helps to achieve the feminist *political goal* of dismantling the oppression of women. For example, the virtue of ontological heterogeneity is a preference for identifying and theorising about difference. Researchers guided by this virtue have investigated whether the efficacy of certain drugs differs with the race and gender of the patients treated with it. In the cases where such differences have been found, the researchers effectively met both feminist cognitive goals (they revealed that previous researchers' assumptions acted to sustain oppression by recommending ineffective treatments for oppressed people) and political ones (they uncovered information about drug efficacy which can be used to improve oppressed peoples' material circumstances) (1994, 477, 1997, 21).

I think that this view is also relativist, because all three of the components of relativism I identified above are present within it. Dependence is present because Longino thinks that epistemic status is relative to a practice (i.e. to a particular scientific methodology and a set of community standards which include theoretical virtues), which is appropriate for a particular cognitive goal (1997, 28–9). She makes this point especially clear in the following passage:

> The alternative virtues are only binding in those communities sharing a cognitive goal that is advanced by those virtues. Their normative reach is, thus, local. In emphasising the provisionality and locality of alternative virtues, this account contrasts quite sharply with accounts offered or implied by advocates of the traditional virtues which, as (purely) epistemic are represented as universally binding.
>
> (1997, 28)

Longino's point here is that the feminist virtues set a practice and a standard of justification for some people – those with feminist goals – but that for other people, with different goals, these standards won't have any normative force. Those people will need to meet other virtues, practices, and standards of justification relative to their own goals. So, justification is *dependent* on a practice.

The above quote also highlights the presence of the second relativist component in Longino's view. In this view, the feminist theoretical virtues and the practices associated with them aren't the only virtues and practices available. There is a plurality of goals and so a *plurality* of practices and of standards for justification.

We get a glimpse of Longino's commitment to the third component of relativism – non-neutrality – when she considers the objection that some hypothetical third set of virtues could serve as a single, objective or

92 *Natalie Alana Ashton*

absolute, standard (1997, 29–30). She identifies two characteristics of theories which might be able to play this role. One is truth, which she says collapses into a theoretical virtue that feminists and traditional epistemologists agree on; empirical adequacy. The other is empirical adequacy itself. As empirical adequacy underdetermines theory choice (this is why theoretical virtues are needed in the first place) (1994, 476–477), she rejects both options. In her own words: "the epistemic is not rich enough to guide inquiry and theory appraisal" (1997, 30). Neutral, value-free justification is insufficient, and there is no absolute or objective epistemic standard which could decisively bind us all independent of our goals.

If Longino is committed to this denial of universal standards, then she won't be able to provide an independent ranking of epistemic practices. And, actually, she doesn't want or try to. She says outright that she's not interested in a "single theory providing a best or definitive account of reality" and instead aims for a view which "does not privilege the feminist or any other set of theoretical virtues" (1997, 32–33). The only epistemic rankings she is interested in are *non-neutral*. So, all three of the components of relativism that I highlighted are present in Longino's view. Despite what she claims, Longino's view is a form of liberatory relativism.

6.4. Objectivity as Regressive

In this section, I'll use Sandra Harding's discussion of 'weak objectivism' as an illustration of regressive anti-relativism.[5] She intends these arguments to show that traditional objectivity is regressive in the sense that I suggest, so in this case (unlike the case of Longino previously) what the view *says* and what I think it *shows* are in agreement with one another. Harding discusses weak objectivity in the context of outlining her own positive view – her take on a view called feminist standpoint theory – so let's begin with the basics of this view.

Standpoint theories have two central theses. First, they say that social factors affect knowledge because differing experiences of social privilege and oppression lead to the development of different *epistemic perspectives* (resources for determining which propositions are justified and which aren't). This is known as the standpoint thesis:

Standpoint thesis: justification depends on 'socially situated' perspectives

According to this idea, subjects have different 'social locations' or different statuses as socially oppressed or socially privileged. For example, black women occupy very different social locations than white men, and these different social locations come with different experiences, which have the potential to enable different epistemic perspectives.

Second, and more specifically, standpoint theorists say that social oppression can lead to *epistemic advantages*, so those who are worse off socially might be better off epistemically. This is known as the inversion thesis (2003) or the epistemic advantage thesis:

Epistemic advantage thesis: social oppression can lead to more, or better, epistemic justification

This advantage thesis comes with several caveats. First, standpoint theorists are careful to point out that epistemic advantage doesn't depend on essential categories; where categories like 'woman' are used, they needn't (in fact shouldn't) be thought of as natural (i.e. biological or pre-social) (Hartsock 1997; Smith 1997; Wylie 2003). Second, the possibility of possessing epistemic advantage is neither a necessary nor a sufficient condition for membership in a social group – it's possible for oppressed people to lack this advantage and for non-oppressed people to have it (Medina 2012). Third, the epistemic advantage isn't automatic. It requires work, in the form of collaborative critical reflection (Fricker 1999: 202–203; Medina 2012; Wylie 2003). And finally, the advantage needn't be global – it's scope can be restricted to certain claims, most plausibly to those about social relations (Harding 1991, 46; Wylie 2003, 37; Fricker 1999, 203).

Beyond these two theses and four caveats, different standpoint theorists cash out their views in different ways – in particular they have different explanations of how the epistemic advantage described in the second thesis arises. Looking at Harding's explanation of this will lead us into her discussion of weak objectivism.

Harding thinks the epistemic advantage that socially oppressed people have comes from their being better placed to identify a certain set of values which can have an effect on scientific practice. On the one hand there are *overt values*, which aren't shared by most researchers and affect science from the outside. Imagine a study on the health effects of tobacco which is funded by a cigarette company – most of us would read such a study cautiously and critically, keeping an eye out for signs of the company's values (such as their interests in avoiding negative perceptions of their products and in turning a profit) affecting the research. All else being equal (i.e. there's no explicit deception going on) these overt values are relatively easy for all researchers to spot.

On the other hand there are *constitutive values*, which are shared by a large proportion of researchers and affect science from within. Because they are widely shared, they can be less salient and so more difficult to spot – at least for some researchers. Harding's explanation of epistemic advantage turns on oppressive values being constitutive in this way. The idea is that people who are affected by these values – e.g. people of colour and white women in the case of racist and sexist values – will

94   Natalie Alana Ashton

find them more salient and so be in a better position to recognise them than people (such as the rich, white, and otherwise privileged men who have historically dominated 'western' science) who aren't.[6]

With this background in place, we can now explore Harding's argument that objectivity is regressive. Harding identifies a guiding principle of 'traditional' science, which is to exclude all social values from the research process. Recalling the definition that I outlined in Section 6.2, we can see that this principle coheres with an objective picture of science. I defined objectivity as the view that epistemic justification is independent of social and individual factors, while this guiding principle says that a certain kind of social factor – social values – should be kept out of scientific research.

Harding's criticism of this objectivity principle is that it undermines itself. Socially oppressed people are less likely to participate in science due to financial, social, and other structural barriers. In recommending that *all* values be kept out of science, the endorsement of this principle prevents the social background and experiences of different scientists from being taken into account and so fails to attend to one important way that certain constitutive values can be identified. These values then reinforce the existing biases and values, which helps to reinforce the barriers keeping oppressed people out of science, and so on, in a vicious cycle which hurts science as well as hurting oppressed people on both an individual and structural level. This means that weak objectivity – in addition to being unhelpful scientifically – is also regressive. So, Harding's argument illustrates the second position one might take towards our central question: regressive anti-relativism.

6.5. Relativism as Regressive

In the previous section, we saw Harding criticise objectivity as regressive. Despite this, she doesn't endorse relativism as a way to support liberatory goals.[7] In fact, she criticises relativism as regressive too. She makes two main arguments in support of this claim. I will discuss each in turn.

6.5.1. Relativism as Weak Objectivity

Harding's first criticism is that relativism amounts to weak objectivity, which we have already seen is regressive. The passage where she puts forward this claim goes as follows:

> Many thinkers have pointed out that judgemental relativism [which Harding equates with the "epistemological claim that there are ... no rational or scientific grounds for making judgements between various patterns of belief and their originating social practices"] is internally related to objectivism. For example, science historian

> Donna Haraway argues that judgemental relativism is the other side of the very same coin from "the God trick" required by what I have called weak objectivity. To insist that no judgements at all of cognitive adequacy can legitimately be made amounts to the same thing as to insist that knowledge can be produced only from "no place at all": that is, by someone who can be every place at once.

There are two key things to note about this passage. Harding thinks (a) that epistemic (or what she calls 'judgemental') relativism is the view that there can be no (rationally grounded, 'cognitively adequate', or otherwise legitimate) judgements between different epistemic frameworks; and (b) that this view is equivalent to the claim that knowledge must come from "no place at all" – i.e. it must be non-situated and value-free. If she's right, then relativism collapses into weak objectivity, which we have already seen is regressive and unsuitable for meeting feminist goals. However, both (a) and (b) are false.

Let's take (b) first. This claim is false because the two views Harding describes are not equivalent. The weak objectivist says that knowledge can be produced "from no place at all", i.e. value-free knowledge is possible. This is a positive claim about the existence of justification in a social vacuum. It is very different from the negative claim she attributes to the relativist, which is that we cannot rank different epistemic frameworks or sets of values.

More importantly for our interests, (a) is also false. The claim that there can be no (rationally grounded) judgements about different frameworks is not a relativist claim. As we saw in Section 6.2, relativists are committed to the non-neutrality claim which says that there is no *system-independent* way to evaluate different epistemic systems. In this view judgements about epistemic frameworks are possible, they are just relative to their own framework or system of values. So, both parts of Harding's first criticism of relativism fail.

6.5.2. Relativism as a Regressive Defence Mechanism

Harding's second criticism of relativism relies on a historical claim. She says that relativism has traditionally been used by members of socially privileged groups as a defence mechanism to enable them to retain their power (1991, 153). Initially she claimed that relativism was exclusively used in this way, although since then she's weakened her claim and acknowledged that both relativism and objectivism have been used for both liberatory and regressive ends (2015, 333). But her general point still stands: some regressives do use relativism in this way (or at least appear to), which suggests that relativism works counter to feminist aims and goals. So, this criticism is worth exploring in more detail.

96   *Natalie Alana Ashton*

I can think of two sorts of cases that illustrate Harding's concern that relativism can be used as a regressive defence mechanism. The first case is of relativist-sounding claims which are used to undermine the claims of the oppressed, for example responding to criticism with lines such as "well, that's one opinion". This strategy appears to allow feminist, anti-racist, and other views to have some level of legitimacy ("of course I can see why *you* might think that"), but it is a regressive strategy because at the same time it attempts to absolve the speaker of the responsibility to properly engage with these views.

I agree with Harding that this kind of move runs counter to feminist aims, but I don't think it's a problem because relativism doesn't warrant it. This strategy seeks to undermine liberatory claims by classifying them as *merely relatively* justified. This only works if we presuppose that there's some other, more legitimate, *absolute* justification to compare the relative justification to. If you don't think such absolute justification exists – as relativists don't – then saying that liberatory claims are *merely* relatively justified isn't an undermining move. It attributes as much epistemic legitimacy to the feminist claims as it is possible to give. Someone who highlights the relativity of a claim's epistemic status in an attempt to undermine it isn't really a relativist; they are an absolutist who is either confused or disingenuous. So this case doesn't demonstrate the regressive nature of relativism, as Harding thinks, but rather the regressive nature of absolutism.[8]

The second case in which relativism is used as a regressive defence mechanism is when it is used as a way to avoid having to justify one's own views. A notorious example of this occurred after President Trump's first press secretary Sean Spicer made a series of false claims in his first official statement in the role. These included the claim that the crowd at Trump's inauguration was larger than the crowd at former President Obama's inauguration, that more people had used the local metro system on the day of Trump's inauguration than on the day of Obama's, and that Trump's inauguration was the first to see the use of floor coverings at the National Mall (Spicer 2017). When the Counsellor to the President, Kellyanne Conway, was asked about these false claims on NBC's *Meet The Press*, she defended them by claiming that Spicer was simply presenting "alternative facts" (Todd 2017).

The idea behind this kind of strategy is to reduce the justificatory burden on oneself. If I say that the facts I'm presenting are 'alternative' facts, then I don't need to prove that yours are false in order to assert that mine are true. As previously though, relativists would take issue with this strategy. Identifying that a set of beliefs are justified relative to a particular system is the beginning of the relativist story, not the end of it, as it entitles your interlocutors to investigate what system your beliefs are supposed to be justified relative to and whether that relativity relationship really does hold, as well as to make (system-dependent) judgements about that system. So whilst the general claim, that there are competing

Relativism in Feminist Epistemologies   97

sets of facts relative to different epistemic frameworks, is endorsed by relativists, the strategy of using this point to avoid the need to provide further justification is not a relativist strategy.

Neither of these cases supports the claim that relativism can be used as a regressive defence mechanism. Both the regressive-defence argument and the relativism-as-weak-objectivity argument have failed, and so Harding's view that relativism is regressive remains unsupported.

6.6. Anti-Relativism as Liberatory

In the last three sections, I discussed views in which – in line with the prevailing opinion in feminist epistemology – (traditional) objectivity is claimed to be regressive. In this section, I'll explore a much less common view, defended by Meera Nanda: that liberatory goals are best met by traditional scientific anti-relativism.[9]

Nanda's (2003) view is informed by the liberation movement resisting the oppression of Dalits (low caste people, also referred to as 'untouchables') and women in India. She describes how caste and gender are part of the oppressive traditional social order in India, which is upheld by Hindu religious beliefs and practices, and discusses the centrality of 'traditional' western scientific values to Bhimrao Ambedkar's challenge to this social order.

Ambedkar, who was originally Hindu, studied under John Dewey in the United States for three years. After returning to India, he publicly converted to Buddhism and launched the Dalit Buddhist movement, which challenges the country's caste system and related oppression (including gender oppression). Nanda emphasises the influence that Dewey and his understanding of 'modern science' has on Ambedkar and his activism and uses this to argue that the traditional western scientific values that feminist epistemologists eschew can actually be crucial to (at least some) liberatory projects. Metaphysical religious beliefs, like those around karma, were effectively challenged by naturalistic, scientific thinking, and so Nanda's claim is that traditional 'western' scientific values are key to the "Dalit-feminist standpoint" and that authors like Harding and Longino who criticise these values undermine the efforts and the liberation of non-western feminists.

Nanda makes a number of other criticisms of Harding, Longino, and "social constructivist critics of science, along with their feminist and post-colonial allies" which I think are unhelpfully sweeping and often only hit straw versions of the intended targets.[10] However, her point that many feminist epistemologists have often overlooked, minimised, or misunderstood the concerns and struggles of women who aren't white and western is true, and her positive contribution to the literature deserves serious consideration.

In the context of this chapter, the aspect of Nanda's work which I find most interesting is the suggestion that Ambedkar's work is an example of

98 *Natalie Alana Ashton*

"objectivity and universality" used for liberatory ends (157). I am not convinced that this is the right way to interpret his project, and in the remainder of this section I will (i) recommend a qualification of the second part of this claim (the one regarding liberation), and (ii) challenge the first part (which regards anti-relativism).

So, first I want to qualify Nanda's claim that the way Ambedkar used science is liberatory. Whilst his work did meet important liberatory goals in the context that Nanda describes – she makes a clear and detailed case for the importance of science to the concrete progress Ambedkar made – it's important to acknowledge that this doesn't show that the scientific values in question are *always* liberatory. In the same way that Nanda cautions against seeing Longino's alternative scientific values as liberatory in all contexts (e.g. in the context of Dalit liberation), we can see that the scientific values which Nanda points to are oppressive in other contexts – e.g. in the western context, as Longino and Harding have argued.[11] Whilst Nanda succeeds in showing that traditional western science can be liberatory, its liberatory potential is restricted to certain contexts.[12]

Second, I want to challenge Nanda's suggestion that Ambedkar's achievements count in favour of anti-relativism. Nanda doesn't say directly that she thinks Ambedkar is an anti-relativist, but she does frame her dissatisfaction with feminist epistemology (which Ambedkar's work is supposed to be an alternative to) as (partly) due to its willingness to challenge science's "objectivity and universality" (157), and she attributes to Ambedkar (and Dewey) the view that "the *content* of modern scientific theories demand[s] universal rational acceptance by *all* people" (158 [italics in original]). This suggests that she takes objectivity and absolutism to be an important part of why Ambedkar's work was capable of supporting liberatory goals in the Indian context, and why (she believes) Longino and Harding's wouldn't be.

However, what Nanda says diverges from what her view shows. Nanda's view of 'modern science' (by which she means the theoretical values characterising traditional western science (158)) as a Dalit-feminist standpoint (177) has considerable similarities to Longino's contextual empiricism, and like that view it also has all of the basic components of relativism. The most obvious component is the second one: Nanda straightforwardly acknowledges a *plurality* of different epistemic frameworks or theoretical values – specifically, the attitude of 'modern science' and the feminist theoretical virtues.

I think that the first component is present too. Nanda seems to accept that both of the sets of values that she considers are successful in different contexts, at least when it comes to meeting liberatory goals (she argues that modern science has been successful in the Indian context, and doesn't dispute that Longino's alternative values have been successful in 'the West'), so she seems to be committed to a kind of liberatory

Relativism in Feminist Epistemologies   99

dependence thesis. And she should also accept *epistemic dependence*, as both frameworks that she discusses have been shown to be epistemically successful (i.e. to have justification depend on them).[13]

The only remaining component is *non-neutrality*. It's difficult to tell what Nanda's stance is on this. On the one hand she says that Ambedkar and Dewey both thought the content of the framework she calls 'modern science' should be rationally accepted by all people, which might be intended as a system-independent evaluation of that (and other) framework(s). On the other hand, the criticisms she actually makes of other frameworks seem primarily to turn on their unsuitability in the specific context that she is discussing. This means that they are system-dependent and so are compatible with non-neutrality. Elsewhere (Ashton forthcoming) I have argued that all coherent versions of standpoint theory require non-neutrality, and so the principle of charity suggests that we presume Nanda does – or at least can – endorse non-neutrality. So, with all three components present, I think that Nanda's view is best understood as a form of liberatory relativism.

6.7. Conclusion

Let's return to the central question that I outlined in the introduction: are feminist projects and goals best served by relativism or by absolutism? I sketched a matrix of four possible positions one could inhabit in response to this question, and each of the preceding four sections explored one of these. We can now update the matrix as follows:

	Liberatory	*Regressive*
Anti-relativism		Weak Objectivity Defence Mechanism 1
Relativism	Longino's Contextual Empiricism Nanda's Modern Science	

Longino and Nanda both took themselves to defend a form of liberal anti-relativism (though Longino would make a distinction between anti-relativism involving objectivity and absolutism, and other non-relativist views, classifying her own view as the latter). I showed that both of them are better understood as arguing for versions of liberatory relativism and so belong in the bottom left portion of the matrix. Harding argued – and I agreed – that her criticisms of weak objectivity show that it can be regressive and belongs in the top right portion. Harding also tried to argue that relativism is regressive. Her first argument for this – that it collapses into weak objectivity – failed (indicated on the matrix by being struck through). Her second argument – that relativism can be used as a regressive defence mechanism – proved unconvincing. One of the strategies we

100 *Natalie Alana Ashton*

considered failed to show the intended conclusion (and again is stuck through), whilst the other turned out to be a form of regressive absolutism.

The result of this is that only the bottom left portion of the matrix (liberatory relativism) and the top right portion (regressive anti-relativism) are occupied. Should we conclude from this that feminist projects are best served by relativism? This answer would be too hasty – especially as Nanda has shown that there can be contexts and cases that we are ignorant of. Instead, at this stage I think we should just conclude that feminist projects *can* be served by relativism, and that the claim that they can be served by anti-relativism is under-supported – which is already a significant departure from the status quo.

Notes

1. Research on this chapter was assisted by funding from the ERC Advanced Grant Project "The Emergence of Relativism" (Grant No. 339382).
2. Authors who have considered the intersection of multiple oppressions in the formulation of standpoint epistemology include Patricia Hill Collins (1986), who has written on the standpoints of black women, and Jose Medina (2012), who argues that we should strive to develop a "kaleidoscopic consciousness" which is always open to the possibility of further standpoints or ways of looking at the world grounded in other intersections of oppression.
3. Though for the record, I only consider absolutism to be the true opposite of relativism.
4. The other theoretical virtues Longino considers are *ontological heterogeneity, complexity, applicability to human need, diffusion of power*, and *empirical adequacy*. This last one is worth noting as it also features in traditional lists of theoretical virtues. It recommends theories which fit with the available data and means that inquiry conducted according to Longino's alternative theoretical virtues is no more 'subjective' or 'pragmatic' than inquiry conducted according to the traditional virtues.
5. Harding makes a distinction between *objectivism*, which she argues is an unhelpful scientific norm, and *objectivity*, which (as we will see shortly) is a version of this norm which she thinks can guide good science.
6. Patricia Hill Collins (1986) made this point first, though she didn't use the term 'constitutive values'. For further discussion of this and the connection to Harding's work, see Ashton and McKenna (2018).
7. Instead she suggests an alternative objective guiding principle for science, *strong objectivity*, which she claims is liberatory. I have argued elsewhere that she is wrong – strong 'objectivity' is actually a kind of liberatory relativism (Ashton forthcoming).
8. A more sophisticated attempt at this same strategy would be to say that the feminist views are justified in the only way possible, but that they are justified relative to a set of values or presuppositions that one doesn't accept – for example, the claim that women are equal to men. This is a legitimate move to make according to relativists, and it also serves one of the feminist cognitive goals that we saw earlier: it helps to reveal the way that gender and assumptions about gender operate in science. So, this would be a relativist strategy, but not one which serves regressive goals particularly well.
9. To be clear: it's not uncommon for epistemologists to think that some form of epistemic objectivity is correct – that's the standard view in traditional

Relativism in Feminist Epistemologies 101

epistemology, and even amongst feminist epistemologists, some modified version of objectivity (such as Harding's 'strong' kind) is the norm. But amongst epistemologists who explicitly share liberatory aims, *traditional* (or 'weak') objectivity is an unusual view.

10. It's beyond the scope of this chapter to expand on this point in detail, but Elizabeth Anderson's (2004) review of the volume in which this chapter first appeared makes some more general points about the problematic ways that many critics engage with feminist epistemology.

11. Nanda might resist this conclusion, as she thinks that there are other problems with Harding and Longino's arguments. As I've said in note 10 previously, I don't think those criticisms are successful, although I don't have time to address them in detail here.

12. My point here is that both Nanda's work and the work of Harding and Longino are subject to this qualification, but I don't mean to imply that Nanda's failure to make it explicit is as egregious as Harding and Longino's (both mention that their work is limited to the feminism of a certain subset of women, but most of the time they tend to talk as though this isn't the case). Emphasising the qualification is important in both cases when we're merely thinking about the issue of relativism, but there are additional reasons to emphasise the qualification in Harding and Longino's work as it creates the imbalance which Nanda is responding to.

13. Nanda might resist this, as I think part of her response to Longino (163–4) is intended to imply that the alternative values will be less epistemically successful than the traditional ones. But the relevant passage reads like a written version of an 'incredulous stare', rather than a systematic critique, and it fails to acknowledge any of the examples of uncontroversial scientific advancement that Longino attributes to her alternative values, so I don't think this undermines my claim that she should accept epistemic dependency.

References

Anderson, E. (2004), "How Not to Criticize Feminist Epistemology: A Review of Pinnick, Koertge and Almeder, *Scrutinizing Feminist Epistemology*," www-personal.umich.edu/~eandersn/hownotreview.html (Accessed November 20th, 2019).

Ashton, N.A. (forthcoming), "Relativising Epistemic Advantage," in *The Routledge Handbook of the Philosophy of Relativism*, edited by M. Kusch, London: Routledge.

Ashton, N.A. and McKenna, R. (2018), "Situating Feminist Epistemology," *Episteme*: 1–20.

Boghossian, P. (2006), *Fear of Knowledge: Against Relativism and Constructivism*, Oxford: Oxford University Press.

Collins, P.H. (1986), "Learning from the Outsider within: The Sociological Significance of Black Feminist Thought," *Social Problems* 33 (6): s14–s32.

Dennett, D. (2000), "Postmodernism and Truth," *The Proceedings of the Twentieth World Congress of Philosophy*: 93–103.

Fricker, M. (1999), "Epistemic Oppression and Epistemic Privilege," *Canadian Journal of Philosophy* 29: 191–210.

Harding, S. (2015), "'Strong Objectivity': A Response to the New Objectivity Question," *Synthese* 104 (3): 331–349.

102 *Natalie Alana Ashton*

———. (1991), *Whose Science? Whose Knowledge?: Thinking from Women's Lives*, Ithaca, NY: Cornell University Press.

Hartsock, N. (1997), "Comment on Hekman's 'Truth and Method: Feminist Standpoint Theory Revisited': Truth or Justice?," *Signs: Journal of Women in Culture and Society* 22 (2): 367–374.

Kakutani, M. (2018), *The Death of Truth*, London: William Collins.

Kimball, R. (1990), *Tenured Radicals: How Politics has Corrupted Our Higher Education*, New York: Harper & Row.

Kusch, M. (2016), "Wittgenstein's On Certainty and Relativism," in *Analytic and Continental Philosophy*, Berlin and Boston: De Gruyter, 29–46.

Longino, H.E. (1994), "In Search of Feminist Epistemology," *The Monist* 77 (4): 472–485.

———. (1997), "Feminist Epistemology as a Local Epistemology," *Aristotelian Society Supplementary Volume* 71 (1): 19–36.

Medina, J. (2012), *The Epistemology of Resistance: Gender and Racial Oppression, Epistemic Injustice, and the Social Imagination*, Oxford: Oxford University Press.

Nanda, M. (2003), "Science as the Standpoint Epistemology of the Oppressed: Dewey Meets the Buddha of India's Dalits," in *Scrutinizing Feminist Epistemology*, edited by C. Pinnick, New Brunswick: Rutgers University Press.

Shapiro, B. (2019), *Facts Don't Care about Your Feelings*, Hermosa Beach, California: Creators Publishing.

Smith, D. (1997), "Comment on Hekman's *Truth and Method: Feminist Standpoint Theory Revisited*," *Signs: Journal of Women in Culture and Society* 22 (2): 392–398.

Spicer, S. (2017), "Spicer: Inauguration Had Largest Audience Ever," *YouTube Video*, 1:13, posted by "CNN," 21 January, www.youtube.com/watch?v= PKzHXelQi_A.

Todd, C. (2017), "Conway: Press Secretary Gave 'Alternative Facts'," *NBC*, 3:39, 22 January, 2017, www.nbcnews.com/meet-the-press/video/conway-press-secretary-gave-alternative-facts-860142147643.

Wylie, A. (2003), "Why Standpoint Matters," in *Science and Other Cultures: Issues in Philosophies of Science and Technology*, edited by R. Figueroa and S. Harding, New York: Routledge, 26–48.

7 Feminist Epistemology and Pragmatic Encroachment

Robin McKenna

7.1. Introductory Remarks

Some have argued that whether you know that p depends on a combination of pragmatic and epistemic factors (Fantl and McGrath 2009; Hawthorne 2004; Grimm 2011; Stanley 2005; Weatherson 2012).[1] These "pragmatic encroachers" tend to focus on a particular pragmatic factor: how much is at stake for an individual. The idea is that, the higher the stakes are for you – the more important it is that you are right – the more evidence you need in order to know. I will call this "stakes encroachment." In my view, there is reason to think that knowledge depends on pragmatic factors other than stakes. In particular, there is reason to think that knowledge depends on social factors such as:

- the subject's social role,
- the subject's social identity, and
- the risk of social injustice.

I will call this "social encroachment."[2] This chapter has two parts. In the first part (§§7.2–4), I will argue for social encroachment and clarify the sort of "social dependence" of knowledge it involves. In the second part (§7.5), I will clarify the relationship between social encroachment and a key idea in feminist epistemologies.[3] At the core of most feminist epistemologies is the idea that the social locations of inquirers make for epistemic differences. One finds this idea in both feminist standpoint theory (Collins 2000, 1986; Harding 1991; Hartsock 1983; Medina 2012; Wylie 2003) and feminist empiricism (Anderson 2004, 1995b, 1995a; Longino 1997, 1994; Nelson 1990).[4] Drawing on Ashton and McKenna (forthcoming), I argue that, while some strands in both feminist standpoint theory and feminist empiricism involve something akin to social encroachment, others don't. This difference corresponds to a difference between two senses in which whether one knows might depend on social factors. Some strands in feminist epistemology are merely committed to social factors playing an enabling role in the production of knowledge;

104 *Robin McKenna*

other strands are committed to social factors also playing a role in justifying our beliefs. I finish by outlining how the debate about pragmatic encroachment could be enriched by incorporating insights from feminist epistemology.

7.2. The Argument From Cases

The first argument for social encroachment is based on cases that purport to show that knowledge depends on a combination of pragmatic and epistemic factors. Such arguments have a common structure. The reader is presented with two cases. The cases differ with respect to some pragmatic factor but are identical with respect to relevant epistemic factors. If it can be shown that there is knowledge in one case but not in the other, knowledge must depend on the relevant pragmatic factor. Here are the cases.

Variation of Social Role

Case 1: Mr. Mulder, who has a keen interest in medicine but is not a medical doctor, reads an article in a reputable newspaper that says that a new drug is safe. He has no reason to think that this information is misleading and good reason to trust this newspaper as it has a good track record when it comes to advances in medical science. Assume that the drug is in fact safe.

Case 2: Dr. Scully, who is a practicing medical doctor, reads the same article. She also has no reason to think this information is misleading in any way and good reason to trust this newspaper.[5]

Intuitively, while Mulder has done all he needs to in order to know that the new drug is safe, Scully has to do more. The thought is that it is enough for a layperson to read about medical advances in a (reputable) newspaper, but a practicing doctor needs to do more. Mulder and Scully's different social roles impose different epistemological requirements when it comes to how they should go about forming beliefs about whether drugs are safe. Mulder can trust the newspaper, whereas Scully needs to check the relevant medical journal articles. If this is right, whether one knows depends on one's social role.

Variation of Social Identity

Case 1: Pam is a manual worker who has good reason to believe that her co-workers are being exploited, though she lacks conclusive proof. She is wondering whether to act on her belief by creating a union. Let's suppose that, if the bosses are taking advantage of the workers, she will be successful in convincing them to join the union, and if the bosses are

Feminist Epistemology, Pragmatic Encroachment 105

not taking advantage of the workers, she will be unsuccessful. Let's also suppose that, because of her position in the company and her gender, Pam faces serious barriers to creating a union: she fears she won't be taken seriously, either by her bosses or her co-workers; she worries that this will get her a reputation as a trouble-maker; etc.

Case 2: Jim also has good reason to believe that the workers are being exploited and is wondering whether to act on his belief. But, because he is male and a manager in the company, he faces fewer barriers to creating a union; he knows he will be taken seriously; he is confident that this will not get him a reputation as a trouble-maker; etc.

In my (and Jason Stanley's)[6] view it is (to put it crudely) easier for Jim to know that his workers are being exploited than it is for Pam. The thought is that Pam's social identity creates barriers to her knowing that don't exist for Jim. Because of her precarious position in the company and her gender, she just needs more evidence than Jim does. If this is right, whether one knows depends on one's social identity.

Variation of Risk of Social Injustice

Case 1: Bob is taking a walk in the forest and hears a noise that could only have come from a large animal. He remembers hearing that the only large animal in this forest is a grizzly bear, but he has no other evidence to back this up. He forms the belief that the animal is a bear.

Case 2: Bob is visiting the local branch office and encounters a female employee, Linda. He remembers hearing that all the women who work in this branch office are administrative assistants, but he has no other evidence to back this up. He forms the belief that the Linda is an administrative assistant.[7]

It is plausible that Bob knows that the animal is a bear. Or, at least, it is plausible if we accept that one can have what Jennifer Lackey (2011) calls "isolated second-hand knowledge," that is, knowledge gained from testimony (second-hand) where one has no other relevant knowledge about the matter (isolated). But I would suggest that it is far less plausible that he knows that Linda is an administrative assistant. We (I take it) want to say that Bob should not believe that Linda is an administrative assistant on the basis of isolated testimony. But the only relevant difference between these cases is what one might call the risk that Bob's belief will cause social injustice. In forming a belief about the identity of the animal there is no risk of Bob perpetrating a social injustice. In forming a belief about Linda's job there is such a risk. If this is right, whether one knows depends on the risk of causing social injustice.[8]

I want to finish this section by emphasizing that, while the argument from the cases provides some motivation for social encroachment, I

106 *Robin McKenna*

don't think it is decisive. It relies on certain intuitions that may not be widely shared, and even if they are shared, there are other ways of accommodating them.[9] However, my aim in this section (and in this chapter) is not to show that social encroachment is *ultima facie* plausible. It is rather to show that, just as there is reason for thinking that knowledge depends on the stakes, there is also reason to think that knowledge depends on social factors.

7.3. The Argument From Knowledge-Action Principles

The starting point of the second argument is the claim that there is a conceptual connection between what one knows and what one may treat as a reason for acting. Take this principle:

PR: S may treat p as a reason for acting iff S knows that p.[10]

The usual argument for principles like PR is that it is supported by ordinary evaluations of the rationality of practical reasoning. For instance, if I turn left on the way to the airport I can justify having done so by saying that I know the airport is in this direction. On the other hand, if I turn left on the way to the airport without knowing that the airport is in this direction, you can criticise me by saying that I do not know that the airport is in this direction. This practice seems to only make sense if a principle like PR is true. What PR tells us is that, if you know that p, there is no "epistemic barrier" to treating p as a reason for acting. This is not to say that there is no barrier at all; p may be irrelevant to the planned action.[11]

Pragmatic encroachers have used PR to argue that knowledge depends on the stakes. Abstracting away from some complications, the argument is simple:

1. Whether S may treat p as a reason for acting depends on the stakes.
2. S may treat p as a reason for acting iff S knows that p (i.e. PR).
3. Whether S knows that p depends on the stakes.

One can construct a structurally identical argument for social encroachment:

1. Whether S may treat p as a reason for acting depends on social factors.
2. S may treat p as a reason for acting iff S knows that p (i.e. PR).
3. Whether S knows that p depends on social factors.

To illustrate how this argument works, consider the cases discussed earlier. Mulder may permissibly treat the proposition that the drug is safe as a reason for acting (e.g. telling a friend about it), whereas Scully

Feminist Epistemology, Pragmatic Encroachment   107

cannot permissibly treat this proposition as a reason for acting. If Mulder were to treat this proposition as a reason for telling a friend about the drug he would be behaving like a good friend, taking an active interest in others' well-being. If Scully were to treat this proposition as a reason for telling a friend about the drug, she would be in dereliction of her professional responsibilities. But the only difference between them is their social role. So whether one may permissibly treat something as a reason for acting depends on one's social role. Thus, if PR is true, whether one knows depends on one's social role.

Or take Pam and Jim. Jim may permissibly treat the proposition that the workers are being exploited as a reason for acting (e.g. creating a union), whereas Pam cannot permissibly treat this proposition as a reason for acting. If Jim were to treat this proposition as a reason for creating a union he would be behaving like a model manager, taking an interest in the welfare of his workers. If Pam were to treat this proposition as a reason for creating a union she would be taking a big risk. But the only difference between them is their social identity – Pam is a woman and employed as a manual labourer, whereas Jim is a man and is middle management. Whether one may permissibly treat something as a reason for acting depends on one's social identity. Thus, if PR is true, whether one knows depends on one's social identity.

Finally, take Bob. It is plausible that Bob may permissibly treat the proposition that the animal is a bear as a reason for acting (e.g. running away), whereas he may not permissibly treat the proposition that Linda is an administrative assistant as a reason for acting (e.g. handing her his expenses form). If Bob were to treat this proposition as a reason for handing her his form, he would run the risk of causing terrible social injustices. Thus, if PR is true, knowledge depends on the risk of causing social injustice.

Before moving on, I want to address two objections. First, one might object that, if Pam were to try to create a union, she would be going above and beyond the call of duty. While supererogatory acts are not required, they are permissible. I agree, but this is no objection to my argument. What is at issue is whether there are epistemic barriers to Pam's treating the proposition that her co-workers are being exploited as a reason for creating a union, not whether she is permitted to try and create a union. My claim is that there are such barriers. Given their respective positions in the company, Pam just needs more evidence than Jim before she can rationally treat her belief that the workers are being exploited as a reason to create a union. If this is right, it tells us something important about why many societies are highly resistant to social change. Social change often requires people to act irrationally, that is, to act on evidence that is insufficient given the situation they find themselves in. Part of Pam's problem is that bringing about the social change she wants requires her to act on evidence that is insufficient. If social

108 *Robin McKenna*

change requires going against rationality, it is no surprise that it can be so difficult to enact.[12]

Second, one might object that I have drawn general conclusions from three cases. But these cases call our attention to a more general phenomenon. Our social roles, social identities and the risk of bringing about social injustice partly determine our responsibilities as inquirers. Doctors have responsibilities that laypeople lack. Because of these responsibilities, they are required to do things that laypeople aren't, like investigate claims about the safety of new drugs for themselves, before they can rationally act. Those who occupy social identities that are oppressed along some dimension have additional responsibilities that those who are privileged along that dimension lack. Pam needs to gather more evidence before she can rationally act, whereas Jim doesn't. Part of Pam's predicament is that bringing about the social change she wants requires not fulfilling these responsibilities.[13] Finally, when deciding what to believe, we have a responsibility to take the social consequences of our beliefs into account. There are reasons for not acting on testimony when it might perpetuate social injustice that are not reasons for not relying on testimony in general.

Like the argument from the cases, the argument from knowledge-action principles provides some motivation for social encroachment, but I do not think it is decisive. The argument relies on PR, and many have rejected such principles.[14] But, again, I am arguing that, just as there is reason to take stakes encroachment seriously, there is also reason to take social encroachment seriously. I take the two arguments I have offered to establish this relatively modest claim.

7.4. Social and Pragmatic Encroachment

This completes my defence of social encroachment. In this section, I will address two issues. First, what is the relationship between social and stakes encroachment? One might think that social encroachment is just a version of stakes encroachment. I will suggest some reasons for resisting this conclusion. Second, if social encroachment is true, knowledge depends on social factors. But "depends" in what sense? As we will see, this issue is important when comparing social encroachment with feminist epistemologies.

In presenting the case for social encroachment, I glossed over an important issue. Is social encroachment just an *instance* of stakes encroachment? That is, does knowledge depend on social factors just because the stakes can depend on social factors? Before suggesting that the answer is "no," I want to highlight that achieving my aims in this chapter doesn't require that social encroachment is anything more than an instance of stakes encroachment. My focus on social encroachment is justified by the fact that it facilitates drawing a connection with

Feminist Epistemology, Pragmatic Encroachment   109

feminist epistemologies, which tend to talk in terms of social factors but not in terms of stakes.

Now let me explain why I think that social encroachment is more than an instance of stakes encroachment. I agree that it isn't a simple task to "isolate" social encroachment from stakes encroachment. The social factors I focus on are all aspects of a subject's social location (where they are positioned in society) and it is difficult to separate the stakes for a subject from that subject's social location. But, while it is important to be mindful of this issue, it isn't an insurmountable problem. I think I can show that social factors drive the requirements on knowledge up (or down) independent of the stakes. Thus, the cases illustrate that knowledge depends on social factors, independent of any dependence on stakes.

We can start with the first case. In the picture I'm working with, our social roles impose different responsibilities on us as inquirers irrespective of whether we are presently (or will soon be) in a high or a low stakes situation. Maybe it is even harder for Scully to know that the drug is safe if it is a drug that she is going to have to decide whether to prescribe than it would be if she is unlikely to need to prescribe the drug. But this just shows that social and stakes encroachment can work together to drive up the requirements for knowledge, not that stakes encroachment "drives" social encroachment.

What about the second case? One might object that, even if it is easier for Jim to know than it is for Pam, this is better analysed in terms of a difference in stakes than in terms of a difference in their social identity. While it is hard to construe the case in such a way that stakes play no role (see previously), there is a problem with this objection. If it is a difference in stakes that is driving intuitions then our intuitions should change if we vary the stakes but keep the social identities fixed. Imagine that for Jim the welfare of his workers is of utmost importance, whereas for Pam the welfare of her co-workers is only important as a small part of a larger struggle against the ruling class. Still, Pam faces barriers to knowing that the workers are being exploited that just don't exist for Jim. It is these barriers that cause the problem for Pam, and these barriers may exist even though Pam doesn't regard it as imperative that she circumvent them. So the objection fails, because varying the stakes doesn't change the intuitions.

Finally, it is perhaps easier to isolate social encroachment from stakes encroachment in the third case. Insofar as we have the intuition that Bob knows that the animal is a bear in case 1, but does not know that Linda is an administrative assistant in case 2, this has nothing to do with the importance for Bob of him being right. The point is that it is impermissible for Bob to believe that Linda is an administrative assistant because of the risk of causing a social injustice. This risk exists whether Bob cares about causing a social injustice or not. Imagine that Bob is entirely

110 *Robin McKenna*

indifferent about perpetuating social injustices. It's all the same to him whether he does or not. There isn't anything "at stake" for Bob in getting Linda's job wrong, but nevertheless it still seems that he isn't permitted to believe that Linda is an administrative assistant. So, even if the first two cases fail to make the case for social encroachment independently of stakes encroachment, the third case can still do the job.

Turning now to the second issue, social encroachers say that knowledge depends on social factors. But "depends" in what sense? We can draw a distinction between two ways in which some property or status F might depend on social factors. Here is Paul Boghossian drawing this distinction in the case of knowledge:

> No one should deny, for example, that knowledge is often produced collaboratively, by members of a social group, and that contingent facts about that group may explain why it shows an interest in certain questions over others. ... [M]embers of a knowledge-seeking group may have certain political and social values and that those values *may* influence how they conduct their work – what observations they make and how well they appraise the evidence that they encounter. ... [W]hat *is* independent of our social make-up is the fact that the fossil record we have discovered constitutes *evidence* for the existence of dinosaurs – contributes to making it rational, in other words, to believe in their existence. That we should have discovered the evidence for the dinosaurs may not be independent of our social context; but *that it is evidence* for that hypothesis is.
>
> (Boghossian 2006, 21–22)

Following Boghossian, let's say that whether S knows that p *causally* depends on social factors iff social factors are an important part of the causal explanation how S came to know (or not know) that p, whereas whether S knows that p *constitutively* depends on social factors iff S knows (or does not know) that p partly in virtue of social factors. The idea behind this distinction is that there are two ways in which whether one knows can depend on some factor F. The first way is causal: F might be part of a causal explanation how you came to know (or not know). Boghossian accepts that social factors can play this causal role (your social and political values may impact on the evidence you have and your appraisal of it). The second way is metaphysical: it might be that one knows (or does not know) that p in virtue of F, because whether one's evidence is sufficient for knowledge depends on F (or because whether the information counts as evidence at all depends on F). Boghossian denies that whether you know depends on social factors in this way.[15]

I think it is clear that, according to any version of pragmatic encroachment, whether you know that p constitutively depends on certain

Feminist Epistemology, Pragmatic Encroachment 111

pragmatic factors.[16] It is no surprise to learn that pragmatic factors have a causal impact on what we know: if you don't care to inquire into something, then you'll know very little about it. Pragmatic encroachment – whether in its stakes or social variety – is the far more controversial view that pragmatic factors (partly) determine how much (or what sort of) evidence we need in order to know. On one way of thinking about stakes encroachment (suggested by Grimm 2011), whether you know constitutively depends on how much is at stake for you because how much is at stake (partly) determines whether your evidence is sufficient for you to know. Paralleling the suggested way of thinking about stakes encroachment, we can say that whether you know constitutively depends on social factors because social factors (partly) determine whether your evidence is sufficient for you to know. Using our cases to illustrate, Scully and Pam don't know because their social roles and identities impose responsibilities on them that they haven't met, and Bob doesn't know that Linda is an administrative assistant because the risk of social harm renders his statistical evidence inappropriate. These social factors don't cause Scully, Pam and Bob to lack knowledge. They lack knowledge partly in virtue of them.

This completes my discussion of the similarities and differences between stakes and social encroachment. I now want to turn to the connection between social encroachment and feminist epistemologies.

7.5. The Situated Knowledge Thesis

At the core of most feminist epistemologies is the situated knowledge thesis: the social locations of knowers are epistemologically relevant. I want to focus on two questions about the situated knowledge thesis:

1. What is the scope of the situated knowledge thesis? That is, is the claim that all knowledge is socially situated (the social locations of knowers are always epistemologically relevant), or is the claim more restricted (the social locations of knowers are sometimes epistemologically relevant)?
2. Does the situated knowledge thesis posit causal or constitutive dependence of knowledge on social factors?

Answering these questions will allow us to explore the connections between social encroachment and feminist epistemologies.

Let's start with the first question. In her excellent overview of feminist epistemology, Elizabeth Anderson says this:

> Mainstream epistemology takes as paradigms of knowledge simple propositional knowledge about matters in principle equally accessible to anyone with basic cognitive and sensory apparatus: "2 + 2 = 4";

"grass is green"; "water quenches thirst." Feminist epistemology does not claim that such knowledge is gendered. Examination of such examples is not particularly helpful for answering the epistemological problems that arise specifically in feminist theory and practice. What is it to know that I am a woman? What is it like to be sexually objectified? Why is it that men and women so often have dramatically divergent understandings of what happened in their sexual encounters? How can we arrange scientific practices so that science and technology serve women's interests? These kinds of questions make other kinds of knowledge salient for feminist epistemology: phenomenological knowledge, *de se* knowledge, knowledge of persons, know-how, moral knowledge, knowledge informed by emotions, attitudes, and interests.

(Anderson 2017)

Anderson is drawing on work in both the feminist standpoint theory tradition and the feminist empiricist tradition here. Feminist standpoint theorists think that those who are oppressed (along some dimension) have an epistemic advantage over those who are relatively privileged (along that dimension). This advantage is only supposed to be with respect to certain phenomena, paradigmatically, social relations (Collins 1986; Harding 1991, 46; Fricker 1999, 203; Wylie 2003, 37). For instance, Patricia Hill Collins (1986) argues that black women have an epistemic advantage over white men with respect to sociology because they have the opportunity to compare multiple perspectives. Collins says that black women, who are "outsiders within" must "assimilate a [perspective] that is quite different from their own" and therefore have the opportunity to develop a kind of "double consciousness" whereas white men can stay within their own dominant perspective (Collins 1986, 26).

Feminist empiricists focus on the role of feminist social values in the production of scientific knowledge, with a strong emphasis on social-scientific research (Anderson 2004; Longino 1994). Helen Longino (1994) cites cases where scientific advances resulted from the application of feminist social values such as a preference for theories that are explanatorily complex (e.g. Barbara McClintock's work on genetic transposition). Anderson (2004) argues that a feminist understanding of divorce provides a more scientifically fruitful way of framing research problems in divorce research and makes it more likely that we will arrive at a good understanding of the impact of divorce on families and the individuals involved.

Anderson's suggestion is therefore that we read these traditions not as proposing that *all* knowledge is socially situated but rather that *some* knowledge is socially situated. Further, this is the sort of knowledge that is important in feminist theory and practice, and the ignoring of which leads to distortion in our philosophical theorizing. So we can

Feminist Epistemology, Pragmatic Encroachment 113

read the situated knowledge thesis as, in part, a methodological injunction. We should focus on a particular kind of knowledge: socially situated knowledge.

We can now turn to the second question. Recall the distinction between causal and constitutive dependence: knowledge causally depends on social factors iff social factors play a significant causal role in the production of knowledge, whereas knowledge constitutively depends on social factors iff social factors partly constitute the production of knowledge. Where does the situated knowledge thesis stand on the question of causal versus constitutive dependence? Drawing on the survey of the literature in Ashton and McKenna (forthcoming), we can say that there are strands in feminist epistemology that seem to only involve causal dependence and strands that seem to involve constitutive dependence. I lack the space for a detailed overview here, so I will merely provide examples from both the feminist standpoint theory and feminist empiricist tradition that seem to fall on each side of this divide.

One common thought in feminist standpoint theory is that our social identities impact on the evidence we have access to. Those who are oppressed may have access to evidence that those who are relatively privileged don't. One finds versions of this idea in classic works in feminist standpoint theory, including Nancy Hartsock (1983) and Collins (1986). Hartsock argues that women's roles as wives and mothers mean they are responsible for a range of tasks that are essential to the functioning of society (e.g. child-rearing) and the household (e.g. cleaning). This means they tend to have a more intimate acquaintance with what is necessary to satisfy our needs than men tend to have. Collins argues that black woman have an epistemic advantage over white men with respect to sociology because their experiences furnish them with evidence that others lack:

> For example, while Black women have and are themselves mothers, they encounter distorted versions of themselves and their mothers under the mantle of Black matriarchy thesis. Similarly, for those Black women who confront racial and sexual discrimination, and know that their mothers and grandmothers certainly did, explanations of Black women's poverty that stress low achievement motivation and the lack of Black female "human capital" are less likely to ring true.
> (Collins 1986, 28)

All Hartsock and Collins need here is the (very plausible) idea that our social identities shape what we can know by shaping the evidence we have access to. This is clearly true, and it is a straightforward instance of causal dependence.[17]

One common thought in feminist empiricism is that we need to look at the causal forces that shape our knowledge. This thought is reminiscent

114 *Robin McKenna*

of Quine (1969). But, where Quine studied (or rather urged epistemologists to study) the psychological processes by which subjects form beliefs, feminist empiricists study the process of knowledge production in social contexts. For example, Elizabeth Anderson (1995a) cites studies showing that the data obtained in anthropological fieldwork depends on the anthropologist's gender. She concludes that, if we want to get accurate data, we need diverse teams of anthropologists. This is also a straightforward case of causal dependence.

While some strands of thought in feminist standpoint theory and feminist empiricism require mere causal dependence, other strands require quite a bit more. Sandra Harding (a prominent feminist standpoint theorist) and Helen Longino (a prominent feminist empiricist) have both called attention to the role played by social values in knowledge production. I am going to argue that, while their views about the role of values differ, they both involve a form of constitutive dependence.

For Harding (1991) women (and other groups who have historically been under-represented in science) are better at identifying *hidden values* (such as assumptions about race and gender) operative in science than men. Take the episode in primatology documented in Wallen (2000, 1990).[18] For decades, primatologists were puzzled by the mating habits of rhesus monkeys. The sexual behaviour of rhesus monkeys peaked at times when females were ovulating, but how did the male monkeys know when to initiate sex? It had been observed that female rhesus monkeys slapped the ground in front of male rhesus monkeys prior to sexual activity, but this observation hadn't been seen as relevant to the question of rhesus monkeys' mating habits. But an influx of female primatologists and broader societal changes led to a questioning of the sexist assumption (females don't initiate sex) that underlay this rejection of the relevance of the observation.

Before the rejection of this sexist assumption, scientists didn't know much about the mating habits of rhesus monkeys. After the assumption was rejected, they did. Did this advance in knowledge causally or constitutively depend on social factors, such as the influx of female primatologists and broader societal changes? Take the observation that female rhesus monkeys slap the ground in front of males. The researchers had access to this observation before and after these societal changes, but it wasn't conceptualised as evidence beforehand. It was rather viewed as difficult to explain in light of the sexist assumption that females don't initiate sex. If we recognise that there's a step that needs to be taken in order to turn observations into evidence, then we can say that these social forces didn't merely cause an increase in our knowledge, but were also partly constitutive of it.

For Longino (1990, 1994, 1997, 2002) the key idea is that feminist social values play a crucial role in justifying scientific theories because they inform a range of methodological decisions, including decisions

Feminist Epistemology, Pragmatic Encroachment 115

about how to decide between theories that seem to do equally well in terms of empirical adequacy. This idea is nicely summarised by Elizabeth Anderson:

> [T]heories do not merely state facts but organise them into systems that tell us what their significance is. Theories logically go beyond the facts; they are 'underdetermined' by all the empirical evidence that is or ever could be adduced in their favour.... The evidential link between an observed fact and a theoretical hypothesis can only be secured by background auxiliary hypotheses. This leaves open the logical possibility that ideological judgments may not be implications of an independently supported theory but figure in the justification of the theory itself, by supplying evidential links between empirical observations and hypotheses.
>
> (Anderson 1995a, 77)

Feminist social values provide the "background assumptions" against which we can take empirical evidence to provide justification for particular scientific theories. This can be illustrated by the episode in primatology discussed earlier. Does the observation that female rhesus monkeys slap the ground in front of males support the hypothesis that the female wants to initiate sex? It doesn't if we're working with certain background assumptions about who initiates sexual activity; it might if we reject these assumptions. We need more than causal dependence to capture this thought. The point is not that background sexist assumptions might cause one to ignore evidence that one would otherwise pay attention to. (Though this is, of course, often the case.) The point is rather that social values provide the framework against which we decide which hypotheses the evidence supports (and the degree to which it supports them). The processes by which scientific theories are justified, and so by which (when it goes well) scientific knowledge is produced therefore constitutively involve social factors.

Finally, we can turn to the question of the relationship between social encroachment and the situated knowledge thesis, and feminist epistemologies more generally. Insofar as it is a methodological injunction, it stands in an interesting relation to social encroachment. Social encroachment – like pragmatic encroachment in general – is a thesis about the nature of knowledge, specifically, the knowledge relation. It says that whether some S stands in the knowledge relation to some p depends on various social factors. As such, it seems to be a thesis about knowledge in general. This prompts a question: can all knowledge be "socially encroached" (or "pragmatically encroached")? Take my knowledge that $2 + 2 = 4$. Can we vary relevant social factors (or the stakes) in such a way that I no longer know that $2 + 2 = 4$? This seems questionable. No matter how this issue turns out, the important point here is that this is

116 Robin McKenna

not an issue that feminist epistemologies need get embroiled in. As Elizabeth Anderson tells us, feminist epistemologists don't want to convince us that our knowledge that $2 + 2 = 4$ is gendered. They want to stop us treating this sort of knowledge as the paradigm, and so constructing our theories of knowledge around it. The core of the feminist epistemological critique of mainstream epistemology is that it has ignored situated knowledge rather than that all knowledge (constitutively) depends on social factors.

Insofar as the situated knowledge thesis is a claim about the way in which our social location impacts on what we know, we have seen that some strands in feminist epistemology involve constitutive dependence of knowledge on social factors, whereas others involve mere causal dependence. So the situated knowledge thesis can be taken in two ways, one of which involves the same sort of social dependence as in social encroachment, the other of which involves a sort of social dependence that can be happily accepted by epistemologists of all stripes. For my part, I think that there are good arguments in the feminist tradition for both forms of dependence (see Ashton and McKenna forthcoming for an overview of some of them), and that these arguments are more compelling than the argument from the cases or the argument from knowledge-action principles presented in this chapter. All told, there is good reason for those interested in pragmatic encroachment – whether for or against – to engage with this literature.

7.6. Concluding Remarks

In this chapter I have tried to do two things. The first was to argue that, just as there is reason to think that knowledge depends on the stakes, there is also reason to think that knowledge depends on social factors. Further, I argued that, while social encroachment and stakes encroachment may be hard to tease apart, there is a case to be made for social encroachment independent of stakes encroachment. The second was to argue that there are some interesting connections, but also some interesting differences, between social encroachment and feminist epistemologies. One difference concerns scope. Where social encroachment is a view about the (social) nature of knowledge, feminist epistemologies tend to encourage us to focus on classes of knowledge – like social-scientific knowledge or knowledge of the social world – that have a clear social dimension. Another difference concerns the sort of social dependence that is at issue. While some projects in feminist epistemology do require the sort of strong constitutive dependence of knowledge on the social countenanced by social encroachers, not all do. Putting this together, we can conclude that there is an important sense in which feminist epistemologies are less radical than social encroachment (and pragmatic encroachment more generally). This should occasion some pause,

Feminist Epistemology, Pragmatic Encroachment   117

given that pragmatic encroachment has been regarded as a central topic in epistemology in the past 20 years, whereas feminist epistemology has very much been confined to the margins.[19]

Notes

1. As a rough first pass, I will say that a factor F is epistemic with respect to p just in case F indicates that p is true, whereas F is pragmatic with respect to p just in case it is not epistemic.
2. Social encroachment isn't new. While the orthodox view in the philosophy of science is that social factors merely play an enabling role in the production of scientific knowledge, some have argued that social factors can also play a role in the justification of scientific theories, for instance by bridging the gap between observational data and theory (see Longino 2002, 1990). This is a form of social encroachment about scientific knowledge. (I briefly discuss this view in §7.5).
3. For attempts to draw connections between pragmatic encroachment and feminist epistemologies, see Kukla (2015) and Stanley (2016).
4. See Intemann (2010) for a helpful discussion of the relationship between feminist standpoint theory and feminist empiricism.
5. Annis (1978) and Wright (2011) use this sort of case to argue that the intuitive correctness of knowledge ascriptions varies with the subject's social role. It is, however, unclear if they want to establish the metaphysical claim that whether a subject knows depends on her social role or the semantic claim that whether she can truly be said to "know" depends on her social role.
6. This case is inspired by a case in Stanley (2015, 254).
7. These cases are inspired by Moss (2018, 230–234), but they are different in that Moss's subject relies on statistical generalizations rather than testimony.
8. This case raises several issues that I lack the space to adequately address. But I would like to highlight two of them. First, why call this 'social encroachment' rather than (following Moss 2018) "moral encroachment"? How one answers this question depends on one's views about the nature of moral facts, but in any event, I see no reason to think that social encroachment and moral encroachment are incompatible. For helpful discussion of moral encroachment see Basu and Schroeder (forthcoming), Fritz (2017), Gardiner (forthcoming) and Pace (2011). Second, why think that the sense of "should" in which Bob should not believe that Linda is an administrative assistant is *epistemic*? As Simion (2018) points out, not every norm that permits or forbids believing under certain epistemic conditions (in this case, having merely statistical evidence) is an epistemic norm. Put roughly, my view is that the norm is epistemic in the sense that it has to do with Bob's responsibilities as an inquirer. While this yields a rather expansive conception of the epistemic domain, I think it is of a piece with viewing epistemology as centrally concerned with the ethics of belief (or, better, inquiry).
9. For relevant discussion of the intuitions supposedly supporting stakes encroachment see Brown (2006), Gerken (2013), Nagel (2008), and Rysiew (2001). For some recent empirical evidence that casts doubt on these intuitions see Rose et al. (forthcoming).
10. While several authors defend principles that connect what one knows with what one may treat as a reason for acting, they differ as to the formulation of these principles. Some (e.g. Hawthorne and Stanley 2008; Williamson

118 *Robin McKenna*

2005) defend a biconditional norm like PR, whereas others (e.g. Fantl and McGrath 2009) only defend the sufficiency direction of PR.

11. This is why Hawthorne and Stanley (2008) restrict PR to actions that depend on p. Because I only discuss actions that depend on the relevant proposition, I ignore this restriction in what follows.

12. While I won't explore this point here, one could take this to be a reason to hold that norms of rationality are a source of what Dotson (2014) calls third-order epistemic oppression.

13. One might worry that social encroachment is in tension with a key idea behind standpoint theory, which is that those who are oppressed along some dimension enjoy compensating epistemic benefits (for more on feminist standpoint theory see §7.5). I take this worry seriously, and adequately responding to it would require a full paper. But let me make two points. First, feminist standpoint theorists hold that the oppressed have an epistemic advantage that the privileged lack, not that there are no epistemic benefits enjoyed by the privileged which the oppressed lack. Second, this epistemic advantage doesn't need to be thought of in terms of (more) knowledge. For instance, Fricker (1999) thinks of it in terms of being better positioned to rectify deficiencies in our existing concepts (or in our wider conceptual schemes), and Medina (2012) thinks of it in terms of being more likely to develop certain intellectual virtues.

14. For relevant discussion see Anderson (2015), Brown (2008), Fassio (2017), Gao (2017), Gerken (2011), Lackey (2010), and Reed (2010).

15. This distinction is essentially equivalent to Haslanger's (1995) distinction between two ways in which gender and racial categories might depend on social factors. I focus on Boghossian because his discussion is primarily about knowledge, not because he was the first to make this distinction.

16. Indeed, some have objected to stakes encroachers that the arguments they cite (in particular, the argument from cases) only show that whether you know causally depends on what is at stake (e.g. Nagel 2008).

17. I want to emphasize that I am not saying that one only finds claims about causal dependence of knowledge on the social in Collins' or Hartsock's work. The point is just that parts of their work exemplify a common strand of thought in feminist standpoint theory, and that particular strand is only committed to causal dependence. For more see Ashton and McKenna (forthcoming, sec. 3).

18. I take this example from Natalie Alana Ashton, who uses it in Ashton and McKenna (forthcoming).

19. Many people have commented on various versions of this chapter. I would particularly like to thank Natalie Alana Ashton, Davide Fassio, Rachel Fraser, Michael Hannon, Nick Hughes, Martin Kusch, Jonathan Schaffer, Alex Skiles, Jason Stanley, Alex Worsnip and audiences in Cardiff, Edinburgh, Oslo and Paris. My work on this chapter was assisted by funding from the ERC Advanced Grant Project "The Emergence of Relativism" (Grant No. 339382).

References

Anderson, C. (2015), "On the Intimate Relationship of Knowledge and Action," *Episteme* 12 (3): 343–353.

Anderson, E. (1995a), "Feminist Epistemology: An Interpretation and a Defense," *Hypatia* 10 (3): 50–84.

Feminist Epistemology, Pragmatic Encroachment 119

———. (1995b), "Knowledge, Human Interests, and Objectivity in Feminist Epistemology," *Philosophical Topics* 23 (2): 27–58.

———. (2004), "Uses of Value Judgments in Science: A General Argument, with Lessons from a Case Study of Feminist Research on Divorce," *Hypatia* 19 (1): 1–24.

———. (2017), "Feminist Epistemology and Philosophy of Science," in *The Stanford Encyclopedia of Philosophy*, edited by E.N. Zalta, Spring 2017 edition, https://plato.stanford.edu/archives/spr2017/entries/feminism-epistemology/.

Annis, D. (1978), "A Contextualist Theory of Epistemic Justification," *American Philosophical Quarterly* 15 (3): 213–219.

Ashton, N.A. and R. McKenna. (forthcoming), "Situating Feminist Epistemology," *Episteme*.

Basu, R. and M. Schroeder. (forthcoming), "Doxastic Wrongings," in *Pragmatic Encroachment in Epistemology*, edited by B. Kim and M. McGrath, Abingdon: Routledge.

Boghossian, P. (2006), *Fear of Knowledge: Against Relativism and Constructivism*, Oxford: Oxford University Press.

Brown, J. (2006), "Contextualism and Warranted Assertibility Manoeuvres," *Philosophical Studies* 130 (3): 407–435.

———. (2008), "Knowledge and Practical Reason," *Philosophy Compass* 3 (6): 1135–1152.

Collins, P.H. (1986), "Learning From the Outsider within: The Sociological Significance of Black Feminist Thought," *Social Problems* 33 (6): S14–S32.

———. (2000), *Black Feminist Thought: Knowledge, Consciousness, and the Politics of Empowerment*, 2nd edition, New York, NY: Routledge.

Dotson, K. (2014), "Conceptualizing Epistemic Oppression," *Social Epistemology* 28 (2): 115–138.

Fantl, J. and M. McGrath. (2009), *Knowledge in an Uncertain World*, Oxford: Oxford University Press.

Fassio, D. (2017), "Is There an Epistemic Norm of Practical Reasoning?," *Philosophical Studies* 174 (9): 2137–2166.

Fricker, M. (1999), "Epistemic Oppression and Epistemic Privilege," *Canadian Journal of Philosophy* 29 (Supplement): 191–210.

Fritz, J. (2017), "Pragmatic Encroachment and Moral Encroachment," *Pacific Philosophical Quarterly* 98 (1): 643–661.

Gao, J. (2017), "Rational Action without Knowledge (and Vice Versa)," *Synthese* 194 (6): 1901–1917.

Gardiner, G. (forthcoming), "Evidentialism and Moral Encroachment," in *Believing in Accordance with the Evidence: New Essays on Evidentialism*, edited by K. McCain, Dordrecht: Springer.

Gerken, M. (2011), "Warrant and Action," *Synthese* 178 (3): 529–547.

———. (2013), "Epistemic Focal Bias," *Australasian Journal of Philosophy* 91 (1): 41–61.

Grimm, S. (2011), "On Intellectualism in Epistemology," *Mind* 120 (479): 705–733.

Harding, S. (1991), *Whose Science? Whose Knowledge? Thinking from Women's Lives*, Ithaca, NY: Cornell University Press.

Hartsock, N. (1983), "The Feminist Standpoint: Developing the Ground for a Specifically Feminist Historical Materialism," in *Discovering Reality: Feminist*

120 Robin McKenna

Perspectives on Epistemology, Metaphysics, Methodology, and the Philosophy of Science, edited by S. Harding and M. Hintikka, Dordrecht: Reidel, 283–310.

Haslanger, S. (1995), "Ontology and Social Construction," *Philosophical Topics* 23 (2): 95–125.

Hawthorne, J. (2004), *Knowledge and Lotteries*, Oxford: Oxford University Press.

Hawthorne, J. and J. Stanley. (2008), "Knowledge and Action," *Journal of Philosophy* 105 (10): 571–590.

Intemann, K. (2010), "25 Years of Feminist Empiricism and Standpoint Theory: Where Are We Now?," *Hypatia* 25 (4): 778–796.

Kukla, R. (2015), "Delimiting the Proper Scope of Epistemology," *Philosophical Perspectives* 29 (1): 202–216.

Lackey, J. (2010), "Acting on Knowledge," *Philosophical Perspectives* 24 (1): 361–382.

———. (2011), "Assertion and Isolated Second-Hand Knowledge," in *Assertion: New Philosophical Essays*, edited by J. Brown and H. Cappelen, Oxford: Oxford University Press, 251–276.

Longino, H. (1990), *Science as Social Knowledge: Values and Objectivity in Scientific Inquiry*, Princeton, NJ: Princeton University Press.

———. (1994), "In Search of Feminist Epistemology," *The Monist* 77 (4): 472–485.

———. (1997), "Feminist Epistemology as a Local Epistemology," *Aristotelian Society Supplementary Volume* 71 (1): 19–36.

———. (2002), *The Fate of Knowledge*, Princeton, NJ: Princeton University Press.

Medina, J. (2012), *The Epistemology of Resistance: Gender and Racial Oppression, Epistemic Injustice, and Resistant Imaginations*, Oxford: Oxford University Press.

Moss, S. (2018), *Probabilistic Knowledge*, Oxford: Oxford University Press.

Nagel, J. (2008), "Knowledge Ascriptions and the Psychological Consequences of Changing Stakes," *Australasian Journal of Philosophy* 86 (2): 279–294.

Nelson, L.H. (1990), *Who Knows: From Quine to a Feminist Empiricism*, Philadelphia, PA: Temple University Press.

Pace, M. (2011), "The Epistemic Value of Moral Considerations: Justification, Moral Encroachment, and James' 'Will to Believe'," *Noûs* 45 (2): 239–268.

Quine, W.V.O. (1969), "Epistemology Naturalized," in *Ontological Relativity and Other Essays*, New York: Columbia University Press, 69–90.

Reed, B. (2010), "A Defense of Stable Invariantism," *Noûs* 44 (2): 224–244.

Rose, D., E. Machery, S. Stich, M. Alai, A. Angelucci, R. Berniūnas, E.E. Buchtel, et al. (forthcoming), "Nothing at Stake in Knowledge," *Noûs*.

Rysiew, P. (2001), "The Context-Sensitivity of Knowledge Attributions," *Noûs* 35 (4): 477–514.

Simion, M. (2018), "No Epistemic Norm for Action," *American Philosophical Quarterly* 55 (3): 231–238.

Stanley, J. (2005), *Knowledge and Practical Interests*, Oxford: Oxford University Press.

———. (2015), *How Propaganda Works*, Princeton, NJ: Princeton University Press.

Feminist Epistemology, Pragmatic Encroachment 121

———. (2016), "Is Epistemology Tainted?," *Disputatio* 8 (42): 1–36.

Wallen, K. (1990), "Desire and Ability: Hormones and the Regulation of Female Sexual Behavior," *Neoroscience & Biobehavioral Reviews* 14 (2): 233–241.

———. (2000), "Risky Business: Social Context and Hormonal Modulation of Primate Sexual Desire," in *Reproduction in Context*, edited by K. Wallen and J. Schneider, Cambridge, MA: MIT Press, 289–323.

Weatherson, B. (2012), "Knowledge, Bets, and Interests," in *Knowledge Ascriptions*, edited by J. Brown and M. Gerken, Oxford: Oxford University Press, 75–103.

Williamson, T. (2005), "Contextualism, Subject-Sensitive Invariantism and Knowledge of Knowledge," *Philosophical Quarterly* 55 (219): 213–235.

Wright, S. (2011), "Knowledge and Social Roles: A Virtue Approach," *Episteme* 8 (1): 99–111.

Wylie, A. (2003), "Why Standpoint Matters," in *Science and Other Cultures: Issues in Philosophies of Science and Technology*, edited by R. Figueroa and S. Harding, Abingdon: Routledge, 26–48.

8 Charity, Peace, and the Social Epistemology of Science Controversies

Sharyn Clough

8.1. Introduction

In previous work in the social epistemology of science (e.g. Clough 2003, 2004, 2011), I have argued against relativist worries about the role of political values in science. Utilizing a pragmatist reading of Donald Davidson's theory of interpretational charity and triangulation (e.g. Davidson 2001, 2004), I argued that political values have empirical content that can be assessed for its strength and relevance in particular science contexts, and that, where relevant and well-supported by evidence, political values, rather than introducing relativism, can actually *increase* the objectivity of the particular scientific theories within which the values are embedded. I have used case studies from epidemiology (Clough 2010) and evolutionary biology (Clough 2002) to show that the inclusion of relevant feminist political values, well-supported by the evidence, can increase objectivity by increasing the empirical adequacy of scientific hypotheses, opening up new avenues for empirical investigation that were previously ignored and explaining more variation in the data than rival hypotheses. I have also used examples where racist political values that were irrelevant and not well-supported by the evidence had an empirically detectable, deleterious effect, that is, they weakened the objectivity of the scientific research within which the racist political values were embedded (Clough and Loges 2008; Clough 2015; Clough and Orozco 2016). However, while I have argued *that* political values have empirical content, and that value-laden claims in science can be objectively assessed, it was not until recently that I was prompted to take the next (pragmatist) step to think about *how* we might deliberate and weigh the evidence for or against value-laden science claims in an explicit way.

In this chapter, I take a small step in that direction and offer a preliminary investigation of the kinds of epistemic practices or virtues needed for objective evidential deliberations about science claims laden by political values. I use examples from Maya Goldenberg's work on deliberations about science claims regarding the safety of childhood vaccines

Charity, Peace, and Science Controversies   123

(e.g. Goldenberg 2016, 2019). I argue for the importance of skills like empathy and epistemic humility in these deliberations, building on feminist pragmatist themes in virtue epistemology, especially the work of Alessandra Tanesini (2016, 2018) and Georgina Campelia (2017), and explicated in terms of peace literacy – a new kind of phronesis or practical wisdom, borrowed from public philosopher Paul K. Chappell (2012, 2017).

Aristotle's emphasis on phronesis and virtue links up well with a pragmatist focus (Pagan 2008). When we view wisdom as a practice rather than a product, then knowing well requires the build-up of particular skills, habits, or virtues, which in turn requires experience, which reinforces the skills, and so on. In this pragmatist view of phronesis, wisdom isn't something we have, it's something we do. Thinking of phronesis in this way pushes back against some of the conceptual distinctions we inherit from the ancient Greek philosophical tradition, e.g. the distinction between techne and episteme. Techne is sometimes conceived as effortful practice in the world, to be contrasted with episteme as purely intellectual or theory-driven. But even Aristotle acknowledged the intellectual elements involved in techne, and pragmatists have worked to uncover in Aristotle the opposite pattern, namely the importance of engaged practice in the world that is needed for a rich intellectual contemplative life (Pagan 2008). Both techne *and* episteme require conscious, intellectual effort and practice (Krakauer 2019), i.e. both involve phronesis as I conceive it here.

The feminist element of the pragmatist approach that I endorse involves claims that, for example, we practitioners of wisdom are embodied in social relations of power (i.e. politics broadly understood) and those political relations are often calibrated according to socially and historically contingent embodied markers such as "gender/sex" and "race" that can be shown empirically to be irrelevant and arbitrary when used as criteria for considering the limits and possibilities of human flourishing. And further, that contingent, irrelevant, and arbitrarily assigned political relations are unjust and in need of melioration (McHugh 2015). These feminist political claims involve a mix of both evaluative and descriptive elements all of which have empirical content that can be objectively assessed (a point I return to in Section 8.2) and all of which are contingent and subject to updating in the face of new evidence (Clough 2013).

At its best, scientific practice is the scaled up, formal version of phronesis as I have characterized it here (Bellolio 2019) and, we feminist pragmatists argue, scientists, as with any and all of us, are embodied in political relations that are often unjust in ways that negatively influence the objectivity of evidential deliberations (Clough and Loges 2008; Clough 2015; Clough and McHugh forthcoming). In cases of scientific claims with controversial policy implications, such as those regarding the safety of childhood vaccines, the political relations at play, on all sides, are various, complex, and often only implicit, making their role barely available to analysis.

The epistemic opacity and complexity introduced by taking political considerations seriously in these kinds of debates can leave the participants (including feminist pragmatists) open to accusations of a self-refuting relativism. As I argue in Section 8.2, I do not find these accusations philosophically compelling, but they sometimes animate public discourse and I think they ought to be addressed. Addressing them involves peeling back a number of assumptions such as the following: if the participants in debates about scientific claims that have controversial policy implications take the time to acknowledge the political considerations at play in establishing what counts as evidence in these debates and how that evidence gets adjudicated (an acknowledgment we feminist pragmatists endorse); *and* if political considerations are understood in the conventional epistemic sense to be unrelated to objective evidential considerations (an understanding we feminist pragmatists reject); then it can seem as if acknowledging the role of political considerations involves the relativist claim that there are no objective (i.e. no nonpolitical) standards of evidence against which the competing scientific claims can be ranked (what Kusch [2020], refers to as the symmetry condition of relativism); so attempting to rank the claims (as feminist pragmatists do) is self-refuting.

I argue that even in debates about complicated cases of politicized science, as with our everyday practices, the fact that we are communicating with each other enough to be party to a debate about scientific claims provides us with the epistemic resources we need to deliberate objectively about the relevant evidence. And unlike the assumptions animating the accusations of relativism outlined earlier, I argue that much of that evidence concerns the political elements of the debate. The only way around is through. Wading in even deeper than we (social epistemologists and scientists alike) are trained to do, practicing our skills of empathy and humility, we can learn to recognize the role of political values embedded in scientific claims; objectively assess the presence and strength of evidence in favor of those values; and course correct as needed.

In the second section of the chapter, I review my pragmatist use of Davidson to argue against relativist worries about political values in science by arguing *for* the objective potential of particular values in particular science contexts. In Section 8.3, I introduce peace literacy as a call for the practice of empathy and epistemic humility in deliberations about evidence generally, and about scientific evidence that has controversial policy implications, in particular. I examine some of the controversies around scientific claims about the safety of childhood vaccines and the issue of what Maya Goldenberg refers to as "vaccine hesitancy" (Goldenberg 2016). In Section 8.4, I examine accusations of relativism

Charity, Peace, and Science Controversies   125

sometimes leveled against vaccine hesitant parents. Some parents who hesitate to vaccinate their children express concern about the objectivity of medical evidence that is affected by the political and financial influences of pharmaceutical companies. When expressing these and similar concerns, these parents are sometimes accused of rejecting the objective role of evidence *simpliciter*, of believing that there is no way to rank competing evidence claims (the symmetry condition again), which would make their resistance to vaccines baseless and self-refuting. I have come to think that this accusation of relativism involves a misreading of the motivations of many vaccine-hesitant parents, and I argue that empathy and epistemic humility are needed to help us navigate the epistemic miasma of current vaccine controversies. The encouragement of empathy and humility might seem to introduce moral and political elements into the epistemic picture that further water down or obscure the objectivity of deliberations about competing scientific claims. I offer reassurance here. Returning to and building off of the pragmatist themes in Davidson's work, I show that the epistemic habits of empathy and humility are in fact *conditions of* objective evidential deliberations.

8.2. Reviewing the Case for the Objectivity of (Some) Values (Some of the Time) in (Some) Scientific Practices

Scientists, scientific practice, and science conventions and institutions are various and the family resemblance holding them together is tenuous; still we think there is something named by "science" and we have good reason to believe that whatever science is, it is shot-through with values of a variety of kinds, including but not limited to political values (see Elliott 2017; de Melo-Martín and Intemann 2018 for a review of the arguments in support of this claim). It seems then that we can no longer use the mere presence of values to discriminate between good science and bad science. If this is correct, then some scientific research can be both value-laden and objective.

As a first-pass definition, I focus on objectivity as a product and expand in Section 8.3 to include objectivity as a process. By "objective scientific research" I mean research that is empirically accurate, that captures as much of the available, relevant evidence as possible, that obscures or discounts as little of the available, relevant evidence as possible, that is based on as representative a sampling of the available, relevant evidence as possible, and/or that explains as much as possible of the variation in the available, relevant evidence at issue. As I explain following, I take values, including political values, to be just as available objectively to each of these evidential kinds of considerations as are the science claims within which those political values are embedded, so the presence of political values in scientific research does not by

126 *Sharyn Clough*

itself reduce the objectivity of the research. Of course, the political values must be relevant and well-supported by the evidence. Goldenberg has called this the "values as evidence" approach (Goldenberg 2013) which contrasts with the approach to objectivity and values promoted by Helen Longino (1990), for example. Longino's account of objectivity focuses on the particular characteristics of science communities needed to ensure that the effects of political values are managed and minimized. I think the characteristics of communities that she outlines are important; however, something like the account I give here is needed if we are to avoid relativism and objectively adjudicate *between* values, rather than merely manage their presence (Clough 2013). For now, in the product-sense of "objective," I will use it as a label for research that is the result of the adequate, attentive capture of the relevant evidence, in formal science contexts and informal everyday phronesis, and argue that we can be objective in this sense regarding claims playing the role of descriptions (facts) or evaluations (values), and, as is more often the case, claims involving some mix of the two.

I recognize that "relevance" is doing a lot of work here. With respect to identifying what counts as relevant evidence, I take this to be a meta question answered by appeal to the same kinds of objective processes that result in the adequate, attentive capture of relevant evidence, only now those processes are aimed at the *kinds* of evidence at issue. In other words, we need evidence to decide the relevance of evidence. This kind of epistemic bootstrapping is not viciously circular as long as the evidence being appealed to isn't the evidence under direct examination. We need to appeal to the evidence of optics, for example, to debate the relevance of different staining techniques in microscopy. I take it that scientists and we social epistemologists of science do this kind of bootstrapping unproblematically all the time. Of course, in the pragmatist account I offer here, the work of adequately, attentively capturing the relevant evidence, and the work of deciding what evidence is relevant, is contingent, historically- and culturally-shaped, and subject to updating in the face of new evidence.

On to Davidson then, and a review of the ways that I use his account to argue that value judgments are beliefs that can be expressed as propositions (sometimes "evaluations" or "value claims") that have empirical content, the evidential strength of which we can objectively assess in all the senses previously listed (Clough 2011). Davidson's argument here builds on his model of interpretational charity and triangulation. In his essay "The Objectivity of Values" Davidson explains:

> How do we tell what the content of a particular moral judgment is? This is a question of interpretation, of the understanding by one person of the utterances of another, since there is no other context in which the content of a judgment can be agreed to or disputed.

Charity, Peace, and Science Controversies   127

> To take up the position of an interpreter is consciously to assume the status anyone with thoughts and attitudes must be in, for the attitudes of a person have a content – are interpretable – only if that person is in communication with others; only interpreters can be interpreted.
>
> (Davidson 2004, 48–49)

Insofar as our value judgments have meaning, then they are beliefs that develop, or they are sufficiently semantically linked to simpler beliefs that develop, through a triangular relationship between us, our interlocutors, and, at the apex of the triangle, the common feature of the world on which our communication is focused. I have sometimes described the triangulation process with the implicit assumption that it is the apex of the triangle that designates the empirical content of the belief, but in good pragmatist fashion, when thinking about wherein the empirical content resides, it is probably better to point to the entirety of the triangular relationship, the entire experience of meaning-making itself. This refiguring helps remind us that the notion of a triangle is an idealization, we are all involved in innumerable relationships of communication with many different origin points, often more than three, operating simultaneously, with shifting apexes (sometime we are the apex of a triangle involving other interlocutors). The notion of a web of belief gets appropriately complicated here. Additionally, the communication does not need to be verbal, the interlocuters don't need to be human, and the process is ongoing.

The main idea is that in the case of simpler beliefs, with which other more complex beliefs link semantically in web-like fashion, the believer (you, say) is one of the points of the triangle, and, to emphasize the importance of the external nature of the meaning-making process and provide an epistemic wedge against relativism, you need at least one interlocutor to establish objectively the empirical content of the belief about which you are communicating. Davidson describes the process of triangulation most clearly in "Three Varieties of Knowledge":

> It takes two points of view to give a location to the cause of a thought, and thus to define its content. We may think of it as a form of triangulation: each of two people is reacting differentially to sensory stimuli streaming in from a certain direction. Projecting the incoming lines outward, the common cause is at their intersection. If the two people now note each other's reactions (in the case of language, verbal reactions), each can correlate these observed reactions with his or her stimuli from the world. A common cause has been determined. The triangle which gives content to thought and speech is complete. But it takes two to triangulate.
>
> (Davidson 2001, 212–213)

128 *Sharyn Clough*

Here's an example. Imagine a young girl learning the truth-conditions of the belief that she's looking at a scientist; i.e. learning, objectively, the meaning of the sentence "That's a scientist." She's in elementary school in a science class with her peers watching a feminist documentary about Rosalind Franklin. She's seen photos of male scientists, but she has never seen a woman in the role of scientist before. In discussion with her peers and her teacher about the film, the penny drops and pointing at Rosalind Franklin in a lab coat, the girl utters the sentence "That's a scientist!" Her teacher nods and smiles. Entirely new career vistas are opened to her. She is enthralled and tells her mom all about it when she gets home from school. Later at the department store with her mom, they pass the cosmetic counter where she sees a woman wearing a lab coat. "That's a scientist!" she exclaims. Her mom, excited by her daughter's new-found career goals, is tempted to encourage the positive momentum, keep it simple, and say "yes," but she sighs and instead tells her daughter "no," doing her best to explain how marketing agencies sometimes use lab coats to build associations in the minds of consumers between cosmetics and the respectable image of science, with the goal of increasing the chances that consumers will buy the cosmetics. She explains that science is about discovery and experimenting, not money and marketing. Or at least it's not supposed to be about money and marketing. The mother sighs again. The little girl frowns.

No matter. The main point is that the girl in our story has inaccurately generalized across instances of women wearing lab coats. She has made an objectively detectable mistake with respect to the truth conditions for the sentence "That's a scientist." Because of the success of feminist political interventions in her science education she no longer associates the concept "scientist" with socially contingent embodied markers like gender that are irrelevant and arbitrary with respect to identifying scientists, but she is still stuck on accidental features concerning clothing, specifically lab coats. She has formed a (non-gendered) stereotype, but a stereotype nonetheless, and has generalized inaccurately on the basis of that stereotype. (She might also now have new mistaken information from her mom concerning the independence between science and commerce, more on that in our discussion of vaccines). However, the externalized triangular process by which she came to form the mistaken truth conditions then allowed her and her mom to trace the origin of the mistake and correct it. The external triangulation through which our beliefs come to have meaning provides the path we follow when objectively (re)assessing the evidential strength of those beliefs.

I have purposely chosen an example of the formation of a belief, "That's a scientist," the genesis of which gave that belief semantic content that, at a glance, seems straightforwardly descriptive but on reflection also contains evaluative elements. It is sometimes hard to tease the descriptive and evaluative realms apart. Philosophers of science attentive to social

Charity, Peace, and Science Controversies 129

epistemology have shown us that the objective assessment of the evidence for our beliefs is a messy process, weakened by innumerable cognitive biases, such as stereotypes, as well as dogmatism and conflicts of interest, but it is important to acknowledge that these weaknesses afflict the assessment of beliefs we might sort as descriptive as much as they afflict the assessment of beliefs we might sort as evaluative (Clough and Loges 2008), and as with this example, they afflict the assessment of beliefs that have both evaluative and descriptive elements.

This is not unrelated to the claim that descriptive and evaluative sorting is largely a function of context. And even within a particular context, no descriptive belief is without evaluative content and, I would add, vice-versa (Clough 2013). For example, here are three claims from the context of scientific research on childhood vaccines that have elements most of us would, I think, sort as descriptive, but note the evaluative layers that lurk beneath the surface:

1. Vaccines are among the most effective and safe public health interventions available to prevent serious disease and death (Institute of Medicine 2013, 1).
2. Vaccines, in rare cases, can cause illness. Most children who experience an adverse reaction to immunization have a preexisting susceptibility. Some predispositions may be detectable prior to vaccination; others, at least with current technology and practice, are not (Institute of Medicine 2013, 19).
3. With the current schedule, children may receive up to 24 immunizations by age 2 years and up to 5 injections in a single visit (Institute of Medicine 2013, 1).

Descriptive claims are supposed to be straightforward candidates for objective assessment, it is the evaluative claims that, on more conventional epistemic accounts, court relativism (of any number of kinds). However, when these three descriptive claims are read together, it becomes clear that for any parent who cares about the safety of their child (i.e. most parents) being presented with these three claims and deciding whether to assent to the prescribed vaccinations requires not just a straightforward assessment of the available evidence for the descriptive elements of the claims regarding the health risk of vaccinating their child or not, but also a meta-assessment of the available evidence for evaluative elements of the claims related to trust in their health-care providers, drug manufacturers, epidemiologists, and immunologists, as well as trust in the sources of information they have about any of these (a level of trust made more difficult by social media and the influence of trolls and bots in online vaccine debates in particular [Broniatowski et al. 2018]). The parents must also run an assessment of the evidence they have for the reasonableness of their trust in the basic social safety net

130   *Sharyn Clough*

in case their child has an unlikely adverse reaction to the vaccine that will require aid beyond what the parents can provide. They must also have the ability to do a meta-evidential comparison of the evidence of the risk of the unlikely but unknown side effects of a vaccine, with the evidence about the risk of the unlikely but more familiar effects of getting, say, measles. This same complexly layered process of assessment goes for any scientist making these claims. Regardless of whether they are parents themselves, scientists and policymakers must be responsive to this broader cluster of considerations when assessing whether there is enough evidence to warrant making the claims on which parents are expected to act.

So, back to the parents. Imagine this is you. You are making this decision in a doctor's office with a crying 16-month-old in your arms after a hurried read of a multi-page informational pamphlet on vaccine safety thrust at you by a nurse who has run off to tend to the next patient – your seven minutes of managed care per appointment are near their end. Might you hesitate? Or might you sigh, cross your fingers, and permit the five scheduled vaccinations out of frustration and exhaustion? In either case, was your decision reached using careful objective deliberation of the three descriptive claims as I've previously described them? Probably not. While the three claims at issue are presented as uncomplicated descriptions, as facts, deliberations about the evidence in support of these claims are often complicated, as previously indicated. (And yet, there is evidence to which we can appeal when assessing these complicated claims – we should not mistake the recognition of epistemic complication for a concession to relativism. More on this in Section 8.5.)

In contrast to these three complicated claims that often get sorted, superficially, as descriptive, here's three more claims in the same policy context, the evidence for which is far less complicated to adjudicate, even though we might sort these claims as evaluative. Note the empirical content to which the evaluative elements are semantically linked, giving the entire claims their meaning:

1a.   Some vaccine researchers have been criminally irresponsible in the conduct of their research.
2a.   Celebrities have no business talking about vaccine efficacy or any other scientific issue unless they also have the relevant medical expertise.
3a.   We need more publicly funded research on childhood vaccine programs.

Regardless of whether you agree or disagree with these more obviously evaluative claims (though I hope you agree), the way you would go about objectively assessing the epistemic strength of your evaluation would involve the semantic linking of your views to claims about responsibility, criminality, celebrity, and conflicts of interest, as well as the evidence you have that informs those concepts.

On my Davidsonian reading, insofar as both the descriptive and evaluative elements of any belief contribute to its meaning, then those elements have empirical content formed through triangulation, or are sufficiently semantically connected to beliefs that do. That is, they are a product of our interactions with each other in the world. Again, because it is in the context of this triangular relationship that the content of our beliefs is more or less directly established, then, it is in the context of this relationship that the evidence for our beliefs can be objectively assessed and mistaken beliefs can be addressed.

The potential for mistakes in our beliefs is the result of the fallible nature of induction. But we can recognize errors, and we can fix them (of course only when we are motivated to do so, which takes empathy and humility, of which more shortly). The results of these fixes are new, and hopefully improved, but still fallible, inductive inferences.

Insofar as this argument about the role of triangulation in the causes of beliefs holds for beliefs sorted as factual *and* evaluative, as well as beliefs with content that can be read as either, or a mix of both, then objectively applying the tools of evidence gathering and justification makes as much sense when considering political values in science as it does when considering those elements of scientific claims that we might sort as more straightforwardly descriptive (within which political values are often embedded).

Taking the pragmatist step into the muck and mire of the actual practice of deliberations about science claims with controversial political implications while avoiding a self-refuting relativism requires the recognition of the existence of a much broader range of claims to which we are responsible as epistemic agents. If I am right, this means that we should expand our understanding of what counts as the kinds of evidence to which scientists and all of us ought be responsive (e.g. expanding what counts as "evidence" to include the experiences that inform not only our descriptive beliefs, but also our political beliefs).

8.3. Taking the Next (Pragmatist) Step

In this section, I discuss *how* evidential deliberations about political values can be effective in science contexts by examining the conditions required for effective deliberation. This is where epistemic humility and empathy begin to make an explicit appearance, and where conceiving of these as social practices, as kinds of phronesis, as habits, helps us see them as a skill set, as literacy, indeed, as *peace* literacy.

The need for taking this next more consistent step in the direction of phronesis, in the direction of moving from analyses of objectivity as a product – as the result of the adequate, attentive capture of the relevant

132　*Sharyn Clough*

evidence – and adding to it, objectivity as a *process*, as habits and skills, became especially obvious to me after encountering studies showing that a significant number of parents who are hesitant to vaccinate their children are affluent, science-literate, white people (e.g. Koerth-Baker 2016). (Full disclosure: I am white, more or less affluent, more or less science-literate, and I just got a booster MMR vaccine for good measure.) It turns out that parental hesitation regarding vaccinations for their children is not always or even often informed by a misunderstanding of the role of evidence or a failure to respect the importance of scientific research. Rather, their hesitation is motivated by an inability to trust the medical establishment or sometimes science as an institution, more generally (Goldenberg 2016). The race and social class of these parents is relevant to the development of my thinking here because I was aware of a number of well-documented reasons for economically-marginalized black people and indigenous people in the US to mistrust medical interventions, and science more generally (e.g. Scheman 2001), but I was not aware of any reasons for economically advantaged, well-educated, white people to be mistrustful. Science as an institution usually worked in our interest (Grasswick 2014). So I was confused. I think my confusion revealed many things, but of relevance to this chapter, my confusion revealed a lack of epistemic humility and a lack of empathy.

My understanding of epistemic humility is based on work in virtue epistemology by scholars influenced by feminism and pragmatism (e.g. Medina 2013; Tanesini 2018). In her essay "Intellectual Humility as Attitude," Tanesini documents the heterogeneity of behaviors, attitudes, and states that often fall under the label "intellectual humility" (2018). Because of this heterogeneity, I will use the term "*epistemic* humility" to refer to just a couple of these, specifically open-mindedness and self-acceptance.

Tanesini writes that self-acceptance is the acceptance of "human limitations and one's own limitations in particular. This dimension of humility is manifested in the awe which is felt by us in the presence of forces that makes us feel small such as the strength of a storm at sea" (2018, 404–405). It is also manifested typically by "the ability to acknowledge one's own errors or shortcomings, rather than deny them … to accept fair criticisms with equanimity and [not be] resentful of them" (2016, 7). These are tall orders, which is precisely why we need to practice them until they become entrenched habits. These habits are an important bulwark against dogmatism. As Elizabeth Anderson has argued, it is dogmatism about our political claims (and our descriptive claims!) that gets in the way of objectivity in scientific research, rather than the mere presence of political claims themselves (Anderson 2004). It might seem that encouraging all of us practioners of phronsesis, including scientists, to acknowledge the possibility of error and recognize our human limitations is a call to give up on the notion of science and scientists as reliable epistemic authorities; a promotion of the view that scientific knowledge

Charity, Peace, and Science Controversies   133

practices are just as good (or just as flawed) as any other; to embrace relativism. As I argue in Section 8.5, diagnosing the problem as one of relativism is a mistake. In fact, the practice of epistemic humility is a condition of objective evidential deliberation.

An important companion to epistemic humility, I have come to realize, is empathy. That I needed to also pay attention to empathy was very much influenced by Chappell (2017), who views empathy as a key capacity in the development of peace literacy. For Chappell, empathy, like other peace skills, is a habit, a phronesis, it takes practice, and it needs to be taught. Empathy is getting new attention in social and moral epistemology (see e.g. Lux and Weig 2017; Betzler 2019; Fagiano 2019; and others in a special issue of the *International Journal of Philosophical Studies* dedicated to empathy); however, it is not a stand-alone capacity. Chappell counsels the development of empathy as a capacity that works best in concert with the development of a number of other cognitive capacities such as imagination, conscience, reason, and hope (Chappell 2012, 2017). Similarly, Jose Medina (2013) argues for imagination/ empathy together with humility and open mindedness, in the formation of what he calls "kaleidoscopic consciousness" (Medina 2013, 200).

As a feminist scholar focused on diagnosing the hierarchies of power that divide us, I had never been confident about the epistemic potential of empathy – a robust capacity for empathy seemed to require the existence of a shared set of human experiences that crossed divisions of political power and I was concerned that whatever shared experiences we could draw from when we empathized with someone, those shared experiences would not be able to overcome the hierarchies that divided us. This lack of confidence might seem ironic given that it was an expression of the very relativism I claimed to eschew when I argued for the potential of shared experience to objectively underwrite the evidential assessment of political values. Regardless, endorsing the epistemic potential in empathy seemed even to me to be a stretch.

Chappell's work reoriented my attention but it was Campelia's 2017 paper "Empathic Knowledge: The Importance of Empathy's Social Epistemology" that put the issue into a familiar epistemic context. Campelia identifies three kinds of rationale underlying concerns about empathy of the sort that were motivating feminists like me and other philosophers concerned about social injustice, bias, and power:

1. That any sufficiently robust degree of knowing how another feels is impossible;
2. That susceptibility to stereotypes renders empathic understanding unreliable; and
3. That empathic activities have a strong potential for false empathy and its attendant interpersonal and societal harms.

(Campelia 2017, 530)

134 *Sharyn Clough*

The second and third of these criticisms find robust support in "Against Empathy" by Jesse Prinz (2011). Believing in the efficacy of empathy requires some confidence in our ability, objectively and reliably, to get outside our own heads and hearts in ways that don't just involve the biased projection of our own concerns onto those who look and act sufficiently like us to motivate our attention. Prinz's essay expresses well the pessimism I had been feeling on this point. In response to these concerns, Campelia argues that if we attend sufficiently to the *social practice* of empathy, to the "interdependent relationality of empathy," then empathy's "epistemic possibility, reliability, and sensitivity to degrees of accuracy are solidified" (531). The emphasis on "social practice" in her analysis was the first pragmatist reminder that my pessimism regarding empathy was misplaced.

In "Empathy on Trial: A Response to Its Critics" (2019), Stephen Morris offers a similar defense of empathy, showing that the biases that afflict our empathic conditioning, inclining us to restrict our focus to the "near and dear," for example, are epistemic habits of mind that can and should be undone. He explains:

> While there is little doubt that empathy is biased in these and other ways, this hardly seems reason in itself for suggesting [as Prinz does] that people should minimize the impact that empathy has over their lives. Rather than seeking to suppress our empathic instincts in light of this bias, it would seem better to use reason to expand our empathy towards individuals whose interests we might otherwise ignore. Such expansion of empathy seems to be a driving force behind numerous societies' greater acceptance of formerly marginalized groups, such as ethnic and religious minorities.
>
> (Morris 2019, 511)

Morris references the work of J. Decety and J. Cowell (2014), who explain how the kind of affective perspective taking that allows us to imagine how others feel "can reduce prejudice and group bias" by bringing about "changes in the way we see others, and those changes generalize to people similar to them, notably members of the same social group to which they belong" (Decety and Cowell 2014, 530).

Campelia provides helpful guidance here. We need to conceive of empathy "as a social epistemic practice *within which knowledge is formed* and *confirmed* with others" (Campelia 2017, 530). Her account overlaps in compelling ways with Davidson's. There is a connection in his model of interpretational charity and triangulation, not just to the elements of active attention that we might sort as epistemic, but also to the kinds of attention we might sort as moral. Think of the empathy underlying the interdependent social practices that enabled the young girl in my earlier example to identify the conditions under which the sentence "That's a scientist" is true.

We can think of empathy as the ability to recognize and see similarities between ours and another's emotional states and points of view, which is actually quite difficult, or it can be caring for others and their emotional states and points of view, which when you think about it for two seconds can also be really difficult. Let's be honest. Neither comes easily, or at least we all know the circumstances where it's hard. And each kind of empathy seems intertwined in complicated ways. We seem to need to care about someone before we will bother to take the energy to recognize them, to see similarities between us and them, and we need to see similarities between us and them before we can care about them. See Figure 8.1.

The reason is because, at a very basic level, identifying similarities, identifying common ground, is made possible by our ability to recognize each other empathically as people with whom we might actually communicate. But to recognize each other empathically as people with whom we can communicate, we need the identification of common ground. Empathy involves a feedback loop between caring for someone and recognizing similarities between ours and other's emotional states and points of view, but there is also a feedback loop between empathy and the identification of common ground. Finding common ground with someone helps us have empathy for them and vice versa.

All of these conditions must be present, arising together in some measure, for communication to be possible. These three features – empathy, common ground, and communication – cycle together. Coordinating all of this takes practice and skill. But we do it more or less successfully, all the time. See Figure 8.2.

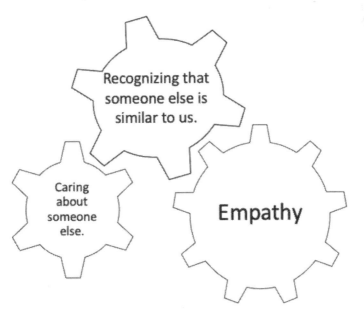

Figure 8.1 Empathy, Recognition, and Care

136 *Sharyn Clough*

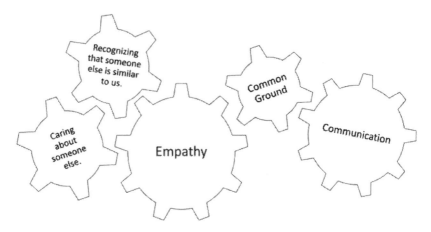

Figure 8.2 Empathy and Communication

So let's do more of it now. Let's return to the project of thinking about the skills of empathy and epistemic humility as conditions of objective deliberation about politically value-laden science, especially in the context of controversial science policy debates about, for example, the efficacy and safety of childhood vaccinations. Let's get back to the case of economically advantaged white people who are "vaccine hesitant."

In "Public Misunderstanding of Science? Reframing the Problem of Vaccine Hesitancy," Goldenberg argues that there are a variety of reasons animating the most recent round of vaccine hesitancy (it is helpful to have historians of epidemiology and health-care policy remind us that this is not a new phenomenon [Goldenberg 2016, 554]). The "science-deficit" explanation for these parents' behavior does not capture an adequate amount of variation in the data and the staying power of this explanation verges on epistemic hubris on the part of scientists (and on the part of those of us social epistemologists, like me, who have been tempted by this explanation).

Goldenberg points out that most parents who are vaccine hesitant know the relevant science (as well as non-experts in any field can "know" the science); and they are indeed compliant with pediatric advice, especially in terms of the admonishments that they become "actively engage[d] in their children's healthcare and [become] experts on their own child" (2016, 566). Goldenberg discusses the research of Leach and Fairhead (2007), who interviewed parents in the UK and found that the parents were eager to discuss evidence and to work as active research partners with pediatricians in their children's health and well-being. These parents' concerns about vaccine safety expressed not a lack of scientific understanding, necessarily, but a mismatch between the individual-levels

Charity, Peace, and Science Controversies 137

of explanation they were seeking (how might this vaccine affect my own particular child's health?) and the population-level of explanation being offered by their doctors. In other words, population-level assurances of vaccine safety did not assuage their concerns for their particular child's safety, in light of the vast amount of evidence the parents had collected on their child's particular health history, immune response, and genetic heritage (Leach and Fairhead 2007, in Goldenberg 2019, 565). This is to say nothing about the growing mistrust in science relative to the increasing influence of pharmaceutical companies in funding the very vaccine research that underwrites these population-level claims about safety.

Parents who hesitate to vaccinate their children aren't necessarily resisting scientific evidence about vaccines, what they are often asking for is *more* evidence, for more research to be done to help diagnose in advance which children will be harmed by vaccine side effects and which not (Goldenberg 2016, 566). (Recall the claim in Section 8.2 that "Most children who experience an adverse reaction to immunization have a preexisting susceptibility. Some predispositions may be detectable prior to vaccination; others, at least with current technology and practice, are not" [Institute of Medicine 2013, 19]; see also Anna Kirkland's *Vaccine Court: The Law and Politics of Injury* [2016] for further discussion of these rare but heartbreaking and currently hard to predict cases of harm.)

Returning again to issues of trust, many parents concerned about the safety of childhood vaccines *do* trust experts, just not the experts you might expect. In her essay "Values and Vaccines" (2016), Maggie Koerth-Baker discusses the puzzling ongoing influence of Andrew Wakefield, whose fraudulent research purported to show links between autism and the vaccine for mumps, measles, and rubella (the MMR vaccine). After he was stripped of his medical license in the UK, Wakefield moved to the US, where "he went on to find fame working with parents who believed their children had been damaged by vaccines" (2016). Koerth-Baker notes that "parents trusted Wakefield in a way that they didn't trust legitimate, factually correct doctors *because he was willing to acknowledge their fears and their philosophical concerns*" (Koerth-Baker 2016, emphasis mine). Here a *lack* of empathy on the part of legitimate pediatric experts has disrupted the objectivity of evidential deliberations.

Failures of empathy and epistemic humility have kept me, but more importantly doctors, epidemiologists, immunologists, and policymakers, from recognizing the kinds of evidence relevant to the decision-making of many of these parents and even from recognizing the evidence used by parents who are *not* vaccine-hesitant. Political and moral issues of trust are playing a role in parental decision-making in either case, and empathy and epistemic humility are required conditions of any objective assessment of the efficacy of their decisions.

138 Sharyn Clough

8.4. Revisiting the Role of Relativism

Every parent who has ever questioned the effectiveness of childhood vaccines cares about their kids' health and safety. Every one. We need to acknowledge that there is a large chunk of common ground here to walk on concerning our care and concern for children. Of the many things up for debate when vaccines are being discussed, no one ever argues that we shouldn't care about the health and safety of kids. But this fact can get lost.

Too often, parents concerned with the safety of vaccinating their children are described as being uninterested in science, truth, facts, or evidence; they hear what they want to hear and deny what they want to deny; they are tired of experts telling them about the efficacy of vaccinations; they are "evidence resistant"; they are symptomatic of a new era of relativism where anyone can be an expert because epistemic authority is no longer valued, every claim to authority is epistemically symmetrical and impossible to rank. I have argued that these kinds of explanations of the phenomenon have important limitations. Recognizing these limits objectively requires humility and empathy. Failures of humility and empathy are the main problems here. Relativistic failures to value truth or evidence, not so much.

Consider that we all share basic needs – food, shelter, peace, love, understanding. As a general rule, people worried about the safety of vaccines do their best to keep their children from playing in traffic, they water their plants, they consume calories in response to hunger, they clothe themselves against the cold. Those of us with fewer worries about vaccines share with those who have more worries a number of true beliefs, that is beliefs for which we all have good evidence. It is this base of shared true beliefs that allows us to communicate our disagreements. Where we disagree is not over the importance of having true beliefs, or the importance of evidence, it's over which beliefs are true, and who to trust as an authority in those cases (most of them) when the evidence is too complex to be evaluated by non-experts.

It is epistemic hubris to frame our very real disagreements as disagreements over the very notion of evidence or truth. It is in our epistemic interest to acknowledge the messiness of evidence gathering and the limited focus of our attention spans and interests; to acknowledge the variety of cognitive biases that plague our own reasoning and evidence gathering; in the case of vaccine hesitancy, to acknowledge the fear that these parents have for their children's safety, especially as features of the broader social safety net are fraying and support for children devolves increasingly on to parents under increasing financial and social strain. I have argued that the epistemic hubris that keeps us from acknowledging these shared features of the world is inter-related with a failure to recognize those with whom we disagree as interlocutors, as members of a

Charity, Peace, and Science Controversies 139

shared world about which we can communicate. This recognition takes empathy. And just as empathy allows us to recognize each other as interlocutors, the fact of our communication as interlocutors reveals our shared commitment to evidence and truth. It is probably no coincidence that the increased polarization of social media keeps us from communicating across lines of empathy. As it gets harder and harder to recognize our similarities, we are losing practice, our muscles of empathy are atrophying, we become more confident about the accuracy of our claims and the inaccuracy of all others, and we communicate less. Empathy and epistemic humility are critical conditions of phronesis, of the engaged practice of objective evidential deliberation, of communication.

8.5. Conclusion

With Anderson (2004), I have argued that when there are problems with political values in science it is not because values exist in or arise from some domain completely unrelated to evidence and are thereby unavailable for empirical examination. Whatever problems there are typically concern the dogmatic way that we sometimes hold on to our evaluative beliefs (and our descriptive beliefs!). Dogmatism about any sort of belief is a kind of epistemic hubris – the opposite of the practice of epistemic humility. One antidote to epistemic hubris is to recognize those with whom we disagree as interlocutors, as members of a shared world about which we can communicate. This recognition takes empathy. And just as empathy allows us to recognize each other as interlocutors, the fact of our communication as interlocutors reveals our common ground. This is the ground we start from as we triangulate on and objectively evaluate the evidence for our beliefs. As Davidson writes, "communication begins where causes converge" (1989, 151). Here is Davidson on common ground:

> Given enough common ground, we can understand and explain differences, we can criticize, compare, and persuade. The main thing is that finding the common ground is not subsequent to understanding, but a condition of it. This fact may be hidden from us because we usually more or less understand someone's language before we talk with them. This invites the impression that we can then, using our mutually understood language, discover whether we share their view of the world and their basic values. This is an illusion. If we understand their words, a common ground exists, we already share their way of life.
>
> (Davidson 2004, 50)

In "Three Varieties of Knowledge" (2001), Davidson likens the practice of communication to a stool with three legs – knowledge of self, others,

140 *Sharyn Clough*

and the world – all three of which have to develop together (over time and with practice) for communication to be effective. I think he would have agreed that we also have to care about each other in order to recognize each other as interlocuters, an epistemic attitude that I have argued takes empathy and epistemic humility. Empathy, common ground, and communication also have to develop together for objective evidential deliberations, for phronesis. I have lost track of the number of legs this gives our stool. Perhaps it is worth switching to a different metaphor – I shall switch here from furniture to pop music. *What's so funny about interpretational charity, peace, love, and understanding?* Nothing. I am confident that Elvis Costello would consider this to be friendly amendments to his ballad. Understanding our interlocutors requires recognizing that they too have beliefs that arise from the evidence of experience. Seeing them as interlocutors requires empathy, maybe even love. Chappell would remind us that together these are the conditions of peace.

References

Anderson, E. (2004), "The Uses of Value Judgments in Science," *Hypatia: A Journal of Feminist Philosophy* 19 (1): 1–24.

Bellolio, C. (2019), "The Quinean Assumption: The Case for Science as Public Reason," *Social Epistemology* 33 (3): 205–217.

Betzler, M. (2019), "The Relational Value of Empathy," *International Journal of Philosophical Studies* 27 (2): 1–26.

Broniatowski, D.A., A.M. Jamison, S. Qi, L. AlKulaib, T. Chen, A. Benton, S.C. Quinn and M. Dredze. (2018), "Weaponized Health Communication: Twitter Bots and Russian Trolls Amplify the Vaccine Debate," *American Journal of Public Health* 108: 1378–1384.

Campelia, G. (2017), "Empathic Knowledge: The Importance of Empathy's Social Epistemology," *Social Epistemology* 31 (6): 530–544.

Chappell, P.K. (2012), *Peaceful Revolution*, New York: Easton Studio Press.

———. (2017), *Soldiers of Peace: How to Wield the Weapon of Nonviolence with Maximum Force*, New York: Easton Studio Press.

Clough, S. (2002), "What Is Menstruation for? On the Projectibility of Functional Predicates in Menstruation Research," *Studies in the History and Philosophy of the Biological and Biomedical Sciences* 33 (4): 719–732.

———. (2003), *Beyond Epistemology: A Pragmatist Approach to Feminist Science Studies*, Lanham, MD: Rowman & Littlefield.

———. (2004), "Having It All: Naturalized Normativity in Feminist Science Studies," *Hypatia: A Journal of Feminist Philosophy* 19 (1): 102–118.

———. (2010), "Gender and the Hygiene Hypothesis," *Social Science & Medicine* 72 (4): 486–493.

———. (2011), "Radical Interpretation, Feminism, and Science," in *Dialogues with Davidson*, edited by J. Malpas, Cambridge, MA: MIT Press, 405–426.

———. (2013), "Pragmatism and Embodiment as Resources for Feminist Interventions in Science," *Contemporary Pragmatism* 10 (2): 121–134.

Charity, Peace, and Science Controversies 141

———. (2015), "Fact/Value Holism, Feminist Philosophy, and Nazi Cancer Research," *Feminist Philosophical Quarterly* 1 (1), http://ir.lib.uwo.ca/fpq/vol1/iss1/7/.

Clough, S. and B. Loges. (2008), "Racist Beliefs as Objectively False Value Judgments: A Philosophical and Social-Psychological Analysis," *The Journal of Social Philosophy* 39 (1): 77–95.

Clough, S. and N. McHugh. (forthcoming), "Where Are All the Feminist Pragmatist Philosophers of Science?," in *The Routledge Handbook of Feminist Philosophy of Science*, edited by S. Crasnow and K. Intemann, New York: Routledge.

Clough, S. and J. Orozco. (2016), "Scientific Sexism and Racism," in *The Encyclopedia of Gender and Sexuality Studies*, edited by N. Naples, Oxford: Wiley Blackwell, doi: 10.1002/9781118663219.wbegss315.

Davidson, D. (2001 [1989]), "A Coherence Theory of Truth and Knowledge," reprinted in his *Subjective, Intersubjective, Objective*, Oxford: Oxford University Press.

———. (2001 [1991]), "Three Varieties of Knowledge," reprinted in his *Subjective, Intersubjective, Objective*, Oxford: Oxford University Press.

———. (2004 [1995]), "The Objectivity of Values," reprinted in his *Problems of Rationality*, Oxford: Oxford University Press.

Decety, J. and J. Cowell. (2014), "Friends or Foes: Is Empathy Necessary for Moral Behavior?," *Perspectives on Psychological Science* 9 (5): 525–537.

de Melo-Martín, I. and K. Intemann. (2018), *The Fight against Doubt: How to Bridge the Gap between Scientists and the Public*, New York Oxford University Press.

Elliott, K. (2017), *A Tapestry of Values: An Introduction to Values in Science*, New York: Oxford University Press.

Fagiano, M. (2019), "Relational Empathy," *International Journal of Philosophical Studies* 27 (2): 162–179.

Goldenberg, M. (2013), "How Can Feminist Theories of Evidence Assist Clinical Reasoning and Decision-Making?," *Social Epistemology: A Journal of Knowledge, Culture and Policy* 29 (1): 3–30.

———. (2016), "Public Misunderstanding of Science? Reframing the Problem of Vaccine Hesitancy," *Perspectives on Science* 24 (5): 552–581.

———. (2019), "Vaccines, Values, and Science," *Canadian Medical Association Journal* 191 (14): E397–E398.

Grasswick, H. (2014), "Climate Change Science and Responsible Trust: A Situated Approach," *Hypatia: A Journal of Feminist Philosophy* 29 (3): 541–557.

Institute of Medicine. (2013), *The Childhood Immunization Schedule and Safety: Stakeholder Concerns, Scientific Evidence, and Future Studies*, Washington, DC: The National Academies Press.

Kirkland, A. (2016), *Vaccine Court: The Law and Politics of Injury*, New York: NYU Press.

Koerth-Baker, M. (2016), "Values and Vaccines," *AEON*, https://aeon.co/essays/anti-vaccination-might-be-rational-but-is-it-reasonable.

Krakauer, J.W. (2019), "The Intelligent Reflex," *Philosophical Psychology* 32 (5): 823–831.

Kusch, M. (2020), "Introduction," in *The Routledge Handbook of Philosophy of Relativism*, edited by M. Kusch, New York: Routledge.

142 Sharyn Clough

Leach, M. and J. Fairhead. (2007), *Vaccine Anxieties: Global Health, Child Health, and Society*, London: Earthscan.

Longino, H. (1990), *Science as Social Knowledge*, Princeton: Princeton University Press.

Lux, V. and S. Weige (eds.). (2017), *Empathy: Epistemic Problems and Cultural-Historical Perspectives of a Cross-Disciplinary Concept*, Basingstoke: Palgrave Macmillan.

McHugh, N. (2015), *The Limits of Knowledge: Generating Pragmatist Feminist Cases for Situated Knowing*, Albany, NY: SUNY Press.

Medina, J. (2013), *The Epistemology of Resistance: Gender and Racial Oppression, Epistemic Injustice and Resistant Imaginations*, Oxford: Oxford University Press.

Morris, S. (2019), "Empathy on Trial: A Response to Its Critics," *Philosophical Psychology* 32 (4): 508–531.

Pagan, N.O. (2008), "Configuring the Moral Self: Aristotle and Dewey," *Foundations of Science* 13 (3–4): 239–250.

Prinz, J. (2011), "Against Empathy," *The Southern Journal of Philosophy* 49: 214–233.

Scheman, N. (2001), "Epistemology Resuscitated," in *Engendering Rationalities*, edited by N. Tuana and S. Morgen, Albany, NY: SUNY Press.

Tanesini, A. (2016), "Teaching Virtue," *Logos and Episteme* 7 (4): 503–527.

———. (2018), "Intellectual Humility as Attitude," *Philosophy and Phenomenological Research* 96 (2): 399–420.

9 Epistemic Responsibility and Relativism

Kristina Rolin

9.1. Introduction

Epistemic relativism is often understood to be a relativism about epistemic justification. *Epistemic justification relativism* involves the view that beliefs are epistemically justified or unjustified only relative to systems of epistemic standards. For the relativist there is more than one such system, and there is no neutral way of choosing between them (Kusch 2017).

In this chapter, I discuss another type of epistemic relativism, relativism about epistemically responsible knowledge claims. While some philosophers understand epistemic responsibility as a virtue that a person can have (Code 1984), I understand it as a relational property holding between the act of making a knowledge claim and an audience. A person can assert "I know that p" in an epistemically responsible or irresponsible way depending on her audience. Different accounts of epistemic responsibility are concerned with the question of when it is epistemically responsible for a person to claim that p rather than with the question of when p is epistemically justified. Insofar as the two questions are connected, accounts of epistemic responsibility aim to clarify how they are connected. *Epistemic responsibility relativism* involves the view that the act of making a knowledge claim is epistemically responsible or irresponsible only relative to an audience and its system of epistemic standards. Like epistemic justification relativism, it is committed to the view that there is no neutral way of ranking different audiences and their systems of epistemic standards.

Epistemic responsibility is of interest to social epistemology because it is an important component in social practices of knowledge seeking, especially in scientific communities (Rolin 2017a, 2017b). Conceptions of epistemic responsibility aim to ensure that scientists are accountable to each other when they are participating in a joint knowledge-seeking practice. According to one account of epistemic responsibility, a person makes a knowledge claim that p in an epistemically responsible way when (i) she provides (or takes steps towards providing) evidence in

144 *Kristina Rolin*

support of p, or (ii) she commits herself to defending p (Williams 2001, 23–24). What counts as evidence of the right kind and amount depends on what the audience is willing to accept without further inquiries or challenges at least for the moment. To be epistemically responsible, the person does not need to cite evidence in support of all her claims. She can put forward a knowledge claim with a commitment to defend it (Brandom 1983, 641). Such a commitment means that she accepts the obligation to defend the claim whenever it is challenged with counterevidence or some other kind of argument. Withdrawing a knowledge claim is an epistemically responsible thing to do when the person is no longer capable of defending it.

Given this account of epistemic responsibility, knowledge claims are epistemically responsible or irresponsible only relative to an audience. Moreover, if systems of epistemic standards vary significantly from one audience to another, as they often do, knowledge claims are epistemically responsible or irresponsible only relative to systems of epistemic standards. This means that a person can claim that p in an epistemically responsible way in one social context, whereas in another social context, her claiming that p in an epistemically responsible way could require another kind or degree of evidence. In yet another social context, her claiming that p could be epistemically irresponsible. There is no such thing as being epistemically responsible in isolation from a social context which involves an audience and its system of epistemic standards. This is because epistemic responsibility is a relational property involving two parties, the person who makes a knowledge claim and her audience. That epistemic responsibility depends on the social context does not yet give rise to relativism about epistemically responsible knowledge claims. Epistemic responsibility relativism involves the further view that there is no neutral way of ranking different audiences and their systems of epistemic standards.

Many social epistemologists want to accept the view that epistemic responsibility is an important component in social practices of knowledge seeking. But they do not generally wish to adopt epistemic responsibility relativism (see also Rolin 2011). If one intends to combine epistemic responsibility with the rejection of relativism, one option is to focus on the audience, its epistemic norms, standards, practices, and institutional arrangements. When the audience is the unit of epistemic appraisal, social epistemologists wish to know whether it has a shared system of epistemic standards. If the audience consists of people with a variety of epistemic standards, it is difficult to know what it takes to meet the epistemic standards of the audience. If the audience shares a system of epistemic standards that is also relatively stable, it is easier to understand what it takes to be epistemically responsible. For this reason, social epistemologists have focused on *epistemic communities* as the preferred units of epistemic appraisal. In virtue of having shared epistemic standards, epistemic communities form the kinds of audiences that are of interest to social epistemology.

According to one influential approach, epistemic responsibility relativism can be refuted by introducing criteria for assessing epistemic communities (e.g. Longino 1990). Such criteria can be epistemically justified by appealing to an instrumentalist account of epistemic rationality. An instrumentalist account involves the view that epistemically well-designed communities are governed by those norms and standards that are conducive to achieving desired epistemic goals (e.g. Giere 1989).

The aim of this chapter is to assess whether an instrumentalist strategy for refuting epistemic responsibility relativism is successful. While I do not object to the instrumentalist account of epistemic rationality, I argue that it involves a trade-off. This is because the norm of epistemic responsibility is not merely an epistemic but also a moral norm. Besides serving epistemic ends, it also serves morally valuable ends, and sometimes the latter trump the former. The trade-off in an instrumentalist strategy is that if one prefers one epistemic community to another on epistemic grounds, then one has to admit that epistemic grounds are not morally neutral. And yet, if one prefers one epistemic community to another on moral grounds, then one has to make a concession to communities that do not come close to being epistemically well-designed. In both cases, there are criteria for ranking audiences and their systems of epistemic standards, and sometimes such criteria may be reasons for choosing between different audiences, but the criteria are not morally neutral.

The chapter is organized as follows. In Section 9.2, I explain why epistemic responsibility relativism is a problematic position for social epistemology. I also introduce the instrumentalist account of epistemic rationality. In Section 9.3, I discuss criteria for assessing epistemic communities. In Section 9.4, I argue that the norm of epistemic responsibility is both an epistemic and a moral norm. In conclusion, I argue that because the norm of epistemic responsibility is both an epistemic and a moral norm, it forces social epistemologists to balance between epistemic and moral goals.

9.2. What Is the Problem With Epistemic Responsibility Relativism?

The problem with epistemic responsibility relativism is that it undermines the norm of epistemic responsibility. The norm of epistemic responsibility captures the view that epistemic responsibility is valuable in social practices of knowledge seeking. The norm of epistemic responsibility states that when a person makes a knowledge claim, she ought to do so in an epistemically responsible way. A person violates the norm of epistemic responsibility when she makes a knowledge claim in an epistemically irresponsible way. Thus the norm of epistemic responsibility implies that a

146 *Kristina Rolin*

person should not make the claim that p when she is not in a position to claim that p in an epistemically responsible way.

To understand how epistemic responsibility relativism can undermine the norm of epistemic responsibility, it is useful to keep in mind the distinction between epistemic norms and standards. Norms, such as the norm of epistemic responsibility, apply to human agents. Norms are behavioral rules that someone is accountable for conforming to. Holding someone to account involves imposing a sanction on them (Kauppinen 2018, 3). Systems of epistemic standards apply to non-agents. Systems of epistemic standards include, typically, standards that make it possible to evaluate evidence, inferences, hypotheses, and theories.

According to epistemic responsibility relativism, what counts as an epistemically responsible knowledge claim depends on the audience and its system of epistemic standards, and there is no neutral way of ranking different audiences and their systems of epistemic standards. The problem with epistemic responsibility relativism is that almost any knowledge claim can be epistemically responsible given a suitable social context. Whenever a person faces the prospect of not being capable of making a knowledge claim in an epistemically responsible way, she can look for another social context in which her knowledge claim could be epistemically responsible. Moreover, she can choose a social context in which a false statement can easily pass for an epistemically responsible claim. Such social contexts can be found in the epistemic bubbles and echo chambers of the internet and social media (Nguyen 2018).

Thus, one implication of epistemic responsibility relativism is that even if a person makes a knowledge claim in an epistemically responsible way, her claim can still be false. I call this the *problem of epistemically responsible false claims*. The problem of epistemically responsible false claims does not need to be disastrous for a social epistemology of scientific knowledge. This is because scientific knowledge claims are rarely justified in a conclusive way, and in many cases, it is possible to raise doubts about their truth. In other words, scientific knowledge claims are fallible. The problem of epistemically responsible false claims is critical when epistemically responsible knowledge claims turn out to be false more often than true. This scenario is conceivable, for example, when the person who puts forward knowledge claims and her audience subscribe to standards that are not truth-conducive.

Another implication of epistemic responsibility relativism is that epistemically responsible knowledge claims can come cheaply. The *problem of epistemically responsible cheap claims* arises when the person who makes the knowledge claim and her audience subscribe to epistemic standards that are so low that it is relatively easy for the person to advance knowledge claims in an epistemically responsible way. Again, the problem of epistemically responsible cheap claims does not need to be critical for social epistemology. In many situations of everyday life, epistemically

Epistemic Responsibility and Relativism   147

responsible cheap claims are not a problem simply because people are not expected to contribute to the advancement of knowledge. The problem of epistemically responsible cheap claims becomes pressing only when inquirers are expected to produce knowledge claims that are novel and significant with respect to a body of scientific knowledge. In such cases, epistemically responsible cheap claims are problematic because they are likely to be trivial or uninformative (or uninteresting in some other ways).

This analysis helps us understand how epistemic responsibility relativism undermines the norm of epistemic responsibility. If epistemically responsible knowledge claims can be false or cheap systemically and not merely incidentally, then it is not clear why inquirers should make an effort to act in epistemically responsible ways. What is the value in conforming to the norm of epistemic responsibility? What good does it do for epistemic communities?

In response to the problem of epistemically responsible false or cheap claims, social epistemologists can attempt to refute epistemic responsibility relativism by introducing the idea of *epistemically well-designed communities* (Kitcher 1993, 303). While the term "epistemic community" refers to any community in which community members pursue similar epistemic goals and share a system of epistemic standards, epistemically well-designed communities are those epistemic communities that are likely to achieve their epistemic goals. In epistemically well-designed communities, epistemically responsible knowledge claims are not likely to be false. They are not likely to be cheap either because community members are expected to make significant contributions to the community's efforts to achieve its goals. Thus, knowledge seekers who care about significant truths and the advancement of scientific knowledge should take their knowledge claims to epistemically well-designed communities and engage feedback from these communities in an epistemically responsible way. Insofar as the norm of epistemic responsibility is epistemically valuable, it is valuable in the context of epistemically well-designed communities.

The idea of epistemically well-designed communities presupposes an *instrumentalist account of epistemic rationality* (Kitcher 1993, 179). According to an instrumentalist account, communities are epistemically well-designed when their norms, standards, practices, and institutional arrangements promote desired epistemic goals, such as significant truth (Kitcher 1993) or empirical success (Solomon 2001). Norms, standards, practices, and institutional arrangements can promote epistemic goals directly, by leading us towards them, or indirectly, by being connected to some other factor that leads us towards them. This is the general form of argument informing the arguments claiming that a distribution of research efforts is epistemically beneficial for scientific communities (Kitcher 1993; Solomon 2001). These authors claim that a distribution

148 *Kristina Rolin*

of research efforts advances the epistemic goals of science indirectly by ensuring that competing theories or methods will receive their share of resources. A distribution of research efforts is thought to be epistemically beneficial in certain phases of inquiry when it is not yet possible to tell which theory (or theories) will be true or most successful empirically, or which method (or methods) will lead to a breakthrough. When competing theories have different epistemic virtues or when different methods have complementary advantages, it is epistemically rational to distribute resources among the theories or the methods, rather than to allocate all available resources to only one theory or method.

An instrumentalist account of epistemic rationality says that a norm, standard, practice or institutional arrangement is epistemically rational when it is a suitable means for achieving desired epistemic goals. As Ronald Giere explains: "To be instrumentally rational is simply to employ means believed to be conducive to achieving desired goals" (1989, 380). An instrumentalist account of epistemic rationality appeals to an objective rather than a subjective sense of instrumental rationality. An objective instrumental rationality consists in "employing means that are not only believed to be, but are in fact conducive to achieving desired goals" (1989, 380). Thus, instrumental epistemic rationality amounts to objective instrumental rationality in the service of desired epistemic ends. Instrumental epistemic rationality is *conditional* since it involves the claim that epistemic norms and standards exert their normative force on inquirers only insofar as the inquirers pursue epistemic goals.

According to an instrumentalist account of epistemic rationality, epistemic goals are the source of normativity. When social epistemologists examine whether particular norms and standards promote epistemic goals, they are concerned with the impersonal goals of scientific communities rather than with individual scientists' personal goals. While individual scientists may be inspired by impersonal epistemic goals – such as the goal of producing true or empirically adequate accounts of some aspects of reality – they are still likely to be motivated as much by their personal goals. Individual scientists' personal goals may be epistemic, non-epistemic or a mixture of epistemic and non-epistemic considerations (Kitcher 1993, 72). Personal epistemic goals are typically more specific than the impersonal epistemic goals of scientific communities. For example, an individual scientist may aim to understand a particular mechanism or to develop expertise on a particular topic in her specialty. Personal non-epistemic goals may include such aims as career advancement, recognition from peers or the aim of helping solve urgent social and environmental problems. In epistemically well-designed communities, the personal (epistemic and non-epistemic) goals of individual scientists and the impersonal (epistemic) goals of scientific communities are aligned so that the pursuit of personal goals serves impersonal goals instead of undermining them (Rolin 2017a).

In sum, I have argued that epistemic responsibility relativism gives rise to the problem of epistemically responsible false or cheap claims. An instrumentalist strategy for solving the problem involves the idea of the epistemically well-designed community. In such a community, the norm of epistemic responsibility is conducive to achieving desired epistemic goals. When social epistemologists adopt an instrumentalist strategy for refuting epistemic responsibility relativism, the challenge is to understand which norms and standards actually promote the epistemic goals of scientific communities. In the next section, I discuss an influential account of epistemically well-designed communities: Helen Longino's critical contextual empiricism (CCE).

9.3. Longino's Account of Epistemically Well-Designed Communities

One way to introduce Longino's account of epistemically well-designed communities is to explain the meaning of each term in CCE: critical, contextual, and empiricism. I will proceed in reverse order. The term "empiricism" in CCE means that experience is the basis of knowledge claims in the sciences (Longino 1990, 219). While Longino acknowledges that different scientific communities may subscribe to different sets of epistemic standards, she emphasizes that the set has to include at least one common standard: empirical adequacy (1990, 77).

In CCE, the term "contextual" refers to three notions of context: the context of particular background assumptions, the context of scientific communities, and the social and cultural context of science. The first notion of context is employed in the argument claiming that evidential reasoning is relative to background assumptions because such assumptions are needed to establish the relevance of empirical evidence to a hypothesis or a theory (Longino 1990, 43). The second notion of context is employed in Longino's social account of objectivity. According to Longino, objectivity of scientific knowledge is a function of a community's practice rather than an individual scientist's observations and reasoning (1990, 74). The third notion of context is used in Longino's analysis of the role of values in science, in which she argues that values belonging to the social and cultural context of science can enter into evidential reasoning via background assumptions (1990, 83). The three notions of context figure in her main argument stating that the social account of objectivity is needed to manage the role of values in science because rules of evidential reasoning cannot guarantee that moral and social values characteristic to a particular social and cultural context are eliminated from the context of background assumptions.

The term "critical" in CCE refers to the view that scientific communities should be governed by norms and standards that facilitate "transformative criticism" (Longino 1990, 76). The notion of transformative

150 *Kristina Rolin*

criticism plays a central role in an instrumentalist justification of norms and standards. Transformative criticism is conducive to achieving epistemic goals because it helps correct false beliefs and biased research, for example, research in which the selection or interpretation of evidence is skewed so that other bodies of relevant evidence or interpretations of evidence are overlooked. Even when criticism does not give scientists a reason to change their views, it can be transformative in other ways. It can improve scientific knowledge by forcing scientists to provide better arguments for their views or to communicate their views more clearly and effectively. Criticism can help scientists avoid dogmatism.

According to Longino, epistemically well-designed communities are guided by four norms, "public venues," "uptake," "public standards," and "tempered equality" (2002, 129–131). The norm of public venues facilitates transformative criticism by requiring that criticism of scientific research have the same or nearly the same weight as original research (Longino 2002, 129). The norm of uptake promotes transformative criticism by requiring that each party to a critical exchange engages with criticism and is willing to revise their view instead of merely "tolerating dissent" (2002, 129–130). The norm of public standards makes transformative criticism possible by requiring that criticism appeals to at least some epistemic standards publicly recognized in the community (2002, 130–131). In well-designed epistemic communities, systems of epistemic standards have been tested for their epistemic success in the actual practice of science. Moreover, individual epistemic standards can be criticized and transformed in reference to other epistemic standards, goals, and values held constant (2002, 131). Finally, the norm of tempered equality of intellectual authority serves transformative criticism in two ways: by disqualifying those communities where certain perspectives dominate because of the political, social, or economic power of their adherents (1990, 78) and by making room for a diversity of perspectives which is likely to generate critical perspectives (2002, 131).

Insofar as the four norms are instrumental for achieving desired epistemic goals, they can be applied as criteria for ranking epistemic communities. Those communities that come close to conforming to the four norms are epistemically better than those communities that fail to meet some or all of the four norms. For example, a community of creationists does not qualify as an epistemically well-designed community because it fails to meet at least two norms, the norm of uptake and the norm of public standards (see also Longino 2002, 158–159). It fails to satisfy the two norms because creationists do not respond to the criticism of the theory of intelligent design. Even though they claim that their religious beliefs are relevant for scientific theories, they refuse to subject these beliefs to critical scrutiny. This is partly because they subscribe to religious goals and values which other members of scientific communities do not accept as goals and values of scientific practices.

Epistemic Responsibility and Relativism   151

Besides providing a basis for ranking epistemic communities, the four norms can be used to criticize the behavior of individual scientists. For example, consider the worry that dissenting scientists succeed in "winning" a scientific debate by creating an atmosphere where other scientists are afraid to express their views openly (Biddle and Leuschner 2015, 269). The norm of tempered equality speaks to this concern by forbidding attempts to intimidate or threaten scientists. Insofar as criticism leads to a transformation in scientific views, the transformation should be an outcome of an open dialogue where participants enjoy equal intellectual authority, and not the result of the exercise of political or economic power (Longino 2002, 131). Furthermore, consider the worry that scientific research is in danger of stagnation because scientists spend a significant amount of their time and energy in repeating their responses to dissenters (Biddle and Leuschner 2015, 262). The norm of uptake speaks to this concern at least partly by demanding that not only the advocates of the consensus view but also dissenters should respond to criticism (Longino 2002, 130). When dissenters are not capable of responding to criticism, they should stop voicing their objections.

In addition to functioning as criteria for ranking epistemic communities, Longino's four norms help us understand why the norm of epistemic responsibility is epistemically valuable in the context of epistemically well-designed communities. The norm of epistemic responsibility does not always promote true beliefs for the person who follows the norm or her audience. Yet, it is likely to promote true beliefs in an epistemically well-designed community in which all community members conform to the norm. This is because in such a social context, the norm of epistemic responsibility advances transformative criticism and transformative criticism is likely to weed out false claims and promote true ones.

Longino's account of epistemically well-designed communities can be interpreted as an application of the norm of epistemic responsibility to epistemic communities. This is because two of the four norms follow from the norm of epistemic responsibility, while two others are necessary to make compliance with the norm of epistemic responsibility feasible for scientists. The norm of uptake follows from the norm of epistemic responsibility because the norm of epistemic responsibility demands that an appropriate challenge receives a response. The norm of tempered equality also follows from the norm of epistemic responsibility because the norm of epistemic responsibility demands that an appropriate challenge be taken seriously independently of who presents it. Things are different for the norm of public venues and public standards. By requiring that those presenting knowledge claims as well as those criticizing the claims have a hearing in the community, the norm of public venues enables scientists to be epistemically responsible. By requiring that those making knowledge claims as well as those

152 *Kristina Rolin*

challenging the claims be aware of the epistemic standards of the community, the norm of public standards enables scientists to be epistemically responsible.

In sum, I have argued that in epistemically well-designed communities, all community members are expected to be epistemically responsible *vis-à-vis* other community members. An instrumentalist defense of the norm of epistemic responsibility can admit that conforming to the norm of epistemic responsibility does not always help a person achieve true beliefs and avoid false ones. For an instrumentalist, what matters is not so much the epistemic success of individuals as the epistemic success of communities. Epistemically responsible behavior is epistemically valuable insofar as it contributes to the epistemic success of communities. The epistemic justification for the norm of epistemic responsibility lies in the claim that when scientists systematically act in epistemically responsible ways towards the other members of their scientific communities, they promote the epistemic goals of their communities, even if not directly, then at least indirectly by facilitating transformative criticism (see also Rolin 2017a).

9.4. The Norm of Epistemic Responsibility as a Moral Norm

Thus far we have seen that an instrumentalist strategy for refuting epistemic responsibility relativism involves the notion of an epistemically well-designed community. Longino's CCE provides one account of an epistemically well-designed community. An instrumentalist does not deny that knowledge claims are epistemically responsible or irresponsible only relative to an epistemic community. Nor does she deny that systems of epistemic standards vary significantly from one epistemic community to another. Instead, she denies the claim that there are no criteria for ranking different epistemic communities and their systems of epistemic standards. According to an instrumentalist, there are criteria for assessing epistemic communities and their systems of epistemic standards. However, such criteria are conditional. This is because the features that turn epistemic communities into epistemically well-designed communities are means for achieving desired epistemic ends.

I shall now argue that an instrumentalist account of epistemic rationality is consistent with the view that some epistemic norms also serve moral goals, and that sometimes moral goals can override epistemic ones. I shall argue moreover that the norm of epistemic responsibility is a moral and not merely an epistemic norm. When people understand the norm of epistemic responsibility as a moral norm, they conform to it because they believe that their actions contribute to the well-being of other human beings.

Epistemic Responsibility and Relativism   153

What exactly makes the norm of epistemic responsibility an epistemic *and* a moral norm? The term "epistemic" in the norm of epistemic responsibility refers to the object that the norm is concerned with, the act of making knowledge claims. The norm states that when a person makes a knowledge claim, she should make it in an epistemically responsible way. That the object of the norm is epistemic does not yet make the norm itself (exclusively) epistemic. Nor does it exclude the possibility that the norm is moral. In order to see why the norm of epistemic responsibility is both an epistemic and a moral norm, we need to consider two questions: one, what is the justification for the norm, and two, what is an appropriate sanction for violating the norm.

Let me discuss first the question of justification. In the last section, I argued that the norm of epistemic responsibility is an epistemic norm in virtue of having an epistemic justification. Its epistemic justification lies in its capacity to promote epistemic goals. The norm of epistemic responsibility promotes epistemic goals indirectly, by facilitating transformative criticism, which in its turn helps scientists eliminate false beliefs and balance biased accounts of the subject matter of inquiry. While the norm of epistemic responsibility may not promote epistemic goals in every social context, it is conducive to achieving epistemic goals in the context of epistemically well-designed communities in which all community members make an effort to be epistemically responsible *vis-à-vis* other community members.

Besides having an epistemic justification, the norm of epistemic responsibility also has a moral justification. The norm of epistemic responsibility is a moral norm in virtue of promoting the well-being of other human beings. By acting in an epistemically responsible way, a person contributes to the well-being of other human beings by showing respect for them, especially in their capacity as knowers. By "respect" I mean the kind of respect that all human beings are owed morally merely because they are human beings, regardless of their social position or individual achievement. As Miranda Fricker argues, our capacity to give reasons, to understand reasons, and to respond to reasons is essential to human value (2007, 44). Thus, if not all human beings, at least all well-functioning adult human beings are entitled *qua* human beings to be taken seriously as an epistemic audience.

Having shown that the norm of epistemic responsibility has both an epistemic and a moral justification, I turn to the second question, the question of which sanctions are appropriate for violating the norm of epistemic responsibility. I argue that the norm of epistemic responsibility is both an epistemic and a moral norm because sanctions for violating the norm have both an epistemic and a moral dimension. An appropriate response by an audience to someone who violates the norm of epistemic responsibility is to deny them credibility. This is the epistemic dimension in the sanction for violating the norm of epistemic responsibility.

154 *Kristina Rolin*

For example, Elizabeth Anderson argues that we should not place our epistemic trust in people who act in epistemically irresponsible ways. As she explains (2011, 146):

> To persist in making certain claims, while ignoring counterevidence and counterarguments raised by others with relevant expertise, is to be dogmatic. To advance those claims as things others should believe on one's say-so, while refusing accountability, is to be arrogant. Dogmatists are not trustworthy, because there is no reason to believe that their claims are based on a rational assessment of evidence and arguments. The arrogant are not trustworthy, because there is reason to believe they are usurping claims to epistemic authority.

The norm of epistemic responsibility is an epistemic norm because it is appropriate to respond to violations of the norm with an epistemic sanction, a reduced level of epistemic trust in the person who advanced knowledge claims in an epistemically irresponsible way.

I maintain that it is equally appropriate to respond to violations of the norm of epistemic responsibility with a *moral* sanction. A moral sanction is typically moral blame which the audience can express in the form of disapproval, resentment, indignation, or contempt (Kauppinen 2018, 5). For example, when a person advances knowledge claims in an epistemically irresponsible way, she may be perceived as someone whose intention is to deceive or mislead her audience. Since this is morally wrong, it is appropriate to respond to her behavior with a moral condemnation. Similarly, when a person who has made a knowledge claim refuses to engage with appropriate criticism, she may be perceived as behaving in a disrespectful way towards the critique. Disrespectful behavior merits a moral disapproval. The norm of epistemic responsibility is a moral norm because violations of the norm call for moral sanctions.

In sum, I have argued that the norm of epistemic responsibility is a hybrid norm with both an epistemic and a moral dimension. Whereas the epistemic dimension involves an epistemic justification for the norm and epistemic sanctions for violating the norm (reduced credibility), the moral dimension involves a moral justification for the norm and moral sanctions for violating the norm (moral blame). That the norm of epistemic responsibility is a moral norm means that a person can have moral reasons for being epistemically responsible. In epistemically well-designed communities, it may not make a difference whether community members are acting in epistemically responsible ways on the basis of moral or epistemic reasons. As long as they act in epistemically responsible ways, they contribute to the epistemic success of the community. However, a moral reason is a legitimate reason to be epistemically responsible also in the context of communities that are less than ideal from an epistemic perspective or *vis-à-vis* individuals who do not play by the rules of epistemically well-designed communities.

Let me use the case of dissenters in science to illustrate this claim. Even if the dissenters do not always conform to the norms of epistemically well-designed communities, there are moral reasons to engage dissent. As Inmaculada de Melo-Martín and Kristen Intemann (2013, 2014) argue, dismissing or discrediting dissenters may send a false message to the public about the nature of scientific knowledge. It may reinforce the misunderstanding that consensus is always an indicator of a scientific theory's being true; that consensus in scientific communities is always unanimous; or that any dissent undermines consensus and its epistemic authority to support public policy. These messages are misleading because consensus in itself does not guarantee that a scientific theory is true; consensus typically involves merely a majority view allowing for the existence of a few doubters; and even when dissent is normatively appropriate it may not undermine consensus views (de Melo-Martín and Intemann 2014, 600–604). By engaging dissent, scientists can offer the public an opportunity to learn about the nature of scientific knowledge. This is morally valuable even when a critical exchange with dissenters is not epistemically fruitful.

That the norm of epistemic responsibility is both an epistemic and a moral norm has implications for epistemic responsibility relativism. In the last section, I argued that an instrumentalist account of epistemic rationality provides social epistemologists with criteria for ranking epistemic communities. The implication is that despite such criteria, it is not self-evident that a person should aim to be epistemically responsible in the context of an epistemically well-designed community rather than in the context of less-than-an-ideal epistemic community. The reason for this is that moral ends can sometimes trump epistemic ones, and they give a person a reason to choose a community that is less than ideal from an epistemic point of view. This is a legitimate move because the norm of epistemic responsibility is a moral norm and not merely an epistemic one.

To summarize, I have argued that an instrumentalist account of epistemic rationality is consistent with the view that some epistemic norms are also moral norms in virtue of serving morally valuable goals. While epistemic goals do not need to be in conflict with morally valuable goals, the two goals can be in conflict, and moral values can override epistemic ones. This means that a person can have a moral reason to be epistemically responsible even when she knows that epistemic responsibility is not likely to serve epistemic ends.

9.5. Conclusion

I have argued that epistemic responsibility relativism is a problematic position insofar as epistemically responsible false or cheap claims are problematic. The problem of epistemically responsible false or cheap claims can be avoided by refuting epistemic responsibility relativism.

156 *Kristina Rolin*

An alternative to epistemic responsibility relativism can be found in an instrumentalist account of epistemic rationality. According to an instrumentalist account, some epistemic communities have a better epistemic design than others. In epistemically well-designed communities, inquirers conform to those norms and standards that are means to achieve desired epistemic goals. Thus, an instrumentalist account of epistemic rationality provides social epistemologists with criteria for ranking epistemic communities and their systems of epistemic standards.

However, the question remains whether the criteria for ranking epistemic communities are neutral. If they are not neutral, what kind of neutrality do they lack? I have argued that the criteria provided by an instrumentalist account of epistemic rationality are merely apparently neutral. If the epistemic justification of epistemic norms and standards depends on an instrumentalist account, epistemic norms and standards are conditional. They are epistemically rational for the inquirers on the condition that the inquirers have made a prior commitment to certain epistemic goals. Epistemic norms and standards may sometimes seem to be unconditional. This is because we do not question the epistemic goals they serve. However, epistemic goals can be questioned on the grounds that they are in conflict with moral goals, and the latter can supersede the former.

The upshot is that the criteria provided by an instrumentalist strategy in order to refute epistemic responsibility relativism are not neutral from a moral point of view. These criteria are decisive only if they are not superseded by moral goals. To claim that some epistemic goals enjoy the status of not-being-superseded-by-moral-goals is to make a moral value judgment.

That moral goals can be in conflict with epistemic goals and override them may strike many readers as a self-evident claim. However, this claim has interesting consequences when we consider norms that are both epistemic and moral, such as the norm of epistemic responsibility. In many cases, we can choose to adopt a moral perspective on our knowledge-seeking practices. In the case of the norm of epistemic responsibility, we do not have a choice. A moral perspective on our knowledge-seeking practices is necessary and not optional.

The hybrid nature of the norm of epistemic responsibility means that a person can have moral reasons to be epistemically responsible in addition to epistemic ones. Moreover, epistemic and moral reasons can pull the person in different directions. Whereas epistemic reasons pull her towards epistemically well-designed communities, moral reasons can pull her towards communities that are less-than-ideal from an epistemic point of view. In both cases, the criteria for choosing among epistemic communities are not morally neutral. When the person prefers one epistemic community to another on epistemic grounds, she has to acknowledge that epistemic grounds are dependent on epistemic goals not superseded

Epistemic Responsibility and Relativism   157

by moral goals. When she prefers one epistemic community to another on moral grounds, she has to be ready to compromise her epistemic standards. An instrumentalist strategy for refuting epistemic responsibility relativism is successful but the success comes with a moral obligation to find an appropriate balance between epistemic and morally valuable goals.

References

Anderson, E. (2011), "Democracy, Public Policy, and Lay Assessments of Scientific Testimony," *Episteme* 8 (2): 144–164.

Biddle, J. and A. Leuschner. (2015), "Climate Skepticism and the Manufacture of Doubt: Can Dissent in Science Be Epistemically Detrimental?," *European Journal for Philosophy of Science* 5 (3): 261–278.

Brandom, R. (1983), "Asserting," *Noûs* 17 (4): 637–650.

Code, L. (1984), "Toward a 'Responsibilist' Epistemology," *Philosophy and Phenomenological Research* 45 (1): 29–50.

de Melo-Martín, I. and K. Intemann. (2013), "Scientific Dissent and Public Policy: Is Targeting Dissent a Reasonable Way to Protect Sound Policy Decisions," *EMBO Reports* 14 (3): 231–235.

———. (2014), "Who's Afraid of Dissent? Addressing Concerns about Undermining Scientific Consensus in Public Policy Developments," *Perspectives on Science* 22 (4): 593–615.

Fricker, M. (2007), *Epistemic Injustice: Power and the Ethics of Knowing*, Oxford: Oxford University Press.

Giere, R. (1989), "Scientific Rationality as Instrumental Rationality," *Studies in History and Philosophy of Science* 20 (3): 377–384.

Kauppinen, A. (2018), "Epistemic Norms and Epistemic Accountability," *Philosophers' Imprint* 18 (8): 1–16.

Kitcher, P. (1993), *The Advancement of Science: Science without Legend, Objectivity without Illusions*, New York: Oxford University Press.

Kusch, M. (2017), "Epistemic Relativism, Scepticism, Pluralism," *Synthese* 194: 4687–4703.

Longino, H. (1990), *Science as Social Knowledge*, Princeton, NJ: Princeton University Press.

———. (2002), *The Fate of Knowledge*, Princeton: Princeton University Press.

Nguyen, C.T. (2018), "Echo Chambers and Epistemic Bubbles," *Episteme*, https://doi.org/10.1017/epi.2018.32.

Rolin, K. (2011), "Contextualism in Feminist Epistemology and Philosophy of Science," in *Feminist Epistemology and Philosophy of Science: Power in Knowledge*, edited by H. Grasswick, Dordrecht: Springer, 25–44.

———. (2017a), "Scientific Community: A Moral Dimension," *Social Epistemology* 31 (5): 468–483.

———. (2017b), "Scientific Dissent and a Fair Distribution of Epistemic Responsibility," *Public Affairs Quarterly* 31 (3): 209–230.

Solomon, M. (2001), *Social Empiricism*, Cambridge: MIT Press.

Williams, M. (2001), *Problems of Knowledge: A Critical Introduction to Epistemology*, Oxford and New York: Oxford University Press.

Part III
Social Epistemology and the Sociology of Scientific Knowledge

10 Sociologism and Relativism

David Bloor

10.1. Introduction

My remit is to describe an intellectual position known as "sociologism."[1] The name is ugly but the position itself is important. The word "sociologism" refers to the claim that knowledge and morality, which are fundamentally social phenomena, have been systematically misdescribed in traditional "philosophical" accounts. Philosophy, at best, is reified sociology. Those who subscribe to a "sociologistic" position are committed to demystifying and decoding philosophical and metaphysical doctrines. Their aim is to reveal the true sociological referent of a philosophical claim and correct the distortions that have arisen. "Philosophy" is to be replaced by the positive science of sociology.[2]

The most famous representative of this approach is Emile Durkheim (1858–1917). His 1912 book, *The Elementary Forms of the Religious Life*, offers a classic statement of sociologism.[3] He began by formulating a sociological account of what was called "primitive" religious thought. He then generalised his analysis to cover the neo-Kantian philosophy that was popular in France at the time he wrote. I shall give a brief account of Durkheim's position. To show its relevance to modern, analytical philosophy, I shall then offer a sociologistic reading of two anti-relativist arguments proposed by the philosopher Crispin Wright. Wright directs one argument against what he calls "traditional" relativism, the other against what he calls "true" relativism.

10.2. Durkheim and Religious Thought

Durkheim was not interested in primitive religions for their own sake. His purpose in studying their exotic totems, taboos, rituals and myths was to draw general conclusions about human nature and society. The anthropological data, he argued, would allow him to investigate a simple case in which general principles would be easily visible. Durkheim saw himself as a scientist whose duty was to penetrate the veil of appearances and reveal the reality behind it. Heat is molecular motion but humans do not experience it as molecular motion. Light is an

162   David Bloor

electromagnetic wave but this is not what humans see. Durkheim wanted to play a role analogous to that of the physicist. His question was: How does the subjective experience of society relate to the objective reality of society?

Durkheim's answer to this question can be given in one word: religion. The elementary function of religion, he said, was to provide a form of collective self-understanding.[4] Religion was the characteristic form in which humans experienced the society in which they lived. It follows, said Durkheim, that primitive religion cannot be dismissed as error and illusion. It is not a mere expression of fear or ignorance in the face of natural forces. Rather, religion furnished a shared representation of a genuine reality, namely social reality. Admittedly, it was a transfigured representation rather than a scientifically accurate representation. Nevertheless, religion provided a practical means to comprehend, protect, navigate and sustain a social structure. For this reason, it must be part of social reality itself. Durkheim's analysis has the intriguing consequence that when the members of a group pray to their gods, they are really praying to themselves.

Using his anthropological data, Durkheim argued that human groups everywhere distinguished between the sacred and the profane. The sacred was held to be mysterious, dangerous and untouchable. The profane was the realm of everyday practicality and causality. The things that were deemed sacred were the central institutions and practices that gave the group its structure and which were symbolised in totems and rituals. The collective good of social order was thus protected by its sacred status.

One expression of the dichotomy between the sacred and the profane was that, everywhere, humans understood themselves as having a dual nature. They felt that they possessed a body and a soul. How did they arrive at the idea of a soul? Durkheim's answer was that the idea of the soul derived from a person's experience of being a member of a group. The soul was their social self, that is, their self as the player of a role, their self as having a status, their self as a social actor. It was their responsible self, informed by the experience of being treated as such by others. No wonder that, while the existence of the soul seemed evident to everyone, nobody could see a person's soul, or could say much about where it was in time and space.

10.3. Durkheim on Morality

Durkheim used the idea of the sacred and profane to shed light on the nature of moral obligation. All societies, said Durkheim, register in some form or other the difference between desiring to do something and being obliged to do it. Everyone experiences the difference between a duty and an inclination. Inclinations and desires arise from within us. Duties and obligations compel us from outside. At the same time duties

Sociologism and Relativism   163

and obligations manage to get inside us, and we can feel the conflict between wants and oughts. But what are these strange external compulsions? What is a moral force?

It was here that Durkheim's sociological analysis made contact with the work of philosophers. He identified two schools of thought whose followers have tried to account for the nature of moral compulsion. One was the Kantian, rationalist tradition; the other was the utilitarian and empiricist tradition. Followers of Kant treated moral obligation as something unique and supernatural. It was something lodged in the soul by God. This account made obligation transcendental and put the basis of morality beyond the reach of science. By contrast, empiricists and utilitarians, such as Mill and Spencer, wanted to keep morality within the bounds of nature and the grasp of science. They were right to want this, said Durkheim, but they failed to identify what was specific to moral obligation as distinct from desire or pleasure or happiness.

In Durkheim's opinion both rationalists and empiricists were wrong because both had grasped only one half of the truth. One had embraced the sacred and the other had embraced the profane, but neither had discovered how to overcome the dualism. Durkheim proposed a synthesis. The reality was that obligation was a social, not an individual, phenomenon. It was a constraint, a norm, collectively affirmed and enforced by the members of a group and thus external to each individual. The seemingly transcendental character of obligation, the way it seemed everywhere and nowhere, was a transfigured response to its social character. Its capacity to reach into the very interior of the individual derived from the innately social character of the human animal. Humans are innately responsive to one another. Both the rationalist and the empiricist accounts were partial because they failed, in their different ways, to do justice to the social.

10.4. Durkheim and Natural Knowledge

Durkheim did not confine his analysis to moral knowledge. He took his sociological argument into the realm of natural knowledge and the human relationship to the material world. We relate to nature, he said, as a collective. Durkheim's position has often been misrepresented by critics so it is important to be clear what he was, and was not, asserting.[5] Durkheim did not espouse a "purely sociological" theory of knowledge.[6] He was well aware of the capabilities of the unaided, individual mind. In the *Elementary Forms* he gave the example of individual animals navigating the terrain over which they hunt or seek water (1961, 491). Their sensory capabilities and their natural cognitive capacities, such as memory, are real and were duly acknowledged. But, argued Durkheim, there is something that human knowledge possesses that animal knowledge does not.

164 *David Bloor*

Durkheim proposed that while animals have cognitive dispositions, humans have cognitive duties, that is, they are subject to constraints which exercise authority over their individual understanding and thought processes. The constraints, he said, were social. In the Kantian tradition these social constraints were ascribed to the a priori categories of thought and forms of intuition. These were said to provide the mental apparatus that shaped and gave a compelling form to our experience of space, time and causality as well as to our moral sense. For Durkheim, the Kantian metaphysics of mind was just a mystified expression of the fact that, when humans interact with nature, they do so by participating in cognitive institutions and conventions.

Consider, for example, the habit of responding to a certain type of object in the environment. A habit, said Durkheim,

> is only a tendency to repeat an act or idea automatically ... it does not at all imply that the idea or act is in the form of an exemplary type, proposed to or imposed upon the mind or will. It is only when a type of this sort is set up, that is to say, when a rule or standard is established, that social action can and should be presumed.
> (1961, 482)

Durkheim's concern was with rules, standards and exemplars, that is, with the structural features of public knowledge rather than private knowledge. Public and private knowledge are qualitatively different: one is objective and one is subjective. Durkheim's focus was on knowledge claims that were collectively accepted as objectively true.

Durkheim again set the claims of the rationalistic, Kantian tradition against those of the naturalistic, empiricist tradition. The Kantians, in their own way, understood that shared knowledge transcended the unaided powers of the individual mind, but they could only offer supernatural answers to Durkheim's questions. Conversely, the empiricists tried to tell the story of knowledge in individualistic, reductionist and psychological terms. Empiricists could explain the pragmatic aspects of knowledge, but not its authoritative aspects.[7] Once again, said Durkheim, it was social phenomena that slipped through the fingers of the philosophers.

The Elementary Forms was published a hundred years ago. Have things changed with the passing of time? Are philosophers now able to offer a superior account of knowledge that would avoid Durkheim's accusation that all they are doing is bad sociology – so bad that they do not even recognise the social when they see it? Let me put this to the test.

10.5. "Traditional" Relativism

In his paper "Fear of Relativism?" Crispin Wright (2008) defines relativism as the claim that whenever we ascribe truth to an assertion we are employing a "standard."[8] There are standards of morality and rationality.

Sociologism and Relativism   165

The truth of the assertion that a person has behaved in a moral or a rational way resides in his or her behaviour having met the relevant standards. For the relativist, truth is always standard-relative and there are no absolute standards. Thus we may expect standards to vary from time to time and place to place.

Before we can assess the tenability of relativism, Wright says that it is necessary to give clear answers to three questions:

1. What is a standard?
2. What does relativity to a standard consist in?
3. What is it to accept a standard?

Wright says that there are "three very natural answers" to these questions (2008, 384). His three answers are as follows:

1. Standards are general propositions.
2. Relativity consists in being logically entailed by such a proposition.
3. Accepting a standard means believing the relevant proposition.

Wright adds an important qualification. He insists that the propositions that embody standards do not simply describe behavioural preferences or tendencies. Rather, those who follow standards apprehend them as something external. They are, he says, "objects of possible consultation" (2008, 381). They are normative "principles" with which the follower "identifies" (2008, 388). Here Wright is following Kant. For Kant a moral act is not just an act that conforms to the moral law; it is an act undertaken out of respect for the moral law. Wright does not use the language of "respect" but he is making the same point.[9] Thus Wright takes account of this qualification when he summarises "traditional" relativism by saying:

> It is a paradigm of the most traditional relativist thinking to hold that there are indeed no defensible absolute notions of morally justified action, or of evidentially justified belief, in exactly this sense: that whether an action or a belief, is justified depends on one's standards, where the standards concerned are conceived as principles governing evaluation, rather than projections of actual patterns of evaluation, and as subject to no objective notion of correctness.
>
> (2008, 381–382)

Here then is Wright's chosen target.

10.6. Wright's Criticism

Now let us see how Wright criticises the form of relativism that he has just identified. He says that, if truth for the relativist is "truth relative

166 *David Bloor*

to a standard," this immediately raises the question of the truth of the standards themselves (2008, 387). The belief in these standards is a belief in their truth, so what does that truth consist in? If the relativist admitted that the truth of a standard is absolute, then this would amount to abandoning relativism as a general account of truth. The relativist would seem to have no alternative but to say that the truth of a standard is itself standard-relative. But this formulation starts a regress which also threatens to render relativism untenable.

Is there any way that the relativist can terminate the regress? Wright explores the possibility that basic standards are reflexively self-validating (2008, 388). If relativity is entailment, and the standard entails itself, then why not say that the standard is true relative just to itself? Wright says that, by this reasoning, every standard would be true because every such proposition entails itself. He therefore dismisses the reflexive argument as hopeless.[10]

Wright concludes that, to avoid a regress, the relativist must accept a second notion of truth other than "true relative to a standard." As Wright puts it: "standard relative truth cannot be the only notion of truth operative throughout ... epistemic and moral evaluation" (2008, 389). Traditional relativism, as defined by Wright, is thus untenable. Is Wright saying that the non-relative truth attributed to standards is a form of absolute truth? Not quite. He thinks that there is a middle ground and that standards may possess a form of truth distinct from either absolute truth or relative truth.[11] Either way, relativism can be dismissed as "nugatory," that is, worthless and futile (Wright 2008, 380).

10.7. Assessing Wright's Argument

How should we assess Wright's argument? The most obvious shortcoming is the failure to explain the, alleged, middle ground between the absolute and the relative. Wright makes passing mention of "minimalist" and "deflationary" accounts of truth (2008, 389), but he does not indicate how they might serve his purpose. A second problem is his equivocation over the word "relative." In the quoted passage he slides from relativism as the denial of absolutism, to relativism as the denial of objectivity. By the end of the paper he is endorsing the idea that relativism implies the absence of all rational constraint on basic standards.[12] There are two errors here. First, Wright assumes that there is no relativist analysis of objectivity. Second, he equates relativism with irrationalism. Durkheim's own work furnishes a counterexample to both these assumptions.[13]

There is, however, a deeper way to challenge Wright's account of relativism. Recall the three questions that he posed about the nature of standards, their relativity and their acceptance. I shall argue that the problems that Wright identifies in the relativist position are not intrinsic to relativism but derive from the answers that he chose to give to his three questions. He called his answers "natural" but they are, in fact, unnatural.

This is where sociologism re-enters the discussion. A sociologist would answer Wright's three questions in a very different way to Wright. Wright says that a standard is a general proposition; a sociologist would say that a standard is a social institution. Wright says that relativity is a form of logical entailment; a sociologist would say that society has a causal impact on the form taken by knowledge and morality. Relativities are causalities. Wright says that acceptance of a standard is belief in a general proposition; a sociologist would say acceptance involves functioning as a competent member of society. In summary:

1. A standard is a social institution.
2. Relativity is social causation.
3. Acceptance is being a competent social actor.

10.8. Test Cases

We can test the merits of these rival sets of answers by looking at examples. Consider the famous "standard metre" which was manufactured and inaugurated in Paris in 1889, amidst much ceremony.[14] Is the standard metre, as Wright would have us say, a species of "proposition?" This does not sound like a revealing description. For Durkheim, by contrast, the standard metre would be just another totem pole. He would tell us to see this totemic object as a public symbol that mediates social organisation and facilitates collective action. He would be right. Materially the standard metre was a metal bar but that fact does not capture what makes it a standard. To understand the status of the standard metre it is necessary to bring into view the people who surround the metal bar and put its existence to a certain kind of use, namely, coordinating their measurements in the workshop or laboratory.

In 1961, Thomas Kuhn offered further insight into this process of coordination in his early (and relatively neglected) paper "The Function of Measurement in the Modern Physical Sciences."[15] Kuhn notes that textbooks and scientific papers frequently contain numerical tables. Typically, the tables display two columns of numbers. One of the columns consists of the predictions derived from a theory. The second column consists of experimental measurements intended to test the theory. Kuhn posed the question: What is the purpose of juxtaposing these two columns of numbers? An answer that readily suggests itself is that these tables show whether the theoretical predictions are accurate. The table shows whether the theory corresponds to the facts. Kuhn does not accept this as an adequate answer. He argues that the tables do not merely show whether the theory corresponds with the facts, they also show what counts as correspondence.

168   *David Bloor*

No one expects the predictions of a theory to be absolutely right just as no one believes that experimental measurements can be absolutely accurate. What is at issue is whether the predictions and measurements are sufficiently close to say that they agree. But what is the criterion of sufficiency and where does it come from? Kuhn's answer is that there is no independent criterion outside the table itself and the use to which it is put. He says:

> I began by asking ... what characteristics the numbers of the table must exhibit if they are to be said to 'agree'. I now conclude that the only possible criterion is the mere fact that they appear, together with the theory from which they are derived, in a professionally accepted text.
>
> (1961, 185)

The numbers, Kuhn said, demonstrate reasonable agreement by "tautology" because they alone "provide the definition of reasonable agreement that has been accepted by the profession" (1961, 185).

If we grant that Kuhn's analysis of scientific knowledge is a form of relativism, then we have the answer to Wright's objection. Wright thinks that the relativist is confronted by a regress that can only be avoided by adopting a non-relativist conception of truth. Kuhn's argument shows what is wrong with this line of reasoning. The regress does terminate, but not in an apprehension of an independent realm of truth. It terminates in a social process, namely, the formation of a group consensus. Kuhn identifies the way in which a consensus crystallises around a paradigm case that functions as a standard. Scientists coordinate their behaviour by reference to the paradigm case and then enrich and extend its applications.

Wright's mistake derives from being in the grip of a false picture of a social process. He talks of propositions when he should be talking about how people coordinate their behaviour and conduct their interactions. Wright's version of the Kantian idea of acting out of respect for a standard should have been expressed, not in terms of a state of mind (such as "belief" or "identification") but, as Durkheim argued, in social terms. What is the social process which generates the sense of a standard as an external thing? The answer is: the ability of competent actors to invoke the standard in the course of criticism, justification and elaboration. It is in this sense that the standard can exists (in Wright's language) as an object of "possible consultation."

The central point is that while standards are, indeed, objects of consultation, they do not exist as independent objects, that is, independent of the discourse in which they are invoked.[16] Similarly with the formation of the consensus that brings standards into existence. It is a performative process of making it true that the standard is a standard by virtue of

Sociologism and Relativism 169

accepting it as a standard. When Wright mentioned, but rejected, the idea of reflexive self-validation he was closer to the truth than he realised. The things referred to when a standard of accuracy is invoked are the references to the standard made by other participants in the discourse and the shared activity it mediates. When behaviour is oriented to a standard, the orientation is to the orientations of other participants. One can see the analogy with Durkheim's insight that, when a group prays to its gods, it is praying to itself.[17]

10.9. "True" Relativism

I now want to take a look at Wright's criticisms of the position he calls "true" relativism.[18] As Wright defines it:

> True relativism is the thesis ... that after the truth-conditions of an utterance have been settled, there can be relativity in the question whether they are satisfied. It is a thesis that engages at the level of content, rather than at the level of speech-acts.
>
> (2006, 54)

What is it for there to "be relativity?" Suppose there is a disagreement. Wright presents the relativist as someone who thinks that three conditions can be satisfied simultaneously. First, the disagreement must be about one and the same proposition, that is, one and the same thought or content. Second, there must be divergent judgements about the truth of this self-same proposition. Third, none of the parties to the disagreement can be said to have made a mistake. Wright doubts if these three conditions can be satisfied simultaneously, at least, not if one adopts a correspondence theory of truth. He therefore doubts if "true relativism" is "fully intelligible" (2005, 54). In short: Once truth-conditions have been settled, there can be no relativity.[19]

Let us consider Wright's claim in the light of Kuhn's example of a standard. Kuhn said that the acceptance of certain numerical tables by the scientific community creates a standard of accuracy. The relativities inherent in this process derive from all the contingent circumstances, aims and interests that generate the consensus about the table and its subsequent application. If these contingencies had been different perhaps different standards would have prevailed. Let us accept for a moment that historical research generates such a causal conclusion. Wouldn't this be an example of relativism in action? I think it would but, according to Wright's definition, it would not be an example of what he calls "true relativism." And indeed, the Kuhn case isn't an example. So what is going on?

The answer is that Wright's definition of so-called "true relativism" is not a definition of any sort of relativism at all. In reality, it is a description of a breakdown of communication and cognitive order. It is a description

170 *David Bloor*

of things going wrong and of a tangle of misunderstandings that needs to be sorted out. It is a description of cognitive confusion, so of course it isn't fully intelligible. Wright has given us, in schematic terms, the parameters within which various strategies of repair must be brought into play. Relativism – by which I mean causal explanation – enters the scene when the historian or sociologist tries to explain why a given strategy of repair prevails or fails to gain credibility.

I speak of strategies because there will always be more than one way to repair an anomaly. One could say: "You understand the proposition in the same way; you make incompatible judgements; so one of you is wrong." Or one could say: "You don't understand the proposition in the same way, so perhaps both of you are right." Such strategies may involve a new division of cognitive labour and reassignment of content. The problem for the social actor is to repair breakdowns by allocating error and by deciding where sameness and difference of meaning lie. The problem for the social analyst is to explain these decisions in a causal way.[20]

Suppose Durkheim had written a book with the title *The Elementary Forms of the Cognitive Life*, rather than *The Elementary Forms of the Religious Life*. He would point out that there is no question of settling truth-conditions, or completing acts of definition, or finalizing the specification of a vocabulary. The task of maintaining cognitive order is unremitting and never-ending. He would not dismiss the appeal to propositions as mere error but would ask us to appreciate their role as primitive accounting devices, a gloss for maintaining order and tracking cognitive responsibility. The philosophers' propositions, he would say, are a transfigured rendering of the social machinery of communication and interaction. If we misunderstand these interactions, propositions will seem to embody a strange power. That is why propositions so often seem to have a mysterious character by comparison with down-to-earth spoken and written sentences. In the imaginary *Elementary Forms of the Cognitive Life*, Durkheim would have said that propositions are the mythical souls of our speech-acts, and souls, as always and everywhere, are symbols of the social.[21]

10.10. Concluding Remarks

The central idea of Durkheim's sociology is that institutions of central significance are transfigured into something mysterious and sacred. He traced this tendency in both the "savage" mind and the "philosophical" mind. Durkheim knew that, if his theory of the sacred were true, then many people would find his analysis abhorrent. They would experience it as sacrilege (Durkheim 1974, 49). The prediction was right.

Today it is the cognitive norms of science that are deemed to be under threat and in need of protection from the profane curiosity of sociological

Sociologism and Relativism   171

enquiry and causal explanation. We should not be surprised that some philosophers are tempted to adopt the role of the guardians of culture and feel moved to do battle with sociologists of knowledge and their corrosive relativism.

I have tried to shed light on these feelings by appeal to Durkheim, but I know that there is much that can be said in criticism of Durkheim's corpus of work. The ethnography is outdated and there are dimensions of social life to which he seemed insensitive, for example: the role of elites, comparative political structures and the role of women in society. He had his blind spots, but his thinking has a power that cannot be denied.

There is also an undeniable grandeur about the Kantian metaphysics that Durkheim criticised. Durkheim himself recognised this. With its compelling categories of thought, Kantian rationalism preserved certain social insights, albeit in a transfigured form. Such grandeur is absent from present-day anti-relativism. What used to be obscure and noumenal is now merely obscure. Despite this, the tradition that goes by the name of "sociologism" still has much to offer those engaged in discussions of relativism. The message is: Whenever relativism is denied – and absolutism implied – look for a social process that has been misdescribed.

Notes

1. Martin Kusch asked me to address the issue of sociologism when he kindly invited me to participate in the conference "Relativism Re-Evaluated" held in Vienna on September 21–23, 2017.
2. Sociologism was part of the professional ideology of the emerging discipline of sociology in the early years of the 20th century. It was a competitor to "psychologism," the ideology of the new discipline of experimental psychology. Both 'isms' were expressions of the more general ideology of scientific naturalism. For an authoritative analysis of psychologism, see Kusch (1995). As far as I am aware there is no corresponding study of sociologism.
3. Durkheim (1961) was originally published in 1912. For a useful selection of Durkheim's writings, see Giddens (1972). The standard critical study of Durkheim is Lukes (1973). For a brief account of Durkheim's work, which acknowledges both its force and its shortcomings, see Parkin (1992).
4. "If religion has given birth to all that is essential in society, it is because the idea of society is the soul of religion" (Durkheim 1961, 466). Notice that, for Durkheim, religion is not the soul of society; society is the soul of religion.
5. The standard criticisms of Durkheim's sociology of knowledge are by Benoit-Smullyan, Dennes, Gehlke, Goldenweiser, Needham, Schaub, and Worsley. For references and a defence of Durkheim, see Bloor (1982).
6. The phrase "purely sociological" is frequently used by critics. It is a position imputed to sociologists rather than one actually embraced by anyone. It would be a nonsensical stance because you cannot have a society without flesh and blood members of the society. You cannot, for example, have a "purely sociological" account of a social institution though of course you may have an account whose main focus is on the sociology and where the biological and psychological dimensions are taken for granted.
7. Durkheim was sympathetic to the pragmatism of the psychologist William James but felt that James had no explanation of the absolute-seeming

172 *David Bloor*

character of truth. This absolutist phenomenology may be false but it still needs explaining. Thus: "this pressure that truth admittedly exercises on minds is itself a symbol that must be interpreted, even if we refuse to make of truth something absolute and extra-human" (1964, 430).

8. Wright (2008). In this paper Wright reviews the anti-relativist arguments put forward by Paul Boghossian in his book *Fear of Knowledge* (2006). Wright says that Boghossian misrepresents the semantics of the relativist's claims and fails to take seriously the idea of relative truth (2008, 387). Nevertheless, he thinks that Boghossian offers an effective criticism of the traditional relativist position. I agree with some of Wright's criticisms of Boghossian but not with Wright's rejection of relativism. For my own response to Boghossian, see Bloor (2007).

9. Wright also notes that, strictly, the logical entailment relation between a standard and an application of the standard requires the help of what he calls "relevant collateral data" (2008, 384). Drawing a determinate conclusion from a standard requires an auxiliary premise. These auxiliary premises introduce a further element of relativity into Wright's account, but one to which he pays no attention.

10. Wright's argument becomes unclear at this point. He imagines the relativist objecting that reflexive self-validation only applies to those standards that have been accepted. Wright says this is "the right reply" (2008, 388) but does not explain why he thinks it is right. He merely says that this reply turns the spotlight onto what the relativist means by "acceptance," and then moves on to this further topic.

11. Belief in a middle ground between "relativism" and "absolutism" is the result of muddled thinking. Logically, of course, the appearance of such middle ground can be manufactured with trivial ease by definitional manoeuvres. Instead of taking the rejection of absolutism as a necessary and sufficient condition for relativism, the rejection can be treated as a necessary, but not a sufficient, condition. Further necessary conditions can then be added at will in order to create the desired middle ground, e.g. by arbitrarily stipulating that relativists subscribe to, say, metaphysical idealism or some form of irrationalism.

12. "The crucial, load bearing idea ... is that of the rationally unconstrained acceptance of (propositions articulating) basic moral and epistemic standards" (Wright 2008, 389). Some authors, following Boghossian, refer to the lack of rational discrimination as the "Equal Validity Thesis."

13. The correct definition is that relativists reject *absolute* standards, not that they reject all standards. For a further discussion of this and other pervasive confusions in the anti-relativist literature see Bloor (2011).

14. For an account of the remarkable rituals that surrounded the creation of the standard metre see Galison (2003, 84ff.).

15. Kuhn (1961). For a sociological reading of Kuhn's argument see Barnes (1982) and Bloor (2016).

16. For a groundbreaking analysis of the self-referential processes that are the basis of social ontology see Barnes (1983).

17. "A society can neither create itself nor recreate itself without at the same time creating an ideal. This creation is not a sort of work of supererogation for it, by which it would complete itself, being already formed; it is the act by which it is periodically made and remade" (Durkheim 1961, 470).

18. Wright (2006).

19. Similar arguments have been put forward by Searle (1995, 166) and by Boghossian (1996, 15).

20. The required causal explanation should be independent of the analyst's own evaluation of the credibility or desirability of what is being explained. This methodological requirement is sometimes called the "symmetry postulate."

The symmetry postulate should not be confused with the Equal Validity Thesis, which is sometimes attributed to relativist sociologists of knowledge.

21. Such a book was written, but not by Durkheim. It appeared in 1953 under the potentially misleading title *Philosophical Investigations*. When we do philosophy, said the author in paragraph 194, "we are like savages, primitive people, who hear the expressions of civilised men, put a false interpretation on them, and then draw the queerest conclusions from it."

References

Barnes, B. (1982), *T.S. Kuhn and Social Science*, London: Macmillan.

———. (1983), "Social Life as Bootstrapped Induction," *Sociology* 4: 524–545.

Bloor, D. (1982), "Durkheim and Mauss Revisited: Classification and the Sociology of Knowledge," *Studies in the History and Philosophy of Science* 13 (4): 267–297.

———. (2007), "Epistemic Grace: Anti-Relativism as Theology in Disguise," *Common Knowledge* 13 (2–3): 250–280.

———. (2011), "Relativism and the Sociology of Scientific Knowledge," in *A Companion to Relativism*, edited by S. Hales, Oxford: Blackwell, 433–455.

———. (2016), "The Pendulum as a Social Institution: T.S. Kuhn and the Sociology of Science," in *Shifting Paradigms: Thomas S. Kuhn and the History of Science*, edited by A. Blum, K. Gavroglu, C. Joas and J. Renn, Berlin: Edition Open Access, 235–252.

Boghossian, P. (1996), "What the Sokal Hoax Ought to Teach Us: The Pernicious Consequences and Internal Contradictions of 'Postmodernist' Relativism," *Times Literary Supplement* 13 December: 14–15.

———. (2006), *Fear of Knowledge*, Oxford: Clarendon Press.

Durkheim, E. (1961), *The Elementary Forms of Religious Life*, translated by J.W. Swain, New York: Collier Books. (The first French edition was published in 1912).

———. (1964), *Essays on Sociology and Philosophy*, edited by K.H. Wolf, New York: Harper Tourchbooks.

———. (1974), *Sociology and Philosophy*, translated by D.F. Pocock, New York: Free Press.

Galison, P. (2003), *Einstein's Clocks, Poincaré's Maps*, New York: W.W. Norton.

Giddens, A. (ed.). (1972), *Emile Durkheim: Selected Writings*, Cambridge: Cambridge University Press.

Kuhn, T.S. (1961), "The Function of Measurement in Modern Physical Science," *Isis* 52: 161–190.

Kusch, M. (1995), *Psychologism: A Case Study in the Sociology of Philosophical Knowledge*, London: Routledge.

Lukes, S. (1973), *Emile Durkheim: His Life and Work: A Historical and Critical Study*, Harmondsworth: Allen Lane.

Parkin, F. (1992), *Durkheim*, Oxford: Oxford University Press.

Searle, J. (1995), *The Construction of Social Reality*, London: Penguin Books.

Wright, C. (2006), "Intuitionism, Realism, Relativism and Rhubarb," in *Truth and Realism*, edited by P. Greenough and M.P. Lynch, Oxford: Clarendon Press, 38–60.

———. (2008), "Fear of Relativism?," *Philosophical Studies* 141: 379–390.

11 Sociologistic Accounts of Normativity

Paul Boghossian

11.1. Introduction

Normative discourse is among the most important and yet most puzzling things that we, human subjects and inquirers, engage in.

Normative talk is *prescriptive*: it makes judgments about how things ought to be, rather than how they are. The most familiar normative judgments are those of *morality*:

1. You ought not to have promised you would attend the conference if you knew you couldn't make it.
2. It is morally right for girls to receive an education.

However, it is vitally important to recognize that judgments of *rationality* are also normative. Thus, we might say:

1. You ought not to believe that smoking is good for you, given the evidence.
2. If you have no reason to doubt your senses, and it visually seems to you as though there is a cat in front of you, then you ought to believe that there is a cat in front of you.

Importantly, normative judgments are not only directed at others, but also at ourselves: each of the other-directed judgments above has a first-person counterpart. This is important in highlighting that we recognize in our own case a distinction between how we are inclined to act and how we *ought* to act.

When we make such judgments, either in their third- or first-person versions, we make them because, in some sense, we believe that they are *correct*. I make judgments (1) – (4), as opposed to their opposites, because I take these judgments to be correct and their opposites to be incorrect. But in what could the "correctness" of a normative judgment *consist*?

In the case of a descriptive judgment, such as

5. Earth is spherical,

Sociologistic Accounts of Normativity 175

we understand well enough in what its correctness consists. Its correctness consists in its truth, which in turn consists in its correspondence with a mind-independent fact – namely, that Earth has a roughly spherical shape. And we understand well enough what it is for this material body to have a roughly spherical shape and how it could have had that property independent of us humans having had any thoughts about it. We understand what it is for such a fact to obtain, and to do so without any help from human minds.

But could we give a similar account of the correctness of normative judgments? Are there human-mind-independent facts about what ought to be done, or what ought to be believed, that sit out there and to which our normative judgments must "correspond" if they are to be correct? Does correctness for normative judgments consist in truth by correspondence to mind-independent fact?

In some periods of human history, belief in supernatural beings was more common than it is these days (although it is still surprisingly strong). Among these supernatural beings, some were gods. In one of the most influential of these super-naturalist views, there was only one God, an almighty being who created the world. In such a monotheistic view, it was perhaps natural to think that normative facts were determined by the dictates of such an almighty being.

Such a view of normative correctness is much less available today in our disenchanted world. More importantly still – it was a totally unworkable idea to begin with, as Plato showed by posing the Euthyphronic question (see Plato, 1961, 10a, and Boghossian, 2017).

11.2. Durkheim and Bloor on Normativity

If God does not determine what is right and wrong, what possibly could? Let me quote here Bloor's description of Durkheim's view, which Bloor sees as the beginning of wisdom on these matters:

> All societies, said Durkheim, register in some form or other the difference between desiring to do something and being obliged to do it.... Inclinations and desires arise from within us. Duties and obligations compel us from outside. At the same time duties and obligations manage to get inside us, and we can feel the conflict between wants and oughts. But what are these strange external compulsions? What is a moral force? ...
>
> [Durkheim] proposed a synthesis. The reality was that obligation was a social, not an individual, phenomenon. It was a constraint, a norm, collectively affirmed and enforced by the members of a group and thus external to each individual. The seemingly transcendental character of obligation, the way it seemed everywhere and nowhere, was a transfigured response to its social character. Its

176   *Paul Boghossian*

capacity to reach into the very interior of the individual derived from the innately social character of the human animal. Humans are innately responsive to one another. Both the rationalist and the empiricist accounts were partial because they failed, in their different ways, to do justice to the social.

(162–163)

According to Bloor's Durkheim, objectivist views of morality are founded on falsehoods: Kantian views because of their alleged reliance on a non-existent God; and utilitarian views because of their alleged failure to distinguish genuine moral obligation from pleasure or happiness. Both of these criticisms seem to me to incorporate serious misconceptions of their targets, but I won't pause over them.

The proposed alternative is an explanation of moral obligation in terms of the acceptance of norms by societies and their enforcement on their members. The individual may experience this societal pressure as though it were a response to the dictates of God, or of objective rationality, or what have you; but in reality, this experience of objective obligation is just a transfigured – that is to say, misleading – experience of what is at bottom a complex form of social pressure, one to which we are responsive because of our innately social natures.

This is a concise statement of a sociologistic view of normativity. And as Bloor emphasizes, Durkheim applied his account not just to morality but to *rationality* as well. It's an entirely *general* account of *normativity*. In doing this, Durkheim shows a coherence rare among theorists of the normative. If you are puzzled as to how there could be any objective facts about normativity, this puzzlement should extend to any sort of normativity, to rationality just as much as to morality.

We can distinguish between two different ways of understanding this sociologistic view of normativity.

On the one hand, it could be understood as a *reductive* view of normativity: to say that X ought to be done or believed is to say that it follows from the norms that we accept that X ought to be done or believed.

On the other hand, it could be construed as an *eliminativist* view of normativity: to say that X ought to be done or believed is to make some objectivist claim that corresponds to nothing real. If we are thinking clearly, we would eliminate such claims in favor of talk about which norms we happen to accept and what they allow or forbid. Such an account would be accompanied by a story about why we were misled into thinking that there was such a thing as objective normativity, a kind of unmasking of the experience of felt compulsion by objective norms as just a transfiguration of the underlying social reality – which is social pressure.

Bloor's remarks definitely suggest the second, eliminativist, view. If the reductive view were meant, Bloor's sociologism would just fall into place as yet another philosophical theory. But Bloor's attitude seems to be, rather, that philosophy, *qua* theory of normativity really *has no subject matter*, and that clearly suggests an eliminativist view. The only real subject matter in the vicinity of philosophy's interest in the normative concerns social structures, strictures and enforcement. That's why Bloor can say, with breathtaking dismissiveness, that he agrees with Durkheim that all that philosophy is doing, at least when it comes to the normative, is bad sociology!

11.3. Bloor on Wright

Bloor goes on to illustrate the virtues of sociologism with a critical discussion of a paper of Crispin Wright's (2008), which is itself a critical discussion of my book *Fear of Knowledge: Against Relativism and Constructivism* (2006).

I will dwell on this part of Bloor's chapter for a bit both because it forms the bulk of Bloor's chapter and because it well illustrates the types of misunderstanding that divide philosophers from their would-be critics in the "sociology of scientific knowledge" (SSK).

Following my own setup, Wright says that, before any assessment of a relativistic view of a given domain can be made, an answer is required to three questions:

A. What is a *standard*?
B. What is it for something to be true *relative* to a standard?
C. What is it to *accept* a standard?

Why do I, and Wright, say that a relativist must supply answers to these three questions? Well, the explanation is simple. A relativist about a given domain, say, morality, is someone who holds that:

> (Moral Relativism) Judgments about morality cannot be absolutely true or false; they are at most true or false relative to the standards accepted by a society. As far as the standards themselves are concerned, there is no question of their correctness.

As we can see from this definition, answers to the three questions are required if we are to properly understand the relativist's position. We need to know what a standard is; what it is for something to be true relative to a standard; and what it is for a particular standard to be the standard of a particular individual or society.

Wright agrees with me in saying that "natural" answers to our three questions are as follows:

A. Standards are general propositions.
B. A particular proposition's being true relative to a standard consists in its being logically entailed by such a general proposition (together with relevant auxiliary facts).
C. Accepting a standard means believing the relevant general proposition.

178   *Paul Boghossian*

Bloor finds the answers that Wright gives to the three questions on behalf of the relativist "unnatural." He prefers the following answers:

A. A standard is a social institution.
B. Relativity is social causation.
C. Acceptance is being a competent social actor.

Bloor's case for preferring these answers is, unfortunately, riddled with misunderstanding.

Against Wright's answer to A, he cites the "standard meter" in Paris. Is the standard meter a proposition, he asks rhetorically? Well, no, it's a metal rod of a certain length.

Doesn't that refute Wright's view that standards are propositions? Well, no, since the standard meter is not a standard in the relevant sense; it's just a metal rod. The standard, the norm, is something that would be formulated as follows:

(Length Norm) The lengths of things should be reported as multiples or fractions of the length of the standard meter.

That's the standard. And that, as you can see, *is* a proposition – indeed, a normative proposition.

But even if this were granted, isn't Bloor right that it's more illuminating to say that a standard is a social institution than that it is a proposition? After all, if something like (Length) is a standard among us, surely that has something to do with our having accepted it as a standard?

No, we need to distinguish the question *what a standard is* (Wright's first question) from the question: *how does a given standard come to have authority over us?*

In talking about standards, you need to be able to say that *there are many possible standards*, only some of which are standards that are operative in a given society. This shows that you can't say that a standard is a norm instituted by a society, since there are many norms that are not instituted by any society. In that sense, a standard is clearly a proposition.

If we then ask what makes one of these possible standards a norm that is operative within a given society, the answer may well be that it is so in virtue of having been socially instituted. What makes it the case that (Length) has the status of a standard or norm is that it has been accepted as a norm by the relevant members of society; as a result, it has the authority of a standard amongst the members of that society.

Bloor says:

> Wright's mistake derives from being in the grip of a false picture of a social process. He talks of propositions when he should be talking

Sociologistic Accounts of Normativity 179

about how people co-ordinate their behaviour and conduct their interactions.

(168)

As I hope I've made clear, there is no conflict between talking about standards as propositions and talking about how some of those propositions become normative for a community by being adopted as standards to be followed.

11.4. Is Sociologism Enough?

But let us ask a more general question: What is it for a possible norm to have *authority* over a person or community?

In principle, it looks as though there is a distinction between a norm *having authority* over some community and that norm having been accepted or endorsed by that community. The two notions are logically distinct.

Although the notions are logically distinct, in some cases they clearly coincide. For example, everyone would agree that (Length) has authority over us only because it has been socially endorsed or accepted. Questions about which units of length to use in reporting about lengths is a *conventional* matter. It is decided upon by social convention.

And, of course, it makes sense that issues about how the length of things should be reported should be a matter of social convention. Standards for reporting on lengths need to be settled one way or another so that we can effectively communicate with one another, but within a broad range of options, it doesn't matter how they're settled. That's why when we come across people who report their lengths in inches and yards, as opposed to meters and centimeters, we don't think of them as making a mistake! We simply think that they have settled on a different conventional standard.

The hard question that interests philosophers is whether *that sort of social institution story* can account for the authority of *all* the norms that intuitively have authority over us.

Sociologism is the view that *any* norm can only come to have authority over an individual by his being part of a society that has come to accept that norm. As Bloor puts it:

> What is the social process which generates the sense of a standard as an external thing? The answer is: the ability of competent actors to invoke the standard in the course of criticism, justification and elaboration. It is in this sense that the standard can exist ... as an object of "possible consultation."

(165)

180 *Paul Boghossian*

Now, Bloor writes as though all of philosophy is committed to the idea that there must be norms that have an authority that is grounded in something beyond societal acceptance. This is one of the many places where he may not be as well-informed about philosophy as he needs to be if he is to be an effective critic of the discipline. I have many colleagues in my own department who are anti-realists about normativity and who would basically agree with Bloor's sociologistic view.

Bloor is right, though, that there are philosophers, myself included, who believe that it is impossible to account for everything that needs accounting for merely by appeal to the sort of authority that social pressure provides.

Take the case of a moral judgment like:

(Torture) It is wrong to torture an innocent child just for your own amusement.

Does anyone really accept that the truth of this norm consists in *nothing* over and above our living in a society that disapproves of such acts? What would we say if we were to come across another society in which the practice of abusing children for fun were accepted? Would we say: "Well, we don't approve of that in our society, but they can do as they please," or would we rather condemn them? Surely, the latter. But with what right would we do that if sociologism is correct and the normative authority of our norms doesn't reach across societal boundaries?

There are, of course, practices about which we do take such a tolerant attitude. For example, (and within certain limits, I suppose) we all take a relativistic attitude towards table manners. But we do not take such a relativistic and tolerant attitude towards (Torture).

Sociologism encourages us to resist applying our own norms to a different society, one that has explicitly disavowed the norms that we find natural. But ordinary moral agents, and not merely professional philosophers, reach across societal boundaries with our norms all the time and would find it intellectually and morally debilitating not to do so. By itself, of course, this observation hardly defeats sociologism. Sociologism need not deny that we are antecedently attracted to an objectivist view of morality. This attachment may be a residue of all sorts of myths. Sociologism seeks to correct our attachment to objectivism by insisting that nothing else is remotely scientifically acceptable.

What I want now to argue, however, is that the correction the sociologistic view is after is impossible to implement coherently. In particular, while it might be coherent to suppose that we could dispense with *moral* judgments with objective purport, it is not coherent to suppose that we could dispense with rationality judgments with objective purport. However, once we have admitted some objective normative facts, we may as well admit as many as there intuitively seem to be.

Sociologistic Accounts of Normativity   181

Consider *any* judgment we might want to make – for example, that Earth is spherical. We make the judgment, presumably, because we think it is justified by the evidence available to us. This is why it would be paradoxical (as Moore 1942 pointed out) for me to assert the following:

> Earth is spherical but I don't have any justification for believing that it is.

But now consider the judgment that Bloor, *qua* proponent of sociologism, wants to make:

> (Rationality) You should not make rationality judgments with objective purport.

Anyone putting forward this judgment would have to be doing so because they thought that (Rationality) itself is the rational thing to think given the considerations they have adduced. There is no other way to understand it. Could the notion of rationality presupposed by this very judgment – the judgment of sociologism itself – be itself simply understood as grounded in social pressure?

Suppose we tried to think of it that way. Bloor says sociologism is the rational thing to believe. In a sociologistic view, that would mean, roughly:

> It follows from the norms and assumptions that my society accepts that we ought to believe sociologism.

There would, however, be two problems with this way of trying to understand the statement of sociologism.

First, it seems false to say that it follows from the norms and assumptions of our society, however exactly that's to be individuated, that sociologism is true. Indeed, if what I've been saying about the objectivist presuppositions of ordinary moral judgments is correct, it would appear that, if society has any view about the matter at all, it is that sociologism is false, certainly as applied to morality.

Second, it follows from sociologism that if some other society were to accept different norms, or make different assumptions, that they would then be perfectly within their rights to reject sociologism. In particular, since there appears to be a community of philosophers who subscribe to different norms, or make different assumptions, they would be, by sociologism's own lights, perfectly entitled to reject sociologism. On what basis, then, are they being criticized by Bloor? Can't he see that, by his own lights, he is not entitled to criticize them?

What this shows, of course, is that Bloor himself does not treat the statement of sociologism in a way that is compatible with his sociologism.

182   *Paul Boghossian*

He regards sociologism as simply true, not just as true relative to his own optional norms and assumptions.

Relativists, as we know, tend to be dismissive of such self-refutation arguments. They often claim that they are just pieces of logical sleight of hand that show nothing serious. I think this attitude is mistaken. Few things could be worse for a view than showing that putting it forward as true is incompatible with its truth.

11.5. Conclusion

If, as I have been arguing, a sociologistic view of normativity is as wrongheaded as I've been claiming, why has it been found so appealing? As far as I can tell, the proponents of sociologism think that their view is forced upon us by taking an appropriately respectful attitude towards the deliverances of basic science. (This would be ironic, if true. The people taken to be most responsible for science-bashing would be seen to be motivated by respect for what they take to be the deliverances of science.)

The train of thought goes something like this: Fundamental physics has shown us that, at bottom, there is nothing but particles and the void. In particular, therefore, there is nothing that could be the source of objective normativity. If there is no such thing as objective normativity, what we experience as objective normativity is just a transfigured version of social pressure. If all there is are various sorts of social pressure, then there can be no criticizing a society which has ended up endorsing a different set of norms than ours.

The basic flaw in this argument is the misguided scientism with which it begins. You can have respect for the great achievements of fundamental physics without supposing that it has given us a complete picture of the world in which we live. There are many important things which physics has not succeeded in explaining and which it may never be able to explain.

One obvious and enormously important example is consciousness. Another big lacuna is something that physics itself relies upon heavily, namely, mathematics. Mathematics concerns numbers and sets which are not among the concrete objects studied by physics, but are rather abstract objects. And physics has not given us any understanding either of the nature of abstracta or of our access to them. Another important gap is that of modality – statements about metaphysical necessity or possibility – of which the statements of mathematics are just one special instance.

In a word, the world we live in is a much more complex and mysterious place than a reductive physicalist picture can do justice to. To account for everything that needs accounting for, we are likely to admit fundamental and irreducible truths about consciousness, abstract objects and modality, at the very least. Once this is recognized, scientistic objections to admitting fundamental and irreducible truths about normative matters will be seen to have lost much of their force.

References

Boghossian, P. (2006), *Fear of Knowledge: Against Relativism and Constructivism*, Oxford: Clarendon Press.

———. (2017), "Relativism about the Normative," *Realism – Relativism – Constructivism: Proceedings of the 38th International Wittgenstein Symposium in Kirchberg* 24: 611–618.

Moore, G.E. (1942), "A Reply to My Critics," in *The Philosophy of G. E. Moore*, edited by P.A. Schilpp. Evanston, IL: Northwestern University, 691–701.

Plato. (1961), *The Collected Dialogues of Plato*, edited by Edith Hamilton and Huntington Cairns, Princeton: Princeton University Press.

Wright, C. (2008), "Fear of Relativism?," *Philosophical Studies: An International Journal for Philosophy in the Analytic Tradition* 141: 379–390.

12 Relativism in the Sociology of Scientific Knowledge Revisited[1]

Martin Kusch

12.1. Introduction

This chapter revisits the relativism of the "Sociology of Scientific Knowledge" (SSK) in light of recent work on relativism in epistemology and the philosophy of language. Many authors have contributed to SSK; I shall focus primarily on the writings of the Edinburgh sociologists Barry Barnes and David Bloor, as well as my own previous contributions.

Relativism in SSK plays two roles: as a substantive position and as a methodology. The latter role is summed up in the "impartiality" and "symmetry" tenets of the "Strong Programme" of SSK:

> It [i.e. the "Strong Programme"] would be *impartial* with respect to truth and falsity, rationality or irrationality, success or failure. Both sides of these dichotomies will require explanation.
>
> It would be *symmetrical* in its style of explanation. The same types of cause would explain say, true and false beliefs.
>
> (Bloor 1991, 7; italics added)

The substantive position is summed up in the following passage:

> For the [SSK-]relativist there is no sense attached to the idea that some standards or beliefs are really rational as distinct from merely locally accepted as such. ... [He] thinks that there are no context-free or super-cultural norms of rationality.
>
> (Barnes and Bloor 1982, 27)

I shall focus primarily on the substantive position and try to defend three theses. First, SSK-relativism is not an instance of recently-much-debated "templates" for relativism. Second, SSK-relativism is therefore not threatened by arguments targeting these template positions. And third, SSK-relativism is nevertheless *in the vicinity* of these templates, and it offers noteworthy sketches of arguments for original relativist claims. In speaking of "recently-much-debated 'templates' for relativism," I am referring primarily to ideas introduced in Paul Boghossian's 2006 study *Fear of*

Knowledge (subsequently "FK"). I shall structure my investigation into SSK-relativism around Boghossian's template for relativism. In so doing I also address his arguments for and against positions that instantiate his template.

The remainder of this chapter is structured as follows. Section 12.2 explains Boghossian's template and its three tenets. For each tenet FK first either reports or invents a relativist argument in its favour before subsequently marshalling an absolutist rejoinder. Sections 12.3 to 12.5 outline and evaluate the case for SSK-relativism relative to Boghossian's template and arguments.

12.2. Boghossian's Template

Boghossian formulates epistemic relativism as a combination of three theses:

1. There are no absolute facts about what belief a particular item of information justifies (epistemic non-absolutism).
2. If a person, S's, epistemic judgements are to have any prospect of being true, we must not construe his utterances of the form "E justifies belief B" as expressing the claim (i.e. the proposition) *E justifies belief B* but rather as expressing the claim: *According to [the] epistemic system, that I, S, accept, information E justifies belief B* (epistemic relationism).
3. There are many fundamentally different, genuinely alternative epistemic systems, but no fact by virtue of which one of these systems is more correct than any of the others (epistemic pluralism).

(FK 73)

Note concerning relationism that it is couched in terms of a *non-relativistic* notion of truth. What is relativized in (2) is not truth but the *content of the proposition*. Using the language of today's philosophy of language, epistemic relationism is thus a form of "(semantic) contextualism," not of "(semantic) relativism" (cf. MacFarlane 2014). (2) also introduces the central concept of an "epistemic system" (subsequently "ES"). An ES is made up of "epistemic principles," such as "*Observation*": "For any observational proposition p, if it visually seems to S that p and circumstantial conditions D obtain, then S is *prima facie* justified in believing p" (FK 84). Finally, epistemic pluralism (3) is tantamount to the thesis of "equal validity": "There are many radically different, yet 'equally valid' ways of knowing the world" (FK 2).

12.2.1. The Argument for Non-Absolutism

According to Boghossian, epistemic absolutism and relativism agree on the *internalist* assumption that "if there are absolute epistemic facts, it must be possible to come to have justified beliefs about what those

186 Martin Kusch

facts are" (FK 75). Boghossian's crucial testcase are facts concerning the superiority of one ES over another. Boghossian's absolutist assumes, and his relativist denies, that we can have epistemically justified beliefs about how our ES compares with others. The relativist's denial is based on the following argument (FK 95–102), which I here present in my own words:

Step 1: We encounter "genuine alternative" ESs. To be a genuine alternative to our ES, another ES must differ from ours in at least one "fundamental" epistemic principle, that is, one epistemic principle, which is not derived from other epistemic principles.

Step 2: When we encounter a genuine alternative to our ES, say "ES_{alt}," we are obliged to justify why we stick to our own ES rather than switch to ES_{alt} (if that is what we choose to do). Call this obligation the "demand for justification."

Step 3: In responding to the demand for justification, we have no choice but to rely upon the resources of our existing ES; after all, it is the only ES we have got. I shall refer to this idea as "ethnocentric justification": epistemic justification of one's own ES cannot but be based upon this very system.

Step 4: Alas, our ES features an epistemic principle, "no-rule-circularity," which blocks the ethnocentric justification of our ES. According to "no-rule-circularity" the justification of a given epistemic rule R must not involve this very R. Generalized for the present case: the justification of our ES must not – on pain of violating no-rule-circularity – use the epistemic resources of our ES.

Step 5: It follows from Step 4 that we cannot have justified beliefs about the epistemic standing of our ES relative to other ESs.

Step 6: Finally, reading Step 5 in the context of the *internalist* assumption ("if there are absolute epistemic facts, it must be possible to come to have justified beliefs about what those facts are"), we must conclude that there are no absolute epistemic facts, and that epistemic relativism is true.

Boghossian is unconvinced. He insists that the demand for justification (Step 2) applies only when we encounter an alternative "impressive enough to make us legitimately doubt the correctness of our own epistemic system" (FK 101). And no-rule-circularity (Step 4) only holds for epistemic principles that have *independently* become doubtful (FK 100). Moreover, and this speaks against both no-rule-circularity and the demand for justification, "each thinker is blindly [default] entitled ... to use the epistemic system he finds himself with, without first having to supply an antecedent justification for the claim that it is the correct system" (FK 99). And finally, Boghossian also gives us the right to dismiss alternative ESs that fail to live up to our demands of "coherence"

(FK 96–7). If Boghossian is on the right track, then Steps 2 and 4 of the relativistic argument are both false.

12.2.2. The Argument for Relationism

Boghossian has the relativist and absolutist agree that ESs consist of "general epistemic principles" which "entail" "particular epistemic judgements." I have already cited the general epistemic principle of *Observation* above, here is an example for a particular epistemic judgement: "If it visually seems to Galileo that there are mountains on the moon, then Galileo is justified in believing that there are mountains on the moon" (FK 85).

Following Gilbert Harman (1996), Boghossian formulates relationism by way of a parallel with "relativism in physics," that is, for instance the relativization of movement to frameworks in Galileo's physics. On this reconstruction, the *un-relativized* claim "The ship moves" is "untrue," that is, either false or incomplete. But the *relativized* claim, "The ship moves relative to framework F," is complete and truth-apt. *Mutatis mutandis* for epistemology: "Otto's belief in ghosts is unjustified" is untrue. And yet, the relativized claim "Otto's belief in ghosts is unjustified according my ES" is complete and truth-apt. In other words, physical and epistemic relativism are cases of "replacement relativism": un-relativized expressions need to be replaced with relativized expressions (FK 83–87).

Boghossian's criticism focuses on the relationship between general epistemic principles and particular epistemic judgements (that, as long as they are un-relativized, are held to be untrue by the relativist). Boghossian allows the relativist different options for fleshing out general epistemic principles and un-relativized epistemic judgements. The former may be thought of as either general propositions or imperatives; and the latter may be rendered – as we have already seen – as either false or incomplete. Boghossian tries to show that none of these renderings works.

Option A (FK 91–93): *general principles are general imperatives; particular un-relativized judgements are untrue.* Here we are to think of general imperatives as ordering us to believe p only if we have the right kind of evidence. According to Option A, (*) "Otto's belief in ghosts is unjustified" needs to be replaced by something like (+) "According to the system of general epistemic imperatives that I accept, Otto's belief in ghosts is unjustified."– Option A runs into difficulty with the intuitive and pre-theoretical thought that judgements like (*) (in their un-relativized form) are "normative"; they express the thought that Otto *ought not to* believe in ghosts. Whatever the relativist offers as a replacement for (*), FK maintains, it ought to preserve this normative character. Unfortunately, (+) does not do so. (+) is not a claim about what anyone ought to believe; it is a claim about what a particular ES

188 *Martin Kusch*

counts as epistemically justified. (+) is a descriptive and not a normative statement.

Option B (85–89): general principles are general propositions; particular un-relativized judgements are untrue. This does not get rid of the problem with normativity. (*) would be replaced with (\$) "According to the system of general epistemic propositions that I accept, Otto's belief in ghosts is unjustified." The replacing proposition fails to preserve the normativity of (*).

Option C (FK 85–86): general principles are general propositions; particular un-relativized epistemic judgements are false. This causes further problems for the advocate of relationism. If particular un-relativized judgements are false, Boghossian holds, then so are epistemic principles *qua* general propositions. This is because particular epistemic judgements like (*) and epistemic principles like *Observation* are propositions "of much the same type" (FK 86): "the epistemic principles ... are just more *general* versions of particular epistemic judgements" (FK 86). Can the relativist bite the bullet and declare general un-relativized principles false? No. This move faces the "endorsement problem": how can we possibly endorse an ES that consists of nothing but false principles?

Option D (FK 87–89): general principles are general propositions; un-relativized particular epistemic judgements are incomplete. Here too the relativist faces the endorsement problem: if particular epistemic judgements are incomplete, then so are the general epistemic principles *qua* propositions. D must treat both as propositions "of much the same type." But saying that one endorses a system of incomplete principles makes little sense. To make matters worse, D also owes us an account of how an incomplete general principle can *entail* particular judgements.

Summa summarum, Boghossian believes that the relativist argument in favour of relationism fails.

12.2.3. The Relativist Argument for Pluralism

I have already mentioned the distinction between "fundamental" and "derived" epistemic principles. A fundamental principle is one "whose correctness cannot be derived from the correctness of other epistemic principles" (FK 67). Recall also the idea of a "genuine alternative to our ES": such alternative differs from our ES in at least one fundamental principle. Boghossian's relativist argues for pluralism by offering plausible historical instances of such alternatives. Such cases are meant to be intuitively plausible cases of "equal validity."

One often cited case is the clash between Galileo Galilei and Cardinal Roberto Bellarmine (Feyerabend 1975; Rorty 1981). Boghossian's relativists describe Galileo's and Bellarmine's disagreement as follows. Bellarmine's ES included the *fundamental* epistemic principle "*Revelation*": "For certain propositions p, including propositions about the heavens,

Relativism in the SSK Revisited   189

believing p is *prima facie* justified if p is the revealed word of God as claimed by the Bible" (FK 69). Galileo's ES did not feature *Revelation*, and nor does ours today. Bellarmine's ES was thus a genuine alternative to Galileo's and our ES(s). Moreover, since *Revelation* was fundamental for Bellarmine, we cannot dislodge it by arguing that is fails to follow from other principles Bellarmine accepted. Ergo: we have no way of refuting *Revelation* in a non-question-begging way. But then, so the relativist reasons, it seems that Bellarmine's ES is as valid as is our own (FK 69).

Boghossian's criticism questions whether Bellarmine's ES really is a genuine alternative to Galileo's and our own. Boghossian tries to make the case for a negative reply by arguing that – on grounds of interpretational charity – we had better not regard *Revelation* as a fundamental epistemic principle in Bellarmine's ES:

Step I: If another ES is incoherent, then we must reject it out of hand (FK 96).

Step II: An ES is incoherent if it features epistemically unprincipled, arbitrary distinctions. If two propositions are treated epistemically differently, then the ES must provide a rationale for this asymmetry (FK 98).

Step III: Assume *Revelation* were a fundamental epistemic principle in Bellarmine's ES. In that case, Bellarmine's ES featured an epistemically unprincipled, arbitrary distinction. It was incoherent (cf. Step II), and we must reject it (in line with Step I).

Step IV: Step III is justified by the following consideration. If *Revelation* had been fundamental for Bellarmine, then he would have used ordinary epistemic principles like *Observation* for "propositions about objects in his vicinity," but *Revelation* for propositions "about the heavens." *Observation* for "earthly matters," *Revelation* for "the heavens." This differential treatment of earthly and heavenly objects was unprincipled. What is worse, Bellarmine himself accepted that *Observation* is often important in forming judgements about the heavens: after all, Bellarmine "used his eyes to note that the sun is shining, or that the moon is half full, or that the clear night-time Roman sky is littered with stars." Bellarmine thus accepted that "the heavens are in a physical space that is above us, only some distance away." Boghossian concludes: "If all this is true, how could he think that observation is not relevant to what we should believe about the heavens, given that he relies on it in everyday life?" (FK 104).

Step V: We thus have a choice. If we assume that for Bellarmine *Revelation* is a fundamental principle, then his ES is incoherent and we have reason to reject it and deny it the status of being as valid as our own. If we treat *Revelation* as a derived principle, then we avoid the incoherence. This is the option interpretational charity calls for. But

190   *Martin Kusch*

then Bellarmine's ES is not a *genuine alternative* to our own: it does not differ from ours in at least one *fundamental* epistemic principle.

Step VI: But how can treating *Revelation* as derived rather than fundamental avoid the incoherence? FK answers as follows: If *Revelation* is derived, then most plausibly it is accepted on the basis of evidence, say, evidence for the belief that the Bible is "the revealed word of the Creator of the Universe." And if that evidence is strong, then "perhaps" there is reason "to override the evidence provided by observation" (FK 104–5).

To sum up, as Boghossian has it, *Pluralism* is not supported by the example of Bellarmine's ES.

12.2.4. An Alternative Template

Finally, and before turning to SSK, I want to flag Crispin Wright's proposal on how to improve on Boghossian's template (Wright 2008). As pointed out earlier, there are (at least) two ways of capturing semantically the relativization central to relativism: relativizing the semantic content of the proposition, or relativizing the truth-predicate. Boghossian does the former, Wright suggests the latter; terminologically, Boghossian commits the relativist to "(semantic) contextualism," Wright to "(semantic) relativism" or "New-Age relativism." The difference between these two positions can also be described by saying that contextualism operates with "thick propositions" and semantic relativism with "thin propositions." Compare the two renderings of the utterance "E justifies belief B":

(Thick proposition) *According to ES$_i$, that I, S, accept, information E justifies belief B.*
(Thin proposition) *E justifies belief B.*

Wright's alternative to the second element of Boghossian's template can thus be formulated as follows:

> B*. Utterances of the form: "E justifies belief B" are not *absolutely* but *relatively* true. They express the "thin" proposition: *E justifies belief B.* Their truth-values are relative to the standards of different contexts in which the proposition is assessed. And there are many different such contexts.

Wright thinks that his reconstruction deals the relativist a better hand than does Boghossian's template. And yet, ultimately Wright too thinks that the relativist position is untenable. A first problem is an infinite regress. If particular epistemic judgements are merely relatively true, that is, true relative to an ES, and if – as Boghossian has argued – particular epistemic judgements and general epistemic principles are "of much the same type" (FK 86) – then general epistemic principles can also at best be relatively true. And if "being relatively true" means "being true relative to a set of epistemic principles," then we need second-order epistemic principles to account for the truth of first-order principles. Alas, in order to account for the relative truth of second-order principles, we need third-order principle ... and so on *ad infinitum* (2008, 388).

The relativist might try to avoid the regress by suggesting that the relative truth of a given general epistemic principle means truth relative to, and determined by, all of the other existing (first-order) principles of a given ES. Wright is not impressed. His reason is (what I will call) the "adoption problem." Assume the relativist is in a situation in which her existing epistemic principles do not yet commit her to either accepting or rejecting a given newly encountered epistemic principle (say of another ES). In such a situation the relativist is dealing with principles "whose basic place in [her] ... epistemic ... system goes with their acceptance being effectively rationally or cognitively unconstrained" (Wright 2008, 388). Unfortunately for the relativist, this crucial condition cannot be met if the relative truth of an epistemic principle is determined by the rest of the epistemic principles that belong to the same ES. An epistemic principle that the relativist encounters for the first time, naturally is not (yet) part of her ES. But then, by the presently considered proposal, it is not even relatively true: it is relatively false. And if it is relatively false, then the relativist is not rationally or cognitively unconstrained in considering it: clearly, she ought *not* to accept it (ibid.).

12.3. From Relationism to Communitarian Finitism

I now turn to relating Boghossian's and Wright's templates and arguments to SSK. I shall begin with the semantic issues.

SSK's theorising about language draws on philosophical ideas that are not centre stage when Boghossian and Wright discuss the semantic aspects of epistemic relativism. SSK's semantic theorising draws on Wittgenstein's "rule-following considerations" (subsequently "RFC") (Wittgenstein 2001). One important aspect of this difference in starting point is that SSK does not offer reflections in terms of *propositions*. Bloor for one does not find propositions a useful tool when discussing meaning in the context of epistemic relativism. Obviously, given constraints of space, I cannot here present a conclusive case for Bloor's, or my own, take on the RFC (cf. Bloor 1983, 1997; Kusch 2002, 2006). I shall be satisfied if I manage to state clearly what the SSK-option amounts to.

There are two main dividing lines with respect to rule-following and meaning: the first separates "individualists" from "communitarians." The individualist maintains that we can, at least in principle, make

192   *Martin Kusch*

sense of the idea that an individual *I* follows a rule *R* in total social isolation. For the communitarian, to make sense of rule-following and meaning, we have to study communal language games in which rules and meanings are attributed to others. Moreover, to declare *I* a follower of *R*, is to give *I* a certain social status.

The second fault line in the literature on rule-following is the difference between "meaning-determinist" and "meaning-finitist" conceptions. The advocates of the former position believe that to follow *R* is to have a(n) (individual or communal) mental state, or a(n) (individual or communal) behavioural disposition, determining which behaviour is correct. The meaning-finitist conceives of particular acts of following *R* as acts of *extending an analogy* with previously learnt exemplars of following *R* correctly. In new circumstances following *R* requires a decision concerning the question which behaviour counts as being most in line with past precedents. This decision will generally be based on a broad range of factors, of which past use is but one. In other words, past use alone underdetermines present and future use.

SSK combines meaning-finitism with communitarianism. It thus holds that the attribution of meaning and rules to others is based on analogies with previously established precedents, as well as on negotiations and the formation of a (temporary) consensus. Finally, SSK's communitarian meaning-finitism is a form of *semantic relativism*: it says that there is not *one correct way* of extending an analogy with previously learnt exemplars. Different individuals or groups may develop language in different ways, and there is no "neutral" perspective from which one of these developments can be declared "right," "correct" or "true" in an absolute sense.

The above sketch suffices as background for discussing how SSK would respond to Boghossian's and Wright's semantic arguments. I shall begin with Boghossian. Remember that he commits the relativist to the idea that utterances of the form "E justifies B" are candidates for truth only if they are taken to express the claim "*According to the ES, that I, S, accept ... E justifies ... B.*" Moreover, if the utterance "E justifies B" is taken to express merely the claim or the proposition "*E justifies B,*" then the utterance is false or incomplete. Boghossian goes on to show that this view runs into problems with normativity, endorsement and entailment.

How could SSK respond? To begin with, it should deny that the utterance "E justifies B" expresses the claim or proposition *According to the ES, that I accept, E justifies B*. After all, SSK takes its lead from Wittgenstein who urges us to focus on how expressions are *used*; and, as Boghossian reminds us, the two formulations have different uses. The first has a normative use, the second does not. Of course, this is not yet a fully convincing answer to Boghossian; the SSK theorists must explain how they can avoid having to formulate their semantic view in the way Boghossian suggests.

Relativism in the SSK Revisited 193

First, it is not obvious that – given Boghossian's own premises – the absolutist can avoid the problems with normativity, endorsement and entailment (cf. Kusch 2009). To see this, we need to ask: Why is only the relativist obliged to insist that the allegiance to a specific ES has to be made explicit? Doesn't the absolutist too have an ES? This system may well be (in the eyes of the absolutist) the one and only correct system, but a system it is nevertheless. If that is true, however, then, by Boghossian's lights, the absolutist must also commit to saying that the utterance "E justifies B" is truth-apt only if it expresses the claim *According to ES ... E justifies B*. Moreover, and still following Boghossian's reasoning *mutatis mutandis*, the absolutist also has reason to take the claim *E justifies B* to be incomplete or false. After all, it is a claim that fails to declare allegiance to the one correct ES. Once this much is accepted, the dialectic advantage of absolutism over relativism disappears. If Boghossian's anti-relationist arguments work against relativism, then they also work against absolutism. This should make it doubtful, even to the absolutist, that Boghossian's reflections on relationism can be on the right track.

Second, SSK theorists do not accept the key premise of Boghossian's rendering of relationism, to wit, that the *conditions of the possibility* of an utterance are part and parcel of the claim the utterance expresses. For the utterance "E justifies B" to be meaningful and truth-apt there has to be a context consisting of previously socially-accepted precedents, a social group with its interests, values and forms of linguistic and epistemic negotiations and the possibility of a consensus on questions of correctness. But this complex context is not part of the claim expressed. Here the SSK theorist can draw on Wright for support. As we saw, Wright is also unconvinced by Boghossian's way of packing the context of an utterance into the relevant proposition.

Third, Boghossian is obviously guided by the thought that *prima facie* someone expressing an un-relativized proposition is thereby committing to absolutism. This is why he thinks the relativist has to insist that "according to ES" must be added to mark the relativistic rendering. SSK theorists *qua* communitarian finitists find this far from obvious. "E justifies B" has its uses in specific (types of) (epistemic) language games. But these language games can be played without committing to either absolutism or relativism. That is to say, the form of the utterance "E justifies B" does not tell us anything about the speaker's absolutist or relativist commitments. Where the speaker stands with respect to relativism or absolutism can only be determined by inquiring about their philosophical views.[2]

Turning from Boghossian to Wright, SSK theorists can accept his idea that, for the relativist, claims of the form "E justifies B" are relatively true – at least when the relevant contexts consist of precedents, negotiations and consensus-formation. And this can be done without falling foul of infinite regresses or the adoption problem.

194 *Martin Kusch*

Take first the objection that New-Age relativism involves an infinite regress. For SSK theorists, claims of the form "E justifies B" are true relative to epistemic precedents and negotiations; these precedents are true relative to further epistemic precedents and negotiations ... and so on. Is this a vicious infinite regress? There is indeed an infinite regress here, but it is *not vicious*. For the SSK theorists such regress in simply an expression of our historical contingency. Historians of science try to understand the history of the processes in which precedents are established and abandoned. There are no first and absolute beginnings to this sequence. When we pass epistemic judgements today, we do so in light of the precedents and negotiations we find ourselves with. We do so without worrying about the potential infinite regress that would result if we aimed for an "ultimate" justification by running back along the historical sequence. Put differently, to couch the historical contingency as an infinite regress is to adopt the absolutist[3] position – it is not an argument for it.

SSK theorists also have an answer to the adoption problem. To avoid the infinite-regress-problem, Wright allows the New-Age relativist to say that a *relatively true* principle is one that the rest of your ES commits you to; and that a *relatively false* principle is one that the rest of your ES does not commit you to. This then allows Wright to highlight a difficulty with respect to those newly encountered principles concerning which your ES is not committed either way. Wright's relativist takes herself within her right to adopt such principles at her pleasure. And yet, given the definition of "relatively false," the newly encountered principles would be false relative to the existing ES.

Wright's argument is easily blocked. The key move is to insist that for a principle p to be *relatively false* is *not* for the rest of the ES to lack any commitment concerning p, but for the rest of the ES to involve a commitment *against* p. In other words, lack of a system commitment concerning p is not a system commitment *against* p. What then should the SSK-relativist say about newly encountered principles concerning which her ES contains no commitments? She should say that the relevant group of epistemic agents needs to make a decision: Does adopting the new principle facilitate epistemic practices? Does it increase overall coherence of the ES? Does it chime with epistemic or other values, or interests of various kinds? If the answer to these questions is positive, then the ES will likely be adjusted in such a way that it does involve support for the newly encountered precedent.

To sum up the discussion of relationism and New-Age relativism, the semantic views of SSK differ from both of the views attributed to epistemic relativism by Boghossian and Wright. And the arguments with which the two philosophers target relationism and New-Age relativism do not affect the communitarian finitism adopted by SSK.

To conclude the discussion of finitism, note that it also has a wider implication concerning the framing of relativism. Central in Boghossian's

Relativism in the SSK Revisited 195

framing is the distinction between two (or more) "systems" of "fundamental" and "derived" rules or principles. Call this view "regularist foundationalism" to mark the fact that it centrally features a *foundation* of fundamental *rules* which enables one to rationally negotiate disagreements amongst empirical claims and derived rules. SSK theorists are suspicious of such hierarchical and rule-centred picture of epistemic practices. SSK follows Thomas Kuhn's (1962) well-known case for the priority of exemplars over rules. That is to say, SSK replaces regularist foundationalism with a position one might call "finitist coherentism": instead of foundational and derived rules, SSK talks of finite numbers of precedents or exemplars. Precedents or exemplars are at the centre of a web of beliefs, values, preferences, actions and instruments. But this does not mean that they are sacrosanct: all it means is that in general actors seek to protect the exemplars from change. Actors prefer to make changes elsewhere in the web.[4]

12.4. Pluralism Reconstructed

I now turn to contrasting Boghossian's and SSK's take on Bellarmine. I have three main comments. The first concerns historical accuracy. If we are to use historical events as material against which to test our philosophical theories then it is important that we get our facts straight. Remember in this light Boghossian's argument that attributing to Bellarmine acceptance of *Revelation* as a fundamental principle is to saddle him with an incoherent system. Allegedly Bellarmine had no justification for letting *Revelation* trump *Observation* when it came to propositions about the heavens. Boghossian insists that arbitrary choices make a system incoherent. And incoherent systems should be rejected.

This reasoning is based on ignorance of the actual historical context (Kinzel and Kusch 2018; Kusch 2017; cf. Biagioli 1993; Blackwell 1991; Finocchiaro 2007; Heilbron 2010; McMullin 2005). Bellarmine did have a twofold justification for using *Revelation* rather than *Observation* for *certain* propositions about the heavens. One reason was the millennia-old opposition between "sublunar" and "celestial" realms. According to the dominant astronomy and physics of the day, these two realms were governed by different laws of nature. Hence it was not arbitrary to think that these two realms might involve different epistemic sources, or at least the same sources to different degrees. Another reason was the equally old distinction between observables and unobservables. Given the astronomical and physical data available to astronomers in Bellarmine's days, the movement of the Earth could not be observed. Nor could it be "demonstrated" by Aristotelian standards; such demonstrations required necessary premises. Bellarmine took the lack of observations and demonstrations in support of Copernicanism to justify doubts about its truth, and "in a case of doubt, one may not

196 *Martin Kusch*

depart from the Scriptures as explained by the holy Fathers" (Bellarmine 1615). Needless to say, this is not a reasoning we today would accept. But this is not what is at issue at this point. The question here is simply whether Bellarmine's uses of *Observation* and *Revelation* would have been arbitrary if he had thought of *Observation* as a fundamental principle. The answer to this question is "no."

My second comment with respect to Boghossian's discussion of *Pluralism* concerns the idea of "equal validity." Boghossian commits epistemic relativism to the idea that all ESs are equally valid. One problem is that Boghossian fails to spell out what exactly "valid" means in this context. Does it mean "valid" in the logical sense? Or does it simply mean "true" or "justified?" A further problem is that *Equal Validity* is not generally a commitment that card-carrying epistemic relativists have been willing to take on. Barnes and Bloor have insisted on this point at least since 1982:

> Our ... postulate ... is not that all beliefs are equally true or equally false, but that ... all beliefs without exception call ... for empirical investigation and must be accounted for by finding the specific, local causes of [their] credibility.
>
> (Barnes and Bloor 1982, 23)

Similar denials can be found in other card-carrying epistemic relativists: Lorraine Code (1995, 202–203), Paul Feyerabend (1975, 189, 1978, 82–84, 1999, 215), Barbara Herrnstein Smith (2018, 26), Hartry Field (2009, 255–256), or Kusch (2019). Note also that Christopher Herbert concludes a lengthy discussion of the issue with the remark: "Nowhere does any 'relativist', to my knowledge, assert that all views are equally valid" (2001, loc. 440).

Of course, absolutist critics of relativism need not be impressed with such denials. They may insist that *Equal Validity* is a *tacit* commitment of the relativist, a commitment that follows from other relativist tenets, tenets the relativist is ready to embrace openly. Maybe such argument can be constructed. But Boghossian makes no effort to do so.

My third comment addresses the question what remains of the very idea of pluralism after we have moved from regularist foundationalism to particularist coherentism, and from *Equal Validity* to its rejection. One victim of these two moves is Boghossian's (seemingly) clear and concise criterion for what constitutes a "genuine alternative" to a given ES: an ES that differs in at least one fundamental principle. This option is off the table when we give up regularist foundationalism.

The main alternative to Boghossian's pluralism, and the alternative SSK favours, is that there is more than one web of precedents, beliefs, values, interests, policies and achievements, and that some such webs differ – and are indeed perceived by their respective actors to differ – in

Relativism in the SSK Revisited 197

fundamental ways. It is hard to quantify such differences in a general way; too many considerations potentially bear upon the question. Still, one rough indication of distance between two webs is the frequency or perceived ease of people "moving" from one such web to another. Another indication is the degree to which advocates of different webs find it important and useful to engage with one another in ways that both sides render as meaningful and reasoned debate. This is messier and more complicated than Boghossian's snappy formula, but this is what our messy social and historical world requires.

12.5. Non-Absolutism and Rule-Circularity

To begin with, it is worth pointing out that for Bloor non-absolutism is the necessary and sufficient condition for relativism: "relativism is the negation of absolutism. To be a relativist is to deny that there is such a thing as absolute knowledge and absolute truth." Absolute knowledge would be knowledge that is "perfect, unchanging, and unqualified by limitations of time, space, and perspective. It would not be conjectural, hypothetical, or approximate, or depend on the circumstances of the knowing subject" (2011, 436–437).

Bloor's and Boghossian's renderings of absolutism are similar enough for us to regard Bloor's and other SSK theorists' arguments against absolute knowledge and absolute truth as considerations challenging Boghossian's absolutism. There are five such arguments. I shall be brief regarding the first four since they do not *directly* challenge Boghossian's reasoning. I mention them here only to indicate that the SSK case for non-absolutism does not exclusively rest on critical reflections concerning rule-circularity.

The first and "flagship" SSK argument for non-absolutism is an induction on the history of science (e.g. Bloor 2011). SSK theorists take it for granted that work on the history and sociology of science has shown that all systems of beliefs are ultimately based on but local and contingent causes of credibility.

In conversations with SSK theorists I have occasionally encountered a second line of thought against absolutism. It is an instance of what cognitive psychologists call the "tool-to-theory heuristic" (Gigerenzer 1991). The starting point is the observation that non-absolutism has proven a highly successful tool in history, sociology and cognitive science of science. The success of this tool needs an explanation. And the best explanation is that non-absolutism is the correct theory concerning the human epistemic and moral predicament. Non-absolutism is thus not just useful; it is true.

A third SSK argument for non-absolutism is that it follows from "naturalism." The naturalist theorist emphasizes that we cannot ever "transcend the machinery of our brains and the deliverances of our sense

198　*Martin Kusch*

organs, the culture we occupy and the traditions on which we depend" (Bloor 2007, 252).

A fourth SSK defence of non-absolutism targets self-proclaimed absolutists' account of, or examples for, absolute facts or absolute knowledge. One concern here is that self-proclaimed absolutists often take for granted that absolutism is the natural philosophical attitude and thus beyond the need for clarification. Boghossian's book is a case in point. Although detailed and complex when it comes to characterizing relativism, FK says very little about (different ways to spell out) absolutism (Bloor 2007, 253).

Finally, and fifth, I turn to considerations that SSK theorists (might) direct against Boghossian's reflections on what he takes to be the relativist's best argument against absolutism. Note to begin with, that the issue of rule-circularity was mentioned already in Barnes and Bloor's first relativist credo, their 1982 paper "Relativism, Rationalism, and the Sociology of Knowledge":

> In the last analysis, he [the SSK relativist] will acknowledge that his justifications will stop at some principle or alleged matter of fact that only has local credibility. The only alternative is that justifications will begin to run in a circle and assume what they were meant to justify.
>
> (Barnes and Bloor 1982, 27; cf. Seidel 2013, 135)

Is this (at least part of) the argument Boghossian is advancing on behalf of the relativist? Not quite: Barnes and Bloor are not arguing that since rule-circular reasoning is prohibited, we are unable to justify our ES. Rather their point is that allowing rule-circular reasoning does not avoid non-absolutism or relativism. That this is indeed what is meant is obvious from Bloor's 2007 discussion of Boghossian's defence of circular reasoning (in order to motivate absolutism). Bloor stresses that circular arguments are unable to establish – in a neutral way – the absolute superiority of our ES over others. If we allow ourselves to reason in a circular fashion, then we must grant the same option also to advocates of other, alternative ESs. Bloor applies these considerations also to the debate between absolutists and relativists: "if absolutists can use circular arguments to justify their position, then relativists can also avail themselves of this move." Bloor invokes similar considerations against Boghossian's "blind entitlement" (Bloor 2007, 261).

Going beyond Bloor's arguments, assume we have indeed been able to show – in rule-circular fashion – that our ES is superior to another ES. Even rule-circularity to one side, why should such historically situated and contingent result give us the confidence that we are at least roughly on the road to absolute knowledge or absolute standards? Why think that our assessment transcends ultimate dependence upon

Relativism in the SSK Revisited 199

local and contingent causes of credibility? Anyone impressed by the already-mentioned considerations in favour of non-absolutism is unlikely to be persuaded otherwise by Boghossian's thought experiment.

Given SSK's Wittgensteinian sympathies, it is also worth pointing out an oddity about Boghossian's "blind entitlement." As Boghossian notes, he takes this idea to be inspired by §219 of Wittgenstein's *Philosophical Investigations*: "When I obey a rule, I do not choose. I obey the rule blindly." I am not convinced that this is in the spirit of Wittgenstein's position. Wittgenstein's remark about obeying a rule blindly is not a remark about an *entitlement*. It is an observation about what we do. Moreover, while Wittgenstein, for instance in *On Certainty,* frequently speaks about our "systems" of beliefs, he does not couch our relationship to such systems in terms of "entitlements." Instead Wittgenstein speaks of this relationship as "something animal" (§359). And "something animal" does not sound like a platform from which to reach absolute standards.

Finally, the issue of rule-circularity in epistemology – or "epistemic circularity" – has been discussed extensively in recent years. Thus even someone who agrees with SSK concerning Boghossian's arguments might still suspect that SSK's non-absolutism runs afoul of other epistemologists' reflections on epistemic circularity. Obviously, I cannot review here the rich literature on this topic. But I shall at least briefly comment on two epistemologists who have been central in this debate.

I begin with William Alston (1986, 1991, 1993), and focus on the latter two book-size studies. Alston argues that we cannot know that our basic sources of beliefs are reliable. The best we can do is come to appreciate that they are "practically" without alternative for us. This makes it "reasonable" for us to rely on them – at least when these practices are psychologically, historically and socially deeply embedded. Interestingly enough, for Alston "mystical perception" qualifies by these criteria. Does this kind of position threaten SSK's non-absolutism? I think not. If practical reasonableness is the best we can get, then there is no reason to assume that we have justified beliefs about absolute epistemic principles – something Boghossian takes to be possible. Indeed, that we are limited to this kind of merely practical endorsement is what some card-carrying relativists (e.g. Street 2011) mean by their denial of absolutism.

Ernest Sosa (2009) distinguishes between "animal" and "reflective" knowledge: the former is externalist-reliabilist; the latter internalist-coherentist: "awareness of how one knows" (2009, 200). Sosa believes that Alston is right only if we think of epistemic justification as linear. But it is "weblike" and delivers "mutually supportive comprehensive coherence." And this enables a "reflective endorsement" of sources of belief. Our basic sources of belief are justified – in a non-circular fashion – insofar as they are based on our coherent "common sense and scientific knowledge of ourselves and the world" (ibid.).

200 *Martin Kusch*

SSK theorists would applaud the distinction between animal and reflective knowledge, albeit Bloor emphasizes as the dividing criterion whether knowledge is based on social-cultural resources or not. Bloor makes room for animal knowledge, knowledge not based on social cultural resources, even in humans (Bloor 1992). But Sosa's attempt to deliver a non-circular justification for our basic sources of belief is unconvincing. If epistemology is part and parcel of our overall web of belief, it too will change: a point stressed in various ways by Feyerabend (1975) or Bas van Fraassen (2002). Nothing is in principle safe from revision. And this thought should make us sceptical about the prospects of reaching justified beliefs about absolute principles. Moreover, it is important to remember that there can be more than one coherent web of "common sense and scientific knowledge of oneself and the world." Remember for example that Alston has a web of beliefs in which mystical perception has a legitimate place. Which one of the competing webs gets to decide on the fundamental epistemic sources?

Finally, consider the "raft" (Sosa 1980) of our common sensed and scientific knowledge of ourselves and the world. How likely is it that this raft drifts towards an ever better grasp of absolute epistemic principles? SSK follows Kuhn in thinking about the development of science in evolutionary terms (Bloor 2007). But for Darwin evolution has no telos. Not to forget that for SSK the selecting environments are (natural-social-cultural) "niches" caused or constituted by our (collective) activities and beliefs. This kind of perspective gives little support to the thought of our getting ever better justified beliefs about absolutes.

12.6. Conclusions

In this chapter I have tried to relate SSK-relativism to recent theorising about relativism in epistemology and the philosophy of language. I have tried to show that Boghossian's template does not fit SSK-relativism and that SSK theorists have a battery of arguments that threaten Boghossian's absolutism. Whatever the merits or weaknesses of my individual arguments, I hope to at least have made plausible that the contemporary debate over epistemic relativism in Anglophone philosophy and the theorizing in SSK are not incommensurable. There is a substantive debate to be had here.

Notes

1. Work on this chapter was made possible by the ERC Advanced Grant Project (#339382): "The Emergence of Relativism: Historical, Philosophical and Sociological Perspectives". For comments I am particularly grateful to David Bloor and Robin McKenna. I have also benefitted from presenting this chapter as a keynote at the 2017 BSPS conference in Edinburgh, as

well as at workshops at the University of Vienna (2017), the Munich School of Philosophy (2017), and Yonsei University (2019).

2. It may well be that the disagreement between Boghossian and SSK regarding semantics goes deeper than the disagreement concerning relativism. Boghossian probably conceives of the task of semantics as formalizing natural language so as to explain our intuitions about the truth or falsity of particular utterances. SSK is skeptical of this project, and finds it unhelpful to think about the language of science. (I am grateful to Robin McKenna for pressing this point in correspondence.)

3. This absolutist position is of course also an expression of meaning-determinism.

4. This coherentism has to be understood in the right way. It is not the traditional coherentism, say, that Michael Williams (2001) targets as too close to traditional foundationalism. That is to say, the coherentism at issue here is not committed to a fixed and context-independent structure of epistemic justifications. The structure of epistemic justification is rather to be thought of as context-dependent and fluid and as not strictly separable from non-epistemic considerations. (I am grateful to Robin McKenna for pressing this point in correspondence.)

References

Alston, W. (1986), "Epistemic Circularity," *Philosophy and Phenomenological Research* 47: 1–30.

———. (1991), *Perceiving God: The Epistemology of Religious Experience*, Ithaca and London: Cornell University Press.

———. (1993), *The Reliability of Sense Perception*, Ithaca and London: Cornell University Press.

Barnes, B. and D. Bloor. (1982), "Relativism, Rationalism and the Sociology of Knowledge," in *Rationality and Relativism*, edited by M. Hollis and S. Lukes, Oxford: Blackwell, 21–47.

Bellarmine, R. (1615), "Letter on Galileo's Theories," *Modern History Sourcebook*, Fordham University, https://sourcebooks.fordham.edu/mod/1615bellarmine-letter.asp (Accessed July 12th, 2019).

Biagioli, M. (1993), *Galileo, Courtier: The Practice of Science in the Culture of Absolutism*, Chicago: University of Chicago Press.

Blackwell, R.J. (1991), Galileo, Bellarmine, and the Bible, Notre Dame: University of Notre Dame Press.

Bloor, D. (1983), *Wittgenstein: A Social Theory of Knowledge*, New York: Columbia University Press.

———. (1991), *Knowledge and Social Imagery*, 2nd edition, Chicago: University of Chicago Press.

———. (1992), "Ordinary Human Inference as Material for the Sociology of Knowledge," *Social Studies of Science* 22: 129–139.

———. (1997), *Wittgenstein, Rules and Institutions*, London and New York: Routledge.

———. (2007), "Epistemic Grace," *Common Knowledge* 12: 250–280.

———. (2011), "Relativism and the Sociology of Scientific Knowledge," in *Oxford Companion to Relativism*, edited by S. Hales, Oxford: Wiley-Blackwell, 433–455.

202 Martin Kusch

Boghossian, P. (2006), *Fear of Knowledge: Against Relativism and Constructivism*, Oxford: Clarendon Press. (Abbreviated as "FK").

———. (2008), "Replies to Wright, MacFarlane and Sosa," *Philosophical Studies* 141: 409–432.

Code, L. (1995), *Rhetorical Spaces: Essays on Gendered Location*, London: Routledge.

Feyerabend, P. (1975), *Against Method: Outline of an Anarchistic Theory of Knowledge*, London: New Left Books.

———. (1978), *Science in a Free Society*, London: New Left Books.

———. (1999), *Conquest of Abundance*, Chicago: University of Chicago Press.

Field, H. (2009), "Epistemology without Metaphysics," *Philosophical Studies* 143: 249–290.

Finocchiaro, M.A. (2007), *Retrying Galileo, 1633–1992*, Berkeley and Los Angeles: University of California Press.

Gigerenzer, G. (1991), "From Tools to Theories: A Heuristic of Discovery in Cognitive Psychology," *Psychological Review* 98: 254–267.

Harman, G. (1996), "Moral Relativism," in *Moral Relativism and Moral Objectivity*, edited by G. Harman and J.J. Thomson, Oxford: Blackwell, 1–64.

Heilbron, J.L. (2010), *Galileo*, Oxford and New York: Oxford University Press.

Herbert, C. (2001), *Victorian Relativity: Radical Thought and Scientific Discovery*, Chicago: Chicago University Press. (Kindle version).

Herrnstein Smith, B. (2018), *Practicing Relativism in the Anthropocene: On Science, Belief and the Humanities*, London: Open Humanities Press.

Kinzel, K. and M. Kusch. (2018), "De-Idealizing Disagreement, Rethinking Relativism," *International Journal of Philosophical Studies* 26: 40–71.

Kuhn, T. (1962), *The Structure of Scientific Revolutions*, Chicago: University of Chicago Press.

Kusch, M. (2002), *Knowledge by Agreement: The Programme of Communitarian Epistemology*, Oxford: Oxford University Press.

———. (2006), *A Sceptical Guide to Meaning and Rules: Defending Kripke's Wittgenstein*, Chesham: Acumen.

———. (2009), "Epistemic Replacement Relativism Defended," in *Epistemology and Methodology of Science: Launch of the European Philosophy of Science Association*, edited by M. Suarez, M. Dorato and M. Redei, Berlin, New York: Springer, 165–176.

———. (2017), "Epistemic Relativism and Pluralism," in *Epistemic Pluralism*, edited by A. Coliva and J.L. Linding Pedersen, London: Palgrave Macmillan, 203–227.

———. (2019), "Relativist Stances, Virtues and Vices," *Proceedings of the Aristotelian Society, Supplementary Volume* 93: 271–291.

MacFarlane, J. (2014), *Assessment Sensitivity: Relative Truth and Its Applications*, New York and Oxford: Oxford University Press.

McMullin, E. (ed.). (2005), *The Church and Galileo*, Notre Dame: Notre Dame University Press.

Rorty, R. (1981), *Philosophy and the Mirror of Nature*, Princeton: Princeton University Press.

Seidel, M. (2013), "Why the Epistemic Relativist Cannot Use the Sceptic's Strategy: A Comment on Sankey," *Studies in History and Philosophy of Science* A 44: 134–139.

Sosa, E. (1980), "The Raft and the Pyramid: Coherence versus Foundations in the Theory of Knowledge," *Midwest Studies in Philosophy* 5: 3–26.

———. (2009), *Reflective Knowledge: Apt Belief and Reflective Knowledge*, Vol. 2, New York and Oxford: Oxford University Press.

Street, S. (2011), "Evolution and the Normativity of Epistemic Reasons," *Canadian Journal of Philosophy* 35: 213–248.

van Fraassen, B. (2002), *The Empirical Stance*, Princeton: Princeton University Press.

Williams, M. (2001), *Problems of Knowledge*, Oxford: Oxford University Press.

Wittgenstein, L. (1969), *On Certainty*, Oxford: Blackwell.

———. (2001), *Philosophische Untersuchungen: Kritisch-Genetische Edition*, Frankfurt am Main: Suhrkamp.

Wright, C. (2008), "Fear of Relativism?," *Philosophical Studies* 141: 379–390.

Contributors

Natalie Alana Ashton is a postdoctoral researcher at the University of Stirling. Before this she was a postdoctoral researcher at the University of Vienna, and before that completed her PhD at the University of Edinburgh. Her research concerns the political and social aspects of epistemology – specifically the effects of oppression and power on epistemic justification. She has published papers on feminist standpoint theory, hinge epistemology, and epistemic relativism, and on the connections between all of these. Her latest work investigates what these topics can tell us about online epistemic environments.

David Bloor is Emeritus Professor in the Sociology of Science at the University of Edinburgh. He has published extensively on the sociology of scientific knowledge and has long defended a relativist stance. This relativism is embodied in the "Strong Programme in the sociology of knowledge." His most recent book is a sociological and historical study of a lengthy and revealing controversy between engineers and physicists concerning the nature of flight: *The Enigma of the Aerofoil: Rival Theories in Aerodynamics, 1909–1930*.

Paul Boghossian is Julius Silver Professor of Philosophy at New York University and Director of its Global Institute for Advanced Study. Elected to the American Academy of Arts and Sciences in 2012, he has written on a wide range of topics including knowledge, meaning, rules, moral relativism, aesthetics, and the concept of genocide. He is the author of *Fear of Knowledge: Against Relativism and Constructivism* (OUP, 2006) and *Content and Justification: Philosophical Papers* (OUP, 2008); and editor, with Christopher Peacocke, of *New Essays on the A Priori* (OUP, 2000). *Debating the A Priori*, a volume of exchanges with Oxford philosopher Timothy Williamson on the topics of a priori and conceptual truth, is forthcoming from Oxford University Press.

Sharyn Clough teaches courses in the study of knowledge, especially scientific knowledge, at Oregon State University. Her research examines the complex ways in which science and politics are interwoven, and the notions of objectivity that can be salvaged once this complexity is acknowledged. She is the director of Phronesis Lab, where she and her team test philosophical hypotheses (Phronesis Lab: Experiments in Engaged Ethics). She is the author of *Beyond Epistemology: A Pragmatist Approach to Feminist Science Studies* and the editor of *Siblings Under the Skin: Feminism, Social Justice and Analytic Philosophy*. In addition, she has written a number of essays on science and political values for journals such as *Social Science and Medicine, Studies in the History and Philosophy of the Biological and Biomedical Sciences, Metascience, Perspectives in Science,* and *Social Philosophy*. She is currently writing a book for a general audience on science and politics.

Annalisa Coliva is Professor and Chair in the Department of Philosophy at the University of California, Irvine. She has written extensively in epistemology, with special reference to the nature of justification and the problem of external world scepticism; on the history of analytic philosophy, particularly on G. E. Moore and Ludwig Wittgenstein; and in the philosophy of mind, mostly on perceptual content, singular thoughts, immunity to error through misidentification, and self-knowledge. Her books include *Moore and Wittgenstein: Scepticism, Certainty and Common Sense* (2010), *Extended Rationality: A Hinge Epistemology* (2015), *The Varieties of Self-Knowledge* (2016), and (with Maria Baghramian) *Relativism* (2019).

Sanford C. Goldberg has been Professor of Philosophy at Northwestern University since 2007. His main areas of research are epistemology, philosophy of language, and philosophy of mind, with a focus on topics at the intersection of these. He is the author of dozens of articles on these topics; his books include *Anti-Individualism* (Cambridge UP 2007), *Relying on Others* (Oxford UP 2010), *Assertion* (Oxford UP 2015), and *To the Best of Our Knowledge* (Oxford UP 2018). He is currently completing a book (tentatively entitled *Conversational Pressure)* at the intersection of epistemology, speech act theory, and ethics, concerning the dynamics of normative expectations in conversation.

Hilary Kornblith is Distinguished Professor of Philosophy at the University of Massachusetts, Amherst. He is the author of *Inductive Inference and its Natural Ground* (MIT Press, 1993); *Knowledge and its Place in Nature* (OUP, 2002); *On Reflection* (OUP, 2012); and *A Naturalistic Epistemology* (OUP, 2014).

Martin Kusch has been Professor of Philosophy of Science and Epistemology at the University of Vienna since 2009. He has published research monographs with OUP, Routledge, MIT Press, and Acumen. His

206   Contributors

main current area of research is epistemic relativism, past and present. He is currently writing two monographs: a defence of epistemic relativism, and a study of the first 20th-century defender of relativism, Georg Simmel.

Robin McKenna is Lecturer in Philosophy at the University of Liverpool. Before coming to Liverpool he worked in Austria (at the University of Vienna) and Switzerland (at the University of Geneva). He completed his PhD at the University of Edinburgh. Most of his work is in epistemology, but he is also interested in the philosophy of language, philosophy of science, and ethics. Within epistemology, he works on various topics in applied epistemology, feminist epistemology, and social epistemology more broadly. Current topics of interest include the epistemology of persuasion, the epistemology of climate change denial (and of "dysfunctional epistemologies" more broadly), epistemic injustice, and social constructivism.

Michele Palmira is a postdoctoral fellow at the University of Barcelona and a senior member of BIAP/LOGOS Research group. His research interests include disagreement, relativism, epistemic rationality, and the nature of inquiry. His work on these topics has appeared in journals such as *Proceedings of the Aristotelian Society, Philosophical Quarterly, Synthese*, and *American Philosophical Quarterly*.

Alexandra Plakias is Assistant Professor of Philosophy at Hamilton College. She received her PhD from the University of Michigan in 2011. Her research focuses on moral psychology and metaethics, and she has published articles on moral disagreement, the role of disgust in moral judgment, and the significance of empirical research for moral theory.

Kristina Rolin is University Lecturer in Research Ethics at the University of Tampere. Besides research ethics, her areas of specialty are philosophy of science and social science, social epistemology, and feminist epistemology. She is interested in the proper role of values in science, the epistemic benefits of diversity in science, collective knowledge, and relations of trust in science. Her journal articles can be found in *Philosophy of Science, Studies in History and Philosophy of Science, International Studies in the Philosophy of Science, Philosophy of the Social Sciences, Hypatia, Episteme*, and *Social Epistemology*. She has also published in interdisciplinary journals, including *Cognitive Systems Research, Perspectives on Science, Science & Education*, and *Science Studies*.

Index

Note: Page numbers in *italics* indicate a figure on the corresponding page.

absolutism 48, 87–90, 185, 194;
  Boghossian's views on 185–187,
  193, 196; denial of 166; implied
  171; non- 197–200; and objectivity
  99; regressive 96, 100
agents 49–50, 55–57, 61, 71–80;
  epistemic 18, 22, 79, 146, 194;
  moral 180
Alston, W. 199–200
'alternative' facts 96
Ambedkar, B. 97–99
analytic epistemology *see*
  epistemology
Anderson, E. 115, 139, 154; on
  anthropology and gender 114; on
  dogmatism 132; on epistemic
  responsibility and trust 154; on
  feminist epistemology 111–112,
  115–116; on political values in
  science 139
animal knowledge *see* knowledge
animals: attitudes toward 59–60;
  beliefs concerning 105, 107, 109;
  Durkheim's views on 163–164;
  human animal 69, 163–164, 176;
  "something animal" 199
anthropology 30, 114, 161–162;
  see also Barrett, C.; Durkheim, E.
Aristotle 71, 123, 195
Ashton, N. A. 99, 103, 113

Barnes, B. 184, 196, 198
Barrett, C. 59
beliefs: auxiliary 59; body of 80;
  connections among 79; and
  convergence 50; and credibility 197;
  and cultural relativism 55; Davidson
  on 131, 139; descriptive 129, 139;

disagreement in 17; empirical 19,
  22; as epistemic intuition 54; and
  epistemic relativism 89, 94, 96, 185;
  and experience 140; expert 33; false
  150, 152–153, 184, 196; first-order
  21; folk 52; formation of 16, 34,
  114; full or partial 12; hinges and
  11–12, 16, 21; and/or knowledge
  61–62, 67; mistaken 131; moral 60;
  and objectivity 49; political 87;
  religious 97, 150; revising 25;
  standards as 166–167, 184; as "state
  of mind" 168; in the supernatural
  175, 187–188; "systems" of 199;
  true 57, 77, 138, 151–152, 196;
  unjustified 69, 77, 187–188; value
  judgements as 126–129, 131;
  see also justified belief
Bellarmine, R. 188–190, 195–196
Bloor, D.: on non-absolutism
  197–198; on normativity 175–177,
  180–181; and Sociology of Scientific
  Knowledge (SSK) 184, 191,
  197–198, 200; on Wright 177–179
Boghossian, P. 48; and Bellarmine
  195–197; *Fear of Knowledge* (FK)
  184–191, 198; on knowledge 110;
  and relationism 187–188; relativist
  argument for pluralism 188–190;
  template 185–195; Wright on
  190–195
BonJour, L. 70
Brandt, R. 59–60
Brink, D. O. 48

Campelia, G. 123, 133–134
Cartesianism 15, 80
Chappell, P. K. 123, 133, 140

208 Index

Chisolm, R. 70
circularity: epistemic 199; "no-rule"
  186; rule- 197–200; vicious 126
Code, L. 196
Coliva, A. 21
common ground 135, 138–140
common sense 51, 199, 200
constitutive dependence *see*
  dependence
constitutive hinge epistemology *see*
  epistemology
contextualism 190; attributor 30;
  liberatory 90
convergence conception 49–50, 54,
  56–57, 63; *see also* objectivity
Copernicanism 195
Cowell, J. 134
critical contextual empiricism (CCE)
  149; *see also* Longino, H.

Dalits, oppression of 97–98
Dancy, J. 48
Darley, J. 52
Darwin, C. 200
Davidson, D. 122, 124; on beliefs 131;
  on common ground 139; pragmatist
  themes 125; "Three Varieties of
  Knowledge" 127, 139; on value
  judgements 126–127
Decety, J. 134
deontologism 35
dependence 89, 91, 99; causal and
  constitutive 110–111, 113–116;
  epistemological 99; social 103
Descartes, R. 80
Dewey, J. 97–99
differential relativistic verdicts 43
doxastic attitudes 18–19, 25
doxastic disagreement 12–13,
  16–18, 26
doxastic justification *see* justification
Dreier, J. 48
Durkheim, E. 161; and Kantian
  metaphysics 164, 168, 171, 176;
  and morality 162–163; and natural
  knowledge 163–164; on normativity
  175–177; and religious thought
  161–162; on standards as a social
  process 168

Egan, A. 56
empathy 123–125, *135*, 135–136,
  136; and epistemic humility

123–140; failure of 137–139; social
  practice of 134; *see also* common
  ground
epistemic absolutism *see* absolutism
epistemic advantages 93
epistemic assessment 32, 40,
  44–45
epistemic circularity *see* circularity
epistemic community 145–147,
  151–157; well-designed 149–156
epistemic dependence 99
epistemic externalists *see* externalists
epistemic humility *see* empathy
epistemic justification *see* justification
epistemic justification relativism 143
epistemic practices 17–18, 21–26, 194;
  Longino on 92; moral and 47; and
  epistemic relativism 30; and science
  claims 122
epistemic rationality 21–27, 33, 156;
  instrumentalist account of 145,
  147–148, 155–156; *see also*
  rationalism/rationality
epistemic relativism 30–31, 44, 47;
  three criteria for 89; *see also*
  relativism
epistemic responsibility 143–149;
  as moral norm 152–155; norm of
  151–156
epistemic responsibility relativism:
  alternative to 156; problem with
  145–149; refuting 157
epistemic strict liability, doctrine of
  36–40
epistemic system (ES) 185–198
epistemology: analytic 67, 69, 79;
  Bayesian approaches to 70;
  constitutive hinge 21–27; cross-
  cultural 51; decision theoretic 70;
  feminist 87, 89, 97–100, 104,
  111–117; hinge 11, 16, 18–27;
  moral 133; naturalistic 66; orthodox
  30–35, 40–41; and standards of
  justification 43; "time-slice" 32;
  virtue 123, 132, 143, 148, 153;
  Yoruba 61; *see also* social
  epistemology
"equal validity" 89, 185, 188, 196
evidential relations *see* knowledge;
  psychologism
evolution 200
externalist-reliabilist *see* knowledge
externalists 32, 67, 78, 81

Index 209

Fairhead, J. 136
false claims 96
Fear of Knowledge (FK)
  see Boghossian, P.
feminist epistemology
  see epistemology
Feyerabend, P. 196, 200
Field, H. 196
finitism 191–195
Fraassen, B. van 200
Franklin, R. 128
Fricker, M. 118, 153

Galileo Galilei 187–189
Geography of Philosophy project 59
Gettier, E. 53–54, 67
God/gods 162–163, 169, 175–176,
  189
Goldenberg, M. 122, 124, 126,
  136–137
Goldman, A. 32, 67–68, 70, 74–75, 78
Goodwin, G. 52–53

Hallen, B. 61–62
Haraway, D. 94–95
Harding, S. 93–100, 114; weak
  objectivity 90, 92
Harman, G. 187
Hempel, C. G. 70
Herbert, C. 196
hinge epistemology *see* epistemology
Hopi 59
Humean sceptic *see* sceptic

Intemann, K. 155

James, W. 38
justification 11, 19, 31, 34, 88–99; and
  belief 181; coherentist 70; demand
  for 186; doxastic 67–69, 71–75, 80;
  epistemic 16, 25, 35, 39, 93–94,
  143, 152–156, 199–200; evidential
  36; instrumentalist 150; internalist
  views about 70, 76; moral 154;
  normativity of 38; propositional
  67–69, 71, 74–75, 78; and
  relativism 198; "ultimate" 194
justified belief 90, 200; conceptions
  of 77; doxastic 75; epistemic 143,
  186–188, 199; and epistemic
  relationism 185; and foundationalist
  requirements 70; Goldman's views
  on 67–68, 78; and knowledge 30;

merely relatively 96; propositional
  71, 74, 78–79; theory of 31, 33–44;
  Wright's views on 165; *see also*
  norms of inquiry

Kahneman, D. 69
Kant, I. 163–165, 168, 171, 176;
  metaphysics 164; neo-Kantian
  philosophy 161
knowledge: achieving 57; animal 200;
  attribution 53–54; Davidson's views
  on 139–140; empathetic 133–134;
  English concepts of 62; and
  epistemically responsible claims to
  143–154; and epistemic practices
  30; and evidential relations 70–71,
  73, 76; externalist-reliabilist 199;
  internalist-coherentist 199; and
  justification 40, 42, 44, 50; and
  morality 161, 167; natural 163–164;
  "no place" of 95; and normativity
  38–40, 42; and norms 16;
  phenomenological 112; and
  propositional justification 68–69,
  78; scientific 149–152, 155, 168;
  second-hand 105; situated 111–116;
  and social factors 92, 103–106,
  108–111; sociologists of 171; three
  varieties of 139–140; Yoruba
  concepts of 61; *see also* Boghossian,
  P., *Fear of Knowledge* (FK);
  Sociology of Scientific Knowledge
  (SSK)
knowledge-action principles 106–108
knowledge-seeking practices
  see practices
Koerth-Baker, M. 137
Kuhn, T. 167–169, 195, 200
Kusch, M. 124, 196

Ladd, J. 59–60
Leach, M. 136
Lewis, D. 56
Longino, H. 90–92, 97–99, 112; and
  critical contextual empiricism (CCE)
  149–152; on objectivity 126
lost hinge disagreement problem
  12–13; solving 13–17

Machery, E. 59, 61
McKenna, R. 103, 113
Medina, J. 133
Melo-Martín, I. de 155

210 *Index*

metaethics 48, 50–52, 54, 56
metaphysics/metaphysical 12, 15, 110; commitments 58–59; doctrines 161; Kantian 164, 171; necessity 182; religious beliefs 97
Moore, G. E. 15, 181
moral agents *see* agents
moral claims 50, 53, 56
moral experience, phenomenology of 48
morality 52–54, 181; Durkheim on 162–163, 176; 'mature folk' 57; and normative judgement 174, 177; and objectivity 52–53, 180; relative 48; and science 163; and society 167, 181; standards of 164; *see also* epistemic responsibility
moral practices *see* practices
moral realism *see* realism
moral relativism *see* relativism
Morris, S. 134

Nanda, M. 97–100
Navajo 59–60
normativity: Bloor on 175–177, 180; Durkheim on 175–177; epistemic 54, 148; of knowledge and justification 38–39, 42, 44; problems with 188, 192; sociologistic accounts of 174–183
norms: of belief 17; cognitive 170; epistemic 55, 58, 144–153, 155–156; moral 51, 145, 153; of rationality 184; social 176, 178–182
norms of inquiry 30; epistemic significance of 31–35; failure to satisfy 36–37, 39, 41–42; and theory of justified belief 31, 33–44

objectivity 48–55; and absolutism 89–90, 99; convergence conception of 49; definition of 88–90; degrees of 55–58; judgements of 53; mind-independence conception of 49; morality's claim to 52; and perception 25–26; as a process 125, 132; as a product 131; as regressive 92–94, 97; relativism vs 57, 80; of science/scientific claims 122, 125–126; and universality 98; of values 124–131; weak 95; *see also* Harding, S.
objectivity assumption 49, 51, 54

orthodox epistemology *see* epistemology

permissivism 31
Peterson, J. 87
phronesis 123, 126, 131–133, 139–140
Plato 175
pluralism 56; epistemic 185; reconstructed 195–197; relativist argument for 188–190
practices 21, 24–25; expert and non-expert 33–34; knowledge-seeking 156; non-neutrality of 89; rationality of 26; religious 97; sacred 162; scientific 112, 125–131, 133, 150; social 39, 45, 55, 94, 131, 134, 143–144; and virtues 91
Prinz, J. 134
psychologism 66–80; and evidential relations 69–72, 74, 79; and relativism 67, 80

Quine, W.V.O. 114

Ranalli, C. 19–20
rational inertia 27; and hinge epistemology 18–21; problem of 13, 17–18
rationalism/rationality 181; concept of 27; extended 22–23; irrationalism/irrationality 12, 72, 166, 184; Kantian 171; narrow 22–23; norms of 184; of practical reasoning 106; standard of 31, 44
realism 47–48, 50; objectivity and 47, 58; Smith's views on 56
relationism 191; argument for 187–188; and communitarian finitism 191–195; epistemic 185
relativism: anti- 88, 90, 92, 94, 97–99; in contemporary analytic philosophy 47; cultural 55; and epistemic authority 138; and ethnography 58–63; and evidential relations 73–74; and feminist epistemology 87–100; liberatory 90–92, 97–99; Longino's views on 91–92; mild 40–44; moral 58–59, 63, 177; and naturalism 66–67; New Age 190, 194; and objectivity 55–57; and political values 122, 124; and psychologism 67, 72,

Index 211

79–80; as regressive 94–97; role of 138–139; self-locating 56; three components of 89, 91–92; truth 13; as weak objectivity 94–95, 97; *see also* absolutism; epistemic relativism; sociologism; Sociology of Scientific Knowledge (SSK)
reliabilists 75, 199
Rosen, G. 49
rule-following considerations (RFC) *see* Wittgenstein, L.
Russell, B. 70

sceptic: Cartesian 15; vs constitutivist 26–27; Humean 19, 21–25
Smith, B. H. 48, 196
social epistemology 143, 145; of science 122, 128–129, 146
sociologism 161, 167, 171, 179–182; of Bloor 176–177, 181
Sociology of Scientific Knowledge (SSK) 177, 184–185, 190–200
Sodipo, J.O. 61–62
Sosa, E. 199–200
Stich, S. 59, 61

Tanesini, A. 123, 132
telos 200
triangulation 122, 126–128, 131, 134
Trump, D. J. 87, 96
trust 16, 19–21, 27, 104, 137–138; and mistrust 132, 137
truth 22; absolute 197; a priori 76; of beliefs 38; Durkheim on 163; and evidence 139; evidentially-constrained accounts of 15; hinges' 14–16, 18; Kuhn on 168; of logic 69; Longino on 92; of normative claims 60; post- 87; and rationality

12; and relativism 13, 56, 59, 182; relativistic notion of 185, 190–191; and standards of justification 43; Wright on 164–166, 168
truth-aptness 16, 50, 187, 193
truth-conditions 128, 169–170
truth-values 55, 57, 190
Tversky, A. 69

vaccines 122, 124–125, 129–130; vaccine hesitance 132, 136–138
value/values: constitutive 93; dispositional theory of 56; epistemic 194; as evidence 126; human 153; judgements 127, 156; moral 155; overt 93; political 110, 122, 124, 126, 131, 133; in science 126, 139, 149, 150; scientific 90, 97–98, 124–131; social 94, 110, 112, 114–115; and vaccines 137
value-free 92, 95
virtue epistemology *see* epistemology
virtues 90–91, 98, 122–123

Wakefield, A. 137
Westernized, Educated, Industrialized, Rich, and Democratic (WEIRD) 58–59
Wittgenstein, L. 11–14, 16; and hinge epistemology 21; rule-following considerations (RFC) 191; and Sociology of Scientific Knowledge (SSK) 192, 199; and Wright 19
Wright, C. 5, 18–21, 161, 164–170; Bloor on 177–179; and Boghossian's template 190–195
Wright, J. 53

Yoruba 61

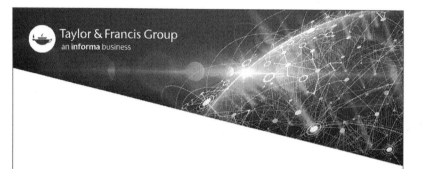

Taylor & Francis eBooks

www.taylorfrancis.com

A single destination for eBooks from Taylor & Francis with increased functionality and an improved user experience to meet the needs of our customers.

90,000+ eBooks of award-winning academic content in Humanities, Social Science, Science, Technology, Engineering, and Medical written by a global network of editors and authors.

TAYLOR & FRANCIS EBOOKS OFFERS:

- A streamlined experience for our library customers
- A single point of discovery for all of our eBook content
- Improved search and discovery of content at both book and chapter level

REQUEST A FREE TRIAL
support@taylorfrancis.com